Discover Your Joy

Daily Splashes of Inspiration for
Living an Abundant Life of Happiness,
Blessings, and Inner Peace

LOUISE PISTOLE

Printed in the United States of America

Published by Author Academy Elite
P.O. Box 43, Powell, OH 43035

Unless otherwise noted, Scripture quotations are taken from the *New International Version, New Living Translation, King James Version, & English Standard Version.* Bible Hub. https://biblehub.com/

Paperback: 978-1-64746-699-2
Hardback: 978-1-64746-700-5
E-book: 978-1-64746-701-2
Library of Congress Control Number: 2021901245

Discover Your Joy
is dedicated to
my Great Aunt Eleanor
who taught me love and grace.

She also taught me to be polite, act like a lady,
and always write thank you notes.

Acknowledgments

These amazing people believed in me, and loved and supported me, throughout this entire journey. I am forever grateful.

My Family: Randy, my husband; Austin, my son, and his awesome family; Susan, my precious sister, and her family; and Martha.

My Team: April Tribe Giauque, Kay Dano, Jill Blackwelder, Pat Simmons, and the entire team and tribe at Author Academy Elite.

My Personal Note To You

Welcome to *Discover Your Joy.*

I am a *JOY*-fanatic! Ten years ago, my minister spoke on the subject of *JOY.* He cautioned us to watch for "*joy stealers.*" His message resonated with me and led me to what became my favorite Bible verse. "Rejoice always." 1 Thessalonians 5:16 NIV. It has taken me on a journey that makes my mind, my heart, and my soul soar with *joy*!

We all have ups and downs in our lives, and I had been through a dark time. The death of my sweet Daddy rocked my world. Daddy was my hero, my soft spot to always land. I was the first girl born into the family in 49 years and Daddy called me his "Princess." But he loved everyone, and he had enough strong tight hugs to accommodate everybody. Daddy had a strong Christian faith and he taught Sunday School to preschoolers for over 40 years. He was a gentle man of few words, but his love consumed everyone around him. Daddy died unexpectedly even though he lingered in ICU for five long weeks. My sister and I sat at the hospital watching, waiting, and praying. And our hearts were shattered when he was gone. There are several beautiful stories of Daddy for you to read throughout this book.

After Daddy's death, my husband and I separated. The day he moved out is probably one of the most difficult memories I have. Suddenly, I was living alone for the first time in my life. What was I supposed to do now? Over the years, our lives had grown apart and marriage just didn't work for us anymore. Somehow, I struggled with reconciling it all in my mind. We didn't immediately divorce. I just felt like divorce was not what God would have us do.

During the years of separation, my life was in limbo. Nothing was settled. For those seven years, I was stuck in a time warp that did not allow me to move forward. Years later, when the divorce was final, it was definitely settled, and I was definitely sad and alone. For the next few years, I poured myself into my business. It kept me busy and occupied.

I was single again for 21 years. During those years, many theories crossed my mind. First and foremost, I wondered if this was God's plan to bring me to a place where I was totally committed to him. I must admit, my faith deepened during those years. I read more. I studied more. I learned more. If this was God's plan, it was working.

Sure, there were happy times and great days, but once I was inspired by my minister, I gradually began to research more about joy. That one word became my lifeline. I purchased books on joy; I read every Bible passage about joy; I covered my walls with sayings about joy. Fifteen years after Daddy's death, I started to discover how truly great my life could be.

Now, I want you to feel the joy that I know. It is a conscious decision to choose joy every day. These *daily splashes of inspiration* will take you through some of my thoughts and feelings. They are short essays yet have enough motivation to inspire you to have a fabulous day. Each inspiration is packed with uplifting and encouraging words of gratitude, happiness, inner peace and joy.

Each day starts with an affirmation. These statements are positive thoughts that can overcome any negative self-talk. Starting the statements with "I" is a powerful way for you to identify with the statement. There's more about affirmations on January 15.

On the first day of each month, there is a simple challenge. Many of the inspirations for that month will relate to the challenge. Then at the end of each month, everything wraps up. Use the Notes page at the end of each month to record your own inspirations and thoughts. Journaling has always been my best friend through great times and tough times. I want you to have a place to write about the good and the not-so-good along your own journey.

Hopefully, these daily inspirations will guide you to *discover joy* in your own life!

Always feel free to email me your thoughts, comments, and stories. My personal email is Louise@LouisePistole.com. I'll surely respond to you.

Wishing you abundant joy always,
Louise

Table of Contents

JANUARY:
WORD OF THE YEAR

Finding Your Joy

JANUARY 1
WORD OF THE YEAR

I put my goal in action.

Several years ago, I started using one word each year as my focus for New Year's Resolutions. With one word, I could adapt as life zigzagged forward.

Here you can almost see what was going on in my life just by the one word I chose for each of the last five years.

Purge	A time to clear mental and physical clutter.
Self-love	Take care of myself and think about things.
Transition	A lot of changes were headed my way.
Focus	Keep my eye on all the newness in my life.
Balance	Balance all the areas of my life.

As I worked through clearing clutter and taking care of myself, I prepared for retirement and a new marriage. In my own mind, I can see how these words seemed to improve with my life each year. I was on the path to joy.

January Challenge: As you look back over prior years, are you able to find yourself in a better place now? Spend some time today thinking about what word would serve you best as you move forward in January and all of the coming year.

What is your word for the coming year that will lead you to discover your own joy?

Today's Joy: I am forever growing in my knowledge, expertise and wisdom.

JANUARY 2
AN AMAZING NEW YEAR

I will follow my joy.

This year is going to be ridiculously amazing!

Goals help keep us focused. And, in order to have my best year ever, I want to concentrate some of my time on self-care. Here are some of my goals.

> This year, I will try to always focus on what is right in my life.
> I resolve to make my life interesting and live in joy.
> I will allow my dreams to direct my heart.
> I will invest in my own joy through self-care.
> I will choose my thoughts with care.
> I will move intently in the right direction for me.
> I will keep my eyes focused on my long-term goals.
> I am willing to change and grow but I will never give up.
> If I am derailed, I will get back on track and keep moving.
> This is my year to shine! All is well!

You can start your new year with joy and laughter by taking care of yourself!

Self-care is one of the best things you can do to find and preserve your inner joy. What are your self-care goals for the coming year?

Today's Joy: This year, I will be aware of my potential.

JANUARY 3
DO UNTO OTHERS

I show gratitude by sharing with others.

Yesterday, I focused on taking care of ourselves in this new year. Today, I want to talk about serving others.

This is my personal commitment.
I will be kind and courteous to everyone I meet.
I will smile and share happiness every day.
I will make time to volunteer for community service.
I will check on my neighbors regularly.
I will show compassion and share my abundance with those in need.
I will perform random acts of kindness.
I will uplift and encourage my tribe of women.
I will love my neighbors as God loves me.
I will pray for my family, friends, neighbors and co-workers.
I will check on friends who are sick or grieving.
I will walk in joy in hopes that others will join me.

Service to others fills you with a rewarding peace. How can you serve others this year? What are your strengths that you can use to help other people?

Today's Joy: "So in everything, do to others what you would have them do to you, for this sums up the Law and the Prophets. " Matthew 7:12 NIV

JANUARY 4
SNOW DAY

Let it snow!

I met a friend today for lunch and when I looked out the window, it was snowing! Totally unexpected and unpredicted SNOW!

The freshness of the new fallen snow is so beautiful. As I finished my coffee and walked outside, there was a sense of calm and peace in the air. The kids were laughing and playing in the snow. Everyone seemed happy and had a smile on their face.

We're all kids at heart and enjoy a quick little snow burst. In the South, we don't see much snow, and everything shuts down at the first sign of a snowflake.

A snow day is definitely a joyful day!

Can you capture the feeling of a day like this? Place it in your memory bank so you can revisit this day when you need a little boost of joy.

Today's Joy: "Kindness is like snow. It beautifies everything it covers."—Kahlil Gibran[1]

JANUARY 5
CHOOSING JOY EVERY DAY

I choose to be joyful.

I try to choose joy every morning as soon as I am awake.

Joy doesn't simply happen. You have to intentionally choose to be joyful and you have to make that choice every day.

Actually, your joy begins with gratitude and being thankful for all you are and all you have. The more grateful you are on a daily basis, the more joyful you will also be.

Joy comes from deep within your soul. It is finding beauty, happiness, and contentment in everyday things on a daily basis.

Once you're in the habit of choosing joy every day, you will start to feel the change in yourself and the world around you.

And, your joy is contagious! As you exude more joy in life, other people around you will begin to also feel more joyful.

How can you choose joy today? What are you grateful for now? Let your gratitude to lead you to enjoy a joyful day.

Today's Joy: "Joy is what happens to us when we allow ourselves to recognize how good things really are."— Marianne Williamson[2]

JANUARY 6
WINTER THOUGHTS

I have sunshine in my heart even on a cold winter day.

It was cold today here on the East Coast. I was content being inside enjoying a cup of cappuccino and reading. These winter days are perfect for making plans for spring. Perhaps you're planning a vacation or what to plant in the garden. I have flower seed catalogs spread out on the table to ponder.

Winter is also a time for slowing down and resting. Your mind has time to clear the clutter and dream of something new when the earth warms again in spring.

The days are shorter and draw us inside earlier in the evening. Huddling by a blazing fire with a good book is the perfect ending to a day.

This time of year, the moon seems fuller and the stars are brighter. As my husband and I stood on the deck last night, he pointed out the constellations in the sky. The night was quiet. Everything was still and peaceful.

How do you enjoy cold winter days and nights? What are you planning for spring?

Today's Joy: "Winter is a season of recovery and preparation."—Paul Theroux[3]

JANUARY 7
A SIGN OF NEW BEGINNINGS

I marvel at the sight.

The holidays are over, the weather here is cold with a chance of snow, and life has settled back into a familiar pattern. I have two large camellia bushes; one is deep red and the other one is cream white. When I look out the back windows and see these two bushes covered in red or white blooms, my heart skips a little ahead

Depending on where you live, camellias bloom through the winter and into the spring. Mine are usually in spectacular full bloom in January each year. Amidst our winter weather, the camellias offer a sign of new beginnings. It is a new year and there is hope for splendid days ahead. I will cut some of the flowers and bring them inside to enjoy their magic here.

What are the first flowers you have blooming in the new year? Let them warm your heart and give you hope for a good year.

It's the end of the first week of January. Do you feel yourself moving closer to joy? Remember to use gratitude every day. Even try to be thankful for the storms in your life. They teach you a lesson, build strength, and help you appreciate better days ahead.

Today's Joy: "Where flowers bloom, so does hope." —Lady Bird Johnson[4]

JANUARY 8
LET YOUR LIGHT SHINE

I will be a light for others.

I enjoyed lunch with Patty this week. She always has a bushel of stories to share.

After a recent medical procedure, she had been dealing with the billing department and the physician's assistant, and it was not a pretty picture.

After much labored conversations she finally told them, "I decided to live this year by letting my light shine before men that they may see my good works and glorify my Father who is in heaven." Then she added, "You're making it difficult for me to fulfill my resolution this year."

It was an interesting story, but I was most impressed that she was purposely living her life to glorify God and let others see him through her actions. And she stood by her resolution even when others were not cooperating.

Are you willing to stand in the face of adversity and proclaim the glory of the Lord? Pray for strength to stand up for what you believe.

Today's Joy: "Let your light so shine before men that they may see your good works and glorify your Father who is in heaven." Matthew 5:16 KJV

JANUARY 9
LISTEN WITH LOVE

I value the friends in my life.

Lola was having coffee with Molly and wanted to pour out her heavy heart to her friend. However, Molly was more engaged with her phone this morning and was only responding with, "Uh huh" every so often. Lola was frustrated that her friend was not listening.

One of the greatest gifts you can give to another person is to be fully engaged when they are talking to you. Put down your cell phone and make eye contact. Pay attention to their facial expressions and body language.

Asking questions is a good way to become engaged with the conversation. Rephrasing what the person said and saying it back to them will reinforce their thoughts.

Also, speaking with love, concern, and empathy shows that you appreciate them sharing with you. It is truly an honor for a friend to have trust in you and to confide in you. Your interest and understanding is like a healing salve. If your heart is in the conversation, your attention will be recognized and appreciated.

Make it your mission to always *listen with love* and compassion. What is your secret to *listen with love* when someone is sharing their heart with you?

Today's Joy: Listening with love is showing kindness.

JANUARY 10
FIRST THINGS FIRST

I will practice staying focused on my project.

It is easy to start something and become distracted. Off to another project we go. Before long, we have numerous things started, but nothing is completed. I am guilty of this, especially first thing in the mornings.

My distractions all come from within myself. I start one thing that makes me think of another thing. First, I'm writing on a new book and before long, I'm planting flowers and pulling weeds. Making dinner can lead to digging through a closet for a box that I just remembered. Whole days can go by and I don't feel like I've accomplished anything.

For this new year, I have purchased a pad of page-size sticky notes with a place for appointments each day of the week and my priorities. I can list my priorities each night and focus on *first things first* each morning.

Try to keep your focus on your "Word of the Year" to stay on track. My word is *balance*, and I'm working on balancing my priorities.

What about you? Do you have a system to handle priorities first? How do you handle distractions? Try to keep your focus on your 'Word of the Year' to stay on track.

Today's Joy: Focus is one of the first steps to success.

JANUARY 11
THE POWER OF WORDS

I speak words of kindness.

One of my favorite guy friends called me on my cell. When I answered, Max said, "I'm feeling pretty down today and so I decided to call the 'Joy Hotline,'" Max knows I'm a joy-fanatic and he made my day by referring to me as the Joy Hotline.

Our words are both powerful and magical. They can crush someone or inspire them. We often say something that we didn't think much about. But it may be the one sentence that sticks with the other person for a lifetime. Good or bad.

Once harsh words are spoken, they *may* not be forgotten. You can only ask for forgiveness.

Let your words be truthful, kind, and gentle. What you say reflects the essence of the person you are in your heart. Illuminate the light in your heart by sharing words of inspiration and encouragement.

What kind words inspire you? Do you make a point to share words of kindness with others?

Today's Joy: "The tongue can bring death or life; those who love to talk will reap the consequences." Proverbs 18:21 NLT

JANUARY 12
JOY IS MY TRUTH AND MY LIGHT

I walk in joy.

What is this joy that I speak of so often?

Joy lives at the epicenter of my heart.
It fuels my emotions and keeps me in a positive place.
Let my truth be heard so others can find their truth.
I know that joy is my truth.

Joy is the light that shines bright in both my heart and my soul.
It illuminates my life and is a watchtower for all to see.
Let my light shine so others see the reflection of light.
I know that joy is my light.

I am abundantly blessed and joyful.
Joy is my daily mantra. Joy is my superpower.

Joy is my truth and my light.

Today's Joy: What is your truth? How do you share your light to the world?

JANUARY 13
ATTITUDE OF GRATITUDE

I am blessed and grateful.

Nadia had struggled financially for a few years. But she recently had learned about using a daily gratitude practice. After a couple of months, she began to notice all the positive things coming her way. Nadia realized her best self culminates with living her life in gratitude.

We are all on a journey to become the best possible version of ourselves. We take classes, read articles, and google topics that are supposed to make us a better person.

An easier approach is being grateful every day which shifts your mindset from negative circumstances to positive outcomes. You will start to focus your thoughts on new possibilities and successes in your life.

Taking time for gratitude every day will reward you with a calm and peaceful mind. Your heart begins to fill with happiness and joy. Your attitude of gratitude will give more meaning and purpose to your life.

What are you thankful for today? Make a mental list of ten things that pop into your mind when you think about gratitude. Warning – making that list just might bring a smile to your face or joy to your heart.

Today's Joy: A moment of gratitude will make your attitude soar!

JANUARY 14
IT'S OK TO ASK FOR HELP

I am not alone.

Ann was feeling desperate. Her husband was coming home late at night and she could tell he had been drinking. She felt like there was no one she could tell. Each day was more difficult than the one before, and she felt all alone. Ann decided it was time for her to call the leader of her Bible Study group and ask for support.

When you are deep in despair, you often feel totally alone. It's like no one else knows or cares about what you are living through. This often happens if you are in an abusive relationship or living with someone who has an addiction. But, in all of these situations and other similar ones, it's always ok to ask for help.

Sometimes, outside people do not realize help is needed or they think you have it all under control. But, find a compassionate friend and share your story. Asking for help is often the bravest thing you can do.

You are strong, but we all have a breaking point. You need assistance long before you reach that breaking point. You need time for your own self-care and self-love.

Take deep breaths, write in a journal, call a friend, and always take your troubles to God in prayer.

Do you know someone who potentially is struggling with desperate issues? What can you do to assist them or encourage them? Will you make a move to help them today?

Today's Joy: "Oh what needless pain we bear, all because we do not carry everything to God in prayer." — **Joseph M Scriven**[5]

JANUARY 15
THE POWER OF AFFIRMATIONS

I love and accept myself.

An affirmation is a positive statement that can change your way of thinking. The repeated affirmation or statement becomes part of your subconscious mind and slowly changes your self-talk from negative to positive.

The affirmations are your first step towards self-improvement and becoming a happier person. But it is the consistency that makes them so powerful and makes them work. The more you use affirmations, the more you will notice positive changes in your life.

You can write any affirmation that resonates with you, and use different ones for different situations. I recommend writing some to use daily and hanging them on your bathroom mirror, so you'll be reminded of the positivity several times each day. You can also write them in your gratitude journal to add power to your thoughts.

Here are a few of my favorites:

> I am calm and peaceful.
> Today will bring me joy and happiness.
> I am perfect just the way I am.

What affirmations resonate with you? Will you use them on a daily basis?

Today's Joy: I prefer to always end my affirmations with *all is well.*

JANUARY 16
JEALOUSY TO GRATITUDE

I will lift up others.

Nancy was obviously jealous over Mary's recent promotion at the office. She was not happy that Mary would now be her immediate supervisor. In her fury, she screamed to Mary, "You do not deserve this promotion. I should be the one who got this job. I know more than you do." Whew! What a statement that was.

Jealousy sometimes occurs because we do not recognize our own value. We often do not appreciate our own uniqueness and self-worth. Was something better in store for Nancy that she did not know about yet? Jealousy is a form of insecurity, lack of self-confidence, and even hatred. We really do not want any of that in our lives. There is no value to us.

There is no good to come of being jealous of another person or their successes or their belongings. We do not know the full story. We do not know the reasons.

It can be difficult to overcome jealousy and it requires a conscious effort. However, if you can get to the point to feel happy for this person and their success, it becomes a form of gratitude.

Congratulate them sincerely and feel the gratitude that exudes from your heart. You already know that the more grateful you are, the more things you have to be grateful for. Their success can also be a win for you.

Do you find yourself jealous of others? Learn to appreciate the goodness in other people. The appreciation will open your heart.

Today's Joy: "Jealousy is the art of counting someone else's blessings instead of your own."—Roy T. Bennett[6]

JANUARY 17
MIRACLES DO HAPPEN

I am worthy of a miracle.

A specialist discovered that my first-grade son had an unknown bone growing in his ear and covering up his ear canal. He was deaf in that one ear. Surgery was the only answer.

I was terrified for my young son. The thoughts of surgery concerned me, but I certainly did not want him to be deaf in one ear. I went home to contemplate and to pray for a miracle.

The fateful day came when we returned to the specialist for a follow-up visit. The doctor performed all the same tests. Finally, he looked at me with unknowing eyes.

The bone was gone! Somehow it had simply disappeared. He was confused, yet amazed, and had no explanation as to how a bone could simply disappear. But there were no signs that a bone had ever been there. Of course, I knew that prayer and miracles go hand-in-hand. We were blessed beyond measure!

Have you experienced a miracle in your life? Sometimes miracles occur and we don't recognize them at the time. Think about all the blessings in your life.

Today's Joy: "Pray without ceasing," 1 Thessalonians 5:17 ESV

JANUARY 18
FIND ONE NEW THOUGHT

I am whole.

Fran felt like a failure. She had lost her job and her home. She did not see any way out of her situation. For Fran, there was no glimmer of hope or any way to become whole again.

No matter how sad you are, how much you are grieving, how lonely you feel or how hopeless life seems, try to find one thought that is even just a little better than the one you are now thinking. Remind yourself of that one thought several times during the next few days until you actually start to feel like that better thought.

Then every day, look for a better thought than the one from the day before. Repeat this new thought until you believe it in your heart. One baby step at a time, you are training yourself to be a happier person.[7]

These positive new thoughts are your pathway to joy.

Even though you are suffering immensely, can you find one positive thought that you can cling to for now? Remind yourself of that particular thought continuously.

Today's Joy: I will survive this problem.

JANUARY 19
MY PERSONAL HOPE

My hope is in my Lord.

One place that I love being is in my gardens. And one particular morning I decided to pull up a plant that had spread and it was time for it to go.

After a while, my eyes began to burn, and I sent my nephew to the store for eye drops. That didn't help. My son then realized that this plant was poisonous and could cause burns and I was getting worse by the minute. As we waited for medical help, I was screaming from the pain in my eyes. My sister said I was literally pulling my hair out. A neighbor who is an RN started giving me pain meds.

I was quickly losing my vision. And even though the pain was excruciating, I fixed my limited eyesight on a recent picture of my two young grandchildren. If I was going to lose my vision, I would etch their photo into my brain.

I was able to get meds to finally stop the pain and even though my corneas were burned, my eyesight was not permanently damaged.

Have you been through a harrowing experience that could be life-altering? What did you do to hold onto your hope?

Today's Joy: Never lose hope and to God be the glory!

I am still and calm.

I love to get up early in the morning before anyone else begins to stir. It is calm and peaceful before the day gets into full swing.

It is a time to read or write, sip coffee and sort through my thoughts. Writing down my thoughts in a journal helps me to focus and brings clarity to my day. Reading devotions reminds me of God's love. When my mind is still, everything seems to fall into place.

Also, I make a list of my many blessings. Today, I am thankful for my husband, my son, and my sister and all the extended and blended families. And in my quiet time today, I have blessed all of them.

As I look out the window, sunbeams are beginning to stream through the trees. Birds are chirping and a new day is about to burst forth.

Do you take time for yourself in the mornings? It will make your day shine a little brighter!

Today's Joy: Positive thoughts during your quiet time can change your day.

JANUARY 21
NATIONAL HUG DAY

I welcome warm hugs.

January 21 is *National Hug Day* and I hope you got lots of hugs today. I'm a hugger person, for sure. Not everyone likes to be hugged so tread lightly until you know your hugs will be well received.

Some years ago, and after a long day of meeting with clients, a new employee said to me, "Do you know that you hug almost everyone who comes in the office?" I was single at the time and clients were my daily source of hugs.

There is a sense of stress relief that comes from receiving a hug, particularly a long hug. It lets the other person know that you care about them. Sometimes this warm embrace is just what the other person needs. And don't forget to hug your pets too!

Are you comfortable giving and receiving hugs? It can be another way to bring a little joy into your life.

Today's Joy: "Sometimes in life you just need a hug. No words, no advice, just a hug to make you feel better." — Author Unknown[8]

JANUARY 22
A MORNING BLESSING

I am blessed beyond measure.

Good morning friends! Good morning world!

I like to begin my day with a morning prayer:

> Thank you, dear Father, for this beautiful day which you have made for us.
>
> The sunshine that warms the earth, the birds that sing in perfect harmony, the lakes and oceans that soothe our soul, thank you for these and all our blessings, we pray.
>
> We come on bended knee to ask your healing mercies on those who are suffering, broken, or in despair. Also, heal those with illnesses; hold them tight in your loving care.
>
> Our hearts are full of gratitude this morning and to you, we give the honor and the glory.
>
> Blessed be this glorious day!
>
> Amen.

Do you start your mornings with a prayer? A simple prayer could include gratitude for your blessings, praises to God, and your prayer requests. It will warm your heart, for sure.

Today's Joy: "Praise the LORD. How good it is to sing praises to our God, how pleasant and fitting to praise him!" Psalm 147:1 NIV

JANUARY 23
CALLS TO DADDY

I love you.

I realize I am aging myself, but here goes. When my sweet Daddy was still living, I would always call him from the kitchen phone as I was leaving on any trip. I called to tell him where I would be, when I would return, and of course, that I loved him.

After Daddy claimed his seat in heaven, I would stop, stand, and stare at that phone on the wall every time I walked out the door. Tears would flood my face and memories would flood my heart.

It's been 25 years and even though the phone is no longer on that wall, I often stop and look at the place where I would spend precious moments with my Daddy.

You've heard it before, but I remind you to not wait until it's too late to place those calls to the ones you love. Even a brief call reminds the other person that you are thinking of them.

Who will you call today? Can you share with them your 'Word of the Year'? It may also encourage them.

Today's Joy: "Those we love don't go away. They walk beside us every day... unseen, unheard, but always near, still loved, still missed, and very dear."—Author Unknown[9]

JANUARY 24
JOY COMES IN THE MORNING

I am safe.

If you have ever been sick and alone at night, you know how long the night can be. It is a miserable feeling and sometimes you wonder it you'll make it till morning when you can call your family or your doctor. I remember having this feeling many times during my single years.

The darkness makes things feel unknown and unnerving. But, somehow, when the morning sun begins to light up the sky, things seem to get better.

Pains and troubles are similar. Things happen in life that brings sadness, grief, or even depression. You might struggle to get through the storms in your life. When you arrive at the other side of the issue, there is usually relief. And finally, you experience the joy that a new morning or a new day brings.

You have to hold on long enough, be patient and believe things will improve in order to know the joy that comes after the darkness has passed.

Have you experienced the feeling of relief after a time of problems? This relief is joy that restores your heart and soul.

Today's Joy: "With the new day comes new strength and new thoughts."—Eleanor Roosevelt[10]

". . . Weeping may endure for a night, but joy cometh in the morning." Psalm 30:5 KJV

JANUARY 25
FOLLOW YOUR NUDGE

I allow God to work through me.

Yesterday, I walked over to check on a neighbor who lives alone and had been in the hospital recently. We sat on her porch and chatted, laughed, and told stories. An hour or so later, I told her I needed to go home and start dinner. Marie replied, "Before you go, I want to tell you something."

She went on to say that she felt better than she had in a long time by having me there. Her heart rate had slowed down and she felt stronger. Then she told me that earlier in the day she had asked a friend to pray for her because she wasn't doing well. But I was amazed when she added, "You are my answer to that prayer."

Something had told me to check on Marie that day. And it turned out to be more than a friendly visit.

Who do you need to check on today? When you feel nudged to call someone or go somewhere, follow the nudge. It may just be what someone else needs.

Today's Joy: "Seek his will in all you do and he will show you which path to take." Proverbs 3:6 NLT

JANUARY 26
PETS ARE FAMILY TOO

I feel nurtured by my pet.

Elle came to me as a rescue kitty and she quickly became Queen of the Estate at my place. It was just the two of us and we were great companions.

Elle was a big cat, all 20 pounds of her along with her long hair. We made regular trips to the groomer for haircuts and last week was no exception. But then, the groomer called and said she was worried and to come quickly. Within a couple of hours, Elle had graduated to pet heaven and she left a huge gaping furry hole in my heart.

For everyone who has ever lost a beloved pet, you know they are more than an animal. These pets are our family. We dote on them; we pamper them; we get up early for feedings or walks; we purchase their favorite foods.

And when they're gone, we are left with a huge furry hole in our hearts. Coming home without our pet being there reminds us of the love we shared. Life must go on, but it's tough getting past the grief and on to the good memories.

Has your heart been broken by the loss of a pet? Our hearts are only broken when true love existed. Be grateful for the time you had together.

Today's Joy: Rest in peace, my sweet Elle. You were beautiful. You were loved. You were always Queen of the Estate.

JANUARY 27
WATERFALLS OF JOY

*I envision a waterfall
overflowing with joy.*

Last year, my husband and I flew to Hawaii for our honey-moon. One day, we took a tour around the island of Maui and through the rainforest. I loved all the gorgeous waterfalls and came home with a gazillion photos of all those waterfalls.

In my mind today, I've replaced all the water in those fabulous waterfalls with joy. Imagine what our lives would look like if we were surrounded by *waterfalls of joy*.

I pictured loving families enjoying time together and everyone taking part in random acts of kindness. Peace and patience babble over the rocks and glisten in the sunlight. Water lilies and ferns grow at the water's edge. This is a place to visit often.

What do you see in your *waterfall of joy*? Just imagining this sight will surely lift your spirits today.

Today's Joy: I am grateful for waterfalls of joy in my life.

JANUARY 28
PRAY FOR OTHERS – PART ONE

I will pray for you.

A chatty lady sat down beside me today at the doctor's office. We noticed how packed the office was and it seemed to be all senior-aged people. One woman appeared to be blind and she was extremely upset with her circumstances. Another lady was so fragile, and I believe she has cancer. A dozen patients wore eyepatches. The room was full of stories, yet everyone was hushed.

When my friendly seatmate was called for her appointment, I began to silently pray for each person waiting to see their doctor. It was the only thing I could do for them, but I also knew, prayer is what they needed more than anything else. The room was quiet and still with little movement. It was easy for me to focus on one person at a time. I believe we are called to pray for others even when we don't know their circumstances.

How do you feel about praying for others when you don't know them? Are you blessed for the opportunity?

Today's Joy: " . . . Pray for each other so that you may be healed . . ." —James 5:16 NIV

JANUARY 29
PRAY FOR OTHERS – PART TWO

My prayers are with you.

My friend, Linda, is an RN and she recently accepted a new position at the hospital. Linda spends her shift sitting in the rooms of patients on suicide watch.

She is not there to care for them; there are other nurses for that task. But Linda's assignment is to watch and make notes of what her patient is doing. It is a quiet and perhaps lonely job.

But, my dear friend says she spends her hours praying for the patient and the patient's family, and all of their needs. How fortunate is this patient to have such a Godly nurse on duty.

What are the opportunities that you have to pray for others in need? We know that prayer is the one thing that can bring perfect healing to everyone in need.

Today's Joy: Use this simple prayer to pray for healing.

> **Dear Father, I come to you now to ask your blessings and healing mercies on this person. In your name and for your glory, I pray. Amen.**

JANUARY 30
KEY TO HAPPINESS

My life is happy and fulfilled.

"There is no key to happiness. The door is always open."—Mother Teresa[11]

We've all read books and listened to videos that promise to provide us the vital keys to happiness. But Mother Teresa offers us a different perspective.

The door to happiness is always open. It's our choice every day to walk through that door and claim happiness as our status.

I spoke with a woman this week who told her story of living a life of disappointment, sadness and frustration. Yet today she coaches women on how to lift themselves up. When I asked her how she made the switch, her response was, "I just decided to be happy." Sometimes it's not quite that easy, but a positive mindset will definitely take you a long way towards living a happy life.

What is your mindset towards happiness? Do you choose happiness on a regular basis?

Today's Joy: Make a decision to choose happiness every day.

JANUARY 31
LIVING AN INSPIRED LIFE

I am on the right path.

An inspired life is limitless. It is filled with possibilities and overflowing with joy. You can open your mind and your heart to the potential. Then, you can purposely affirm to yourself, "I choose to live an inspired life full of joy."

Your life is busy, and you cannot wait for all the stars to line up before you embark on this journey. It's OK to start small, but I do encourage you to dream BIG!

What is your passion? What is your calling in life? Use these questions to find your purpose and shift your life to add inspiration and spark.

Empower yourself by knowing your vision. Then, follow your creative self to see where it takes you. Give yourself permission to go with the flow of the day.

Taking time to dream, explore, and discover. This is living an inspired life full of joy!

January Challenge Follow-Up: What is your 'Word of the Year' from the inspiration on January 1st? Are you already using your Word to move forward this year? Do you feel at least one step closer to discovering your own joy?

Today's Joy: "To live inspired is to be moved by the breath of the Divine."—Karletta Marie, Creator of Daily Inspired Life[12]

DISCOVER YOUR JOY

WORD OF THE YEAR

Finding Your Joy

FEBRUARY:
THE MONTH OF LOVE

Sharing Love, and Joy

FEBRUARY 1
SISTERLY LOVE

I cherish my sister.

Do you have a sister that you love and adore?

"A sister is someone more special than words. She's love mixed with friendship; the best things in life." –Douglas Pagels, *What is a Sister*[1]

This quote exactly says what I feel about my little sister. Sazzy is six years younger than me but in so many ways, we are closer than a lot of twins.

I believe it is our heart and soul connection that keeps us so close. If you have a sister, you probably understand what I am saying. Sometimes our close sisters are not sisters by blood. Instead, they are sisters by choice.

Whether your sisters are by blood or by choice doesn't really matter. Just having this connection with a sister means you always have a shoulder to lean on when times are tough, and you have someone to celebrate with when times are great.

February Challenge: February is the month of love. Make a point of letting people know you love them – your family, friends, and others in your circle.

Today's Joy: A sister is a best friend for life.

FEBRUARY 2
AN ANSWER TO PRAYER

*I take all of my cares
to God in prayer.*

Jeremiah 33:3 NIV says, "Call to me and I will answer you and tell you great and unsearchable things you do not know."

I want to break this verse in two parts for you. First, "Call to me and I will answer you." What a beautiful promise that is from our Lord. How many times have you wanted someone to talk with, someone to tell your troubles to, or someone to lean on? By praying to God, he has said he will answer you. That is a powerful verse full of promise.

The second part of the verse is also interesting to me. He will "tell you great and unsearchable things you do not know." Does that intrigue you? I want to know everything that God has to tell me.

Will you call on your God today and see what answers he is waiting to share with you?

Today's Joy: "In seasons of distress and grief, my soul has often found relief."—William Walford[2]

FEBRUARY 3
A BEAUTIFUL DAY

I cherish beautiful days.

It was a glorious day here in North Carolina. Today is February 3 and the temperature was 75°. Just three days ago, we had snow. And that's how our weather fluctuates.

The snowy day was lovely, and this sunny day was fabulous. Having a beautiful day, though, isn't always about the weather. Your sunny attitude will brighten your day and everyone around you.

As you look at each day, you will surely find something that is beautiful.

- A phone call from a friend
- Dandelions from a child
- A card in your mailbox
- A good report from the doctor
- The sun is shining

Even if your whole day wasn't beautiful, look for the beauty hiding in the pockets of your day. You might be surprised.

What did you find in your day that made you smile?

Today's Joy: "Give every day the chance to become the most beautiful day of your life." —Mark Twain[3]

FEBRUARY 4
LIVE IN AUTHENTICITY

I have the courage to be myself.

Windy Gail Boatright says,

> My daily goal in life is to live in authenticity.
>
> Authentic: (in existentialist philosophy) relating to or denoting an emotionally appropriate, significant, purposive, and responsible mode of human life.
>
> I am responsible for my feelings and emotions. I cannot expect anyone else to give me what I do not freely give myself. I cannot feel one way and act another. That is not being genuine and truthful.
>
> All I want is [to be] genuine and truthful in all my relationships. It hurts to care for people who don't care for me, but it happens. Every. Single. Day.
>
> I won't be hardened. I won't become insensitive. I don't need to attract any more souls like that in my life.[4]

What does living an authentic life mean to you? How would an authentic life look compared to the life you are living today?

Today's Joy: "I have to be what I need others to be." — Windy Gail Boatright*from same source

FEBRUARY 5
LOVE

I strive to convey love to everyone.

In 1 Corinthians 13:4-7 NIV it says,

> Love is patient, love is kind. It does not envy, it does not boast, it is not proud. It does not dishonor others, it is not self-seeking, it is not easily angered, it keeps no record of wrongs. Love does not delight in evil but rejoices with the truth. It always protects, always trusts, always hopes, always perseveres.

This is a favorite verse and one that often comes to mind when we think of a wedding. Actually, it applies to everyone and at all times.

We love different people in different ways. And some people are hard to love at all but keep this familiar verse close to your heart.

During this month of love, consider reaching out more and sharing your love.

Compare your words and actions to these verses about love. Are your words loving? Are your actions kind? Are you seeking the best for everyone?

Today's Joy: "And now these three remain: faith, hope and love. But the greatest of these is love." 1 Corinthians 13:13 NIV

FEBRUARY 6
START A JOY JAR

I have joyful memories.

Think back to a time when you needed a little happy boost. Here's a fun and quick tip.

Reading happy notes will always bring a smile to your face. You get bonus points if those notes trigger the memory of a pleasant event.

Grab a big jar or vase or bowl—something that is pretty to you or holds special meaning. Gather some colorful notepads and pens.

Then, start writing down good things that come your way, no matter how large or small. Write one thing on each note and place it in your Joy Jar. Be sure to put your jar in a prominent place so you'll be more likely to use it every day.

When your spirits are low, you can pull out a few reminders of all the amazing things in your life. Reading them is sure to lift your mood. Your notes will provide inspiration, confidence, and hope!

Reading them will also remind you of all you have to be grateful for and boost your gratitude-meter!

What are you grateful for today? Did you find a spark in your Joy Jar?

Today's Joy: Joyful memories fill my soul.

FEBRUARY 7
PATIENCE IS A VIRTUE

I am calm and patient.

Judy was waiting for Lola to arrive for their coffee date. When Lola arrived, and before she had an opportunity to explain her delay, Judy started, "Where were you? Why are you so late? I have other things to do instead of just waiting around on you."

Patience is one of the fruits of the spirit as presented in Galatians 5:22.

It is not just the ability to wait, but the ability to keep a good attitude while waiting.

True patience begins by finding the peace and patience within yourself. Sometimes, this is harder than being patient with other people. However, try to keep the faith that everything will come to you at the right moment.

Put your trust in God's perfect timing. In today's world, we want things to happen instantaneously. But sometimes, that is not what's best for you. Perhaps there's a lesson to be learned while you wait. Whatever the reason is for your wait, embrace it and just know, it will surely be worth the wait.

Are you a patient person? Or do you need to practice taking a deep breath and waiting until the time is right?

Today's Joy: "A person's wisdom yields patience; it is to one's glory to overlook an offense." Proverbs 19:11 NIV

FEBRUARY 8
ORGAN DONOR

I will share with another person.

Can you imagine the feeling of knowing your life literally depends on someone else?

Being an organ donor can be a difficult decision. Harder still, may be the decision to donate the organs of someone you love when their days to live are few.

I have several friends who were the recipients of an organ transplant. They've managed to live full and beautiful lives due to the generosity of someone else.

My own brother received a transplant, and it gave him another twelve years of life. Those happened to be the happiest years of his life.

Being an organ donor turns sorrow into hope. It is a way to literally give life to someone else. According to WebMD, there are far more people in need of a transplant than there are people willing to donate an organ.[5]

Save a life! Give a gift! Donate life!

Have you thought of becoming an organ donor? It's a decision to make now rather than later. It is the ultimate gift of love.

Today's Joy: Life is for sharing.

FEBRUARY 9
THE JOY OF MEMORIES

*I cherish the memory
of my loved one.*

Losing someone you love is one of the hardest facts of life. The grief and the empty hole in your heart can leave you feeling sad or even depressed for a long time.

When my Daddy passed away, no one could have told me how much it would hurt. My heart was broken.

Gradually, and over a period of time, you start to feel a bit better. It's a long road, for sure, and there are setbacks along the way.

But finally, you reach a place where you can find joy in the memories of your loved one. Take time to reminisce and cherish your memories always.

Today, I love telling stories about my Daddy. My sister and I regularly start sentences with, "Our Daddy would have said." It's always a lovely memory.

Which one of your loved ones have gone on to heavenly heights? What are your memories of that person? A scrapbook of photos and mementos is a great way to find joy in your precious memories.

Today's Joy: "The deeper that sorrow carves into your being, the more joy you can contain."— Khalil Gibran[6]

I am grateful for each day.

How many times have you wished for more hours in a day?

Time is constantly fleeting. It is one thing that, once it is past, you can never retrieve it. You can get more water, more trees, and more food. However, the one resource that you cannot replenish is time.

Stop for a moment and consider that this hour or this day, once it is gone, cannot be replaced. And time seems to go by quickly.

I remember the days the grandkids were born and now they're both in high school. We don't think much about the hours or the days as they pass. But when we stop and look back over the last year or the last five years, we wonder where the time went.

We must make good use of every moment of every day. This resource, called time, will not pass this way again.

What can you do to make each day count? What can you do so you won't have regrets about the time that slipped quietly away?

Today's Joy: "Time is your most precious gift because you only have a set amount of it. You can make more money, but you can't make more time." —Rick Warren[7]

I live an abundant life.

Were you ever in Girl Scouts? Did you learn their motto? Here are some mottos, or simply ideals, for everyday living.

> Give thanks every day.
> Always be kind.
> Hold onto hope.
> Believe in miracles.
> Replenish your soul.
> Trust your heart.
> Live in peace.
> And always choose joy!

These are my mottos/ideals for living an abundant life. Reading over them, it seems like a tall order for daily living. However, once you accomplish even one, all the others will fall into place.

Start by giving thanks. It's hard to believe something so simple can have such a monumental impact on your life. Get in the habit of starting your day with gratitude, then say a simple *thank you* for little things throughout the day, and always end your day with a gratitude list.

What are your thankful for today? Who are you grateful to have in your life?

Today's Joy: The more thankful you are, the more blessings you will receive.

One kind word can change someone's entire day.

Lola made a quick stop at the Post Office. As she was ready to enter, she noticed someone behind her and as always, Lola held the door for the woman. Nancy Naysayer snapped at Lola saying, "I'm not disabled. I can open the door for myself."

As you go about your day with a smile on your face and joy in your heart, you may encounter a similar joy stealer. They will be the ones who will tell you everything that is wrong with the world. Just be kind and polite and wish them a nice day. Try not to let their attitude or their bad day steal your own joy.

Joyce Meyer says, "Watch out for the joy stealers; gossip, criticism, complaining, fault finding and a negative judgmental attitude."[8]

As Joyce says, "joy stealers are not always people." Feeling overwhelmed and distracted, dealing with chaos and confusion, or regrets and guilt will also sap your joy.

Keep choosing joy every day, enjoy the journey, and allow joy to remain in your heart. How will you deal with any joy stealers that cross your path?

Today's Joy: I am abundantly joyful!

Repeat this affirmation to yourself several times during the day. Each time you say it, you'll go up the joy-meter another notch!

FEBRUARY 13
RED ROSES

Happy Valentine's Day, almost

Are flowers one of the first thoughts that come to your mind for Valentine's Day?

Red flowers, particularly roses, are commonly thought to convey feelings of true love. Try to imagine how many thousands of red roses are sold on Valentine's Day. My Mom managed a florist for many years, and I remember the flurry that ensued.

"The rose speaks of love silently in a language known only to the heart."[9] The author is unknown, but it is surely a beautiful thought. So many men, especially, send red roses to their sweetie to proclaim their forever love.

Besides the classic roses, there are other red flowers that are also quite elegant. Think of red tulips, that are gorgeous, and fun-loving red poppies.

So, on this special Day of Love, choose a red flower, not only for your "other half" but for anyone you love. Our challenge for February is tell someone you love them. Who can you share your love with today?

Today's Joy: "Nature always wears the colors of the spirit."—Ralph Waldo Emerson[10]

FEBRUARY 14
A VALENTINE MEDITATION

I am loved.

Who do you love on this special day that is set aside to proclaim love?

Valentine's Day is known as a day of love, especially for sweethearts. However, love is a universal language. Hopefully, you're in a space to also love your kids, your parents, your siblings, co-workers, neighbors, and virtually, all mankind.

There are different kinds of love and you will not feel the same way about everyone, but you can love everyone in some manner.

Try saying this verse to yourself with a prayerful mind:

> Create in me a pure heart, O God and renew a steadfast spirit within me. Psalm 51:10 NIV

This verse speaks to me, clears my heart, and fills me with enough love to share with everyone.

Take time to reach out to those who may be feeling lonely or in despair. Call a friend whom you haven't spoken to in a while. Share your love!

Wishing you a day filled with love and joy! Happy Valentine's Day!

Today's Joy: "Love is patient, love is kind. It does not envy, it does not boast, it is not proud." 1 Corinthians 13:4 NIV

FEBRUARY 15
SPREAD LOVE TODAY

*I spread love and joy
everywhere I go.*

Lola had a long list of errands to run and she wanted to be as efficient as possible. First stop was the dry cleaners where she held the door open for other customers. On to get gas and she smiled across the lanes at other drivers also filling their tanks. For the next few hours, Lola shared compliments, made small talk, and spread love at her every stop.

Spreading your love and kindness may be just what another person needs today. It is a simple act for you but it could make a major difference in another person's life. It costs you nothing to be kind and loving to everyone you meet.

As others feel your positive energy, your love will radiate happiness and peace to the people you encounter. You will also feel your own spirits being lifted. Your smile will become wider and your happiness will begin to soar.

Mother Teresa reminds us, "Spread love everywhere you go. Let no one ever come to you without leaving happier."[11]

How can you spread love today?

Today's Joy: Leave footprints of love and kindness along your path.

FEBRUARY 16
KEEP PADDLING

I know I can do it.

Nadia had trained long and hard to run her first marathon. The day arrived and she kept up her speed and her breathing the first few hours. But gradually, she began losing her momentum. Could she keep going? Could she finish the marathon?

Imagine your life as a stream or a river. When life gets tough, just keep paddling your canoe. It will always be easier for you to paddle downstream rather than upstream. However, the important thing to remember is to never give up—never stop paddling.

No matter what hurdle you are facing, believe you can master it. And keep going. By continuing along in a forward motion, you are proving to yourself that you are strong. You are confident. And you can accomplish this feat.

It's when you stop or even slow down to a crawl that you lose momentum. It's the momentum that motivates you to keep going.

It's probably not an easy endeavor, but when you complete it, you'll realize it was worth the work and the struggle that you endured.[12]

What struggles have you overcome by believing in yourself and continuing forward?

Today's Joy: Magic happens when you keep paddling.

FEBRUARY 17
IS MY SOUL ASLEEP

I choose to be awake and aware.

I got up this morning and went about my day. But now, it is nightfall, and I can barely remember anything that happened this day.

Could it be that my soul fell asleep? If I have no feelings or memories of the day, did my soul fall asleep? I must awaken; I must awaken my soul.

Carly Marie says, "I am grounded. My spirit is grounded deep in the earth. I am calm, strong, centered and peaceful. I am able to let go of fear and trust that I am eternally safe. I am worthy of all things beautiful."[13]

I know I can awaken my soul by enjoying the moments, being curious about the world around me and being aware of what is yet to be. My heart and soul easily align opening me up to enormous possibilities. I know the purpose of my life is to be joyful.

Are your heart and soul awake and aligned? Are you open to new possibilities?

Today's Joy: I am moving in the direction that my soul leads me.

FEBRUARY 18
TODAY IS A FRESH START

I am enough.

Today is a new day! It's a fresh start! The splendor of the sunrise reminds you that a new morning has arrived.

Try to put all the stress and troubles of yesterday behind you and move forward today with a new spirit. Clear out any leftover clutter from previous days and approach today with positive thoughts and expectations. Embrace the opportunities that a new day offers.

Now, take a deep breath and look in the mirror at yourself. Smile and tell yourself, "I am doing enough. All is well." Repeat this mantra several times during the day. Each time you say it, your smile will be a little bigger and your confidence will begin to soar.

Today is your opportunity to make a difference. Try to encourage someone, be kind, count your blessings and most of all, enjoy your day. Let today be the start of something new.

Do you feel the exhilaration of a fresh start today?

Today's Joy: "This is the day the LORD has made. We will rejoice and be glad in it." Psalm 118:24 NLT

FEBRUARY 19
SECRET INGREDIENT

I choose the secret of love.

Do you have a secret ingredient you use in your favorite recipes?

A wonderful chef friend made my family a delicious dinner. When I asked about the flavor of one particular dish, her response was, "The secret ingredient is love."

When your Mom and grandmother made certain dishes, didn't they always have a special flavor? Often you couldn't replicate the dish even with the exact recipe.

Our lives are also comprised of a secret ingredient. I believe it is also love, just like in our favorite recipes.

E. Corona wrote, "And the bravest of souls are those who choose love. Over and over."[14]

By living a life of love, our hearts are also full of gratitude, hope, and joy.

Will you choose the secret ingredient for your life? Will you choose love?

Today's Joy: "When you have nothing but love, you have everything."—John Kuypers[15]

FEBRUARY 20
FRIENDSHIP

I cherish my friendships.

Proverbs 27:9 NLT tells us, "The heartfelt counsel of a friend is as sweet as perfume and incense."

If you have a special, sweet friend in your life, you know this is true. I met my sweet friend, Molly, over forty years ago. She definitely refreshes my soul, and she does it on an almost daily basis.

Molly has been there through the down times and the great times. Her love and support have been by my side constantly. She is always there to listen to me and to pray for me.

Today is her birthday. Happy Birthday, my dear sweet Molly! I love you!

Do you have a constant supportive friend that is always there for you? If so, let them know how much they mean to you and your life.

Today's Joy: "Many people will walk in and out of your life, but only true friends will leave footprints in your heart." —Eleanor Roosevelt[16]

FEBRUARY 21
LOVING YOURSELF

I love myself just the way I am.

This morning, I learned of a 16-year-old girl who just passed away from suicide. It is such a heart-breaking story that stirs so many emotions. Many times, suicide is the result of not believing you are good enough.

Love is a powerful force. And it begins by loving yourself totally and unconditionally, but that's not always easy to do.

Write down any of the things that you don't like about yourself. Consider if anything on your list is something you might work on changing. Or perhaps, tell yourself it's ok and learn to accept it. No one is perfect and you don't need to be, look, or act like anyone else.

You are unique. Love yourself for it. Every day, tell yourself, *I am loved just the way I am. I am proud to be me. I am enough.*

What would happen if you loved yourself first and foremost?
Can you gently embrace your imperfections?
How would you feel if you focused on your positive traits?

Today's Joy: "To fall in love with yourself is the first secret to happiness."—Robert Morely[17]

I embrace new habits.

"I am happy, and I have friends, but I don't feel joyful," Mary confided in me. She wondered what she needed to do to bring more joy into her life.

Being happy comes from good circumstances in your life. But anything could happen and suddenly you're no longer happy.

Joy is a feeling deep within your heart and soul that is not disrupted by an unpleasant day. Joy will sustain you when you make it a habit.

Set aside a specified time when you can consciously focus on joy for twenty-one days. Every day, practice gratitude by writing down ten things you are thankful for. Recite affirmations several times during the day such as, *Today I choose joy.* Banish any negative thoughts that come up and replace them with positive ones.

Then, at the end of twenty-one days, check in with yourself to see if you feel more joyful. My guess is your response will be a resounding, "Absolutely!"

Today's Joy: There is joy in my soul today!

FEBRUARY 23
A STROKE OF LUCK

I will trust God's perfect timing.

"Remember that sometimes not getting what we want is a wonderful stroke of luck," said Dalai Lama.[18] More likely, though, is that God had a better plan.

I dated a guy for a number of years that I thought marrying him would make my life complete. He was smart, well-known and well-liked, and he adored me! Things didn't work out for us and we went our separate ways.

Within a couple of years, I started to realize all the reasons why we would not have made a good couple. And, I was thankful that life had separated our paths.

I believe things work out the way they are supposed to, and that most things happen for a reason. Sometimes, it is hard for us to see the silver lining when our lives take unexpected twists and turns.

But I know God is in control, and he has my best interest at heart.

Looking back, when did life take an unexpected turn in your life, but things turned out better than expected?

Today's Joy: "For I know the plans I have for you declares the Lord, plans to prosper you and not to harm you, plans to give you hope and a future." Jeremiah 29:11 NIV

FEBRUARY 24
WINDOW OF YOUR HEART

I see love.

Imagine a window to look inside of your heart. What would you see? Is it filled with love, kindness, happiness, and joy? Is there gratitude for all of your blessings?

When all this goodness fills your heart, it is reflected in your daily life. Your life is full of gratitude, helping others, and spreading love.

Take a few minutes to examine your heart. Ask God to help you remove any anger, guilt, or other negatives so that you will have a pure heart. Go forward and out into the world as if everyone you meet can look into the window of your heart.

Are you pleased with what others see when they look into the window of your heart? What can you do to improve the view?

Today's Joy: "Eyes are the windows to the soul. A smile is the mirror of the heart."—Janna Cachola[19]

GENEROSITY IS LOVE

The happiest people are the givers.

"The generous will themselves be blessed, for they share their food with the poor." Proverbs 22:9 NIV.

Even though this verse talks of sharing food, there is so much more that we can share with those in need. They may also need shelter, medical care, and even just someone to care.

There is a lady in our city that regularly combs the streets at night to serve our homeless. She goes out armed with food and drink, warm hats, gloves, and blankets, and a heart full of prayers. Her generosity is overflowing with love.

Serving others is not only helping those in need, but graciously sharing our bounty with others. We come away with a warm feeling in our heart.

Today, I encourage you to seek out the homeless shelters, the soup kitchens, and anywhere else you can donate or volunteer. Be generous with both your time and your dollars. Giving fills your life with joy!

Where can you share your generosity with others? Be sure to tell them you love them.

Today's Joy: "It is not how much we give but how much love we put into giving."—Mother Teresa[20]

FEBRUARY 26
MOON AND STARS

I patiently wait for nightfall.

As long as I remember, I've loved the moon. Even as a child, I remember saying a nursery rhyme about the moon. Today, I am still intrigued by the magic of the moon.

On a clear night when the moon is full, you can see outside as if streetlights were everywhere. What a brilliant sight it is! One of my favorite places to view the full moon is over the ocean. As the waves rush in, the beach is illuminated by the bright moon.

And along with the moon are the twinkling stars! There's more magic by wishing upon the first star you see at night. The darker the night, the more brilliant the light from the moon and the stars.

Embrace the night sky! Wish upon a star! And adore the handsome Mr. Moon!

Do you enjoy searching the night sky for magic? Does it bring back any childhood memories?

Today's Joy: "The moon is the reflection of your heart and the moonlight is the twinkle of your love." —Debasish Mridha[21]

FEBRUARY 27
LOVE AND MARRIAGE

I will love you always and forever.

What can you do to keep your marriage intact "until death do you part?" I am not a marriage counselor at all, but I've picked up a few tidbits along the way. And I'm a newlywed myself.

In my parent's generation, divorce was a rarity. But today, statistics show that almost half of the marriages in the US end in divorce.

- I believe you have to start the process of keeping your marriage together from the day you say, "I do" and not waiting until problems appear.
- Marriage is about love and respect, and it requires patience.
- Try to do something nice for your spouse every day. Ask them what you can do to help them have a good day.
- Respond to comments they make. It is an invitation to engage in a conversation with your spouse.
- End every day with, "I love you."

What are the special things you do for your spouse and your marriage?

Today's Joy: "A good marriage isn't something you find. It's something you make."—Gary L Thomas[22]

I will always love you.

My parents were married in 1948. Times were different and their love was grand.

Daddy would write my Mom a sweet note every day and leave it on the kitchen table. Short and sweet yet overflowing with true love. Mom kept all those love notes and now, I have them.

Mom was a marvelous cook and she loved to cook for Daddy. Daddy enjoyed every meal she made. They were married 46 years before death parted them.

Love stories like theirs are not what you hear about today. Times were slower; families spent lots of time together. They ate most meals together. Their air-conditioning was found outside under a shade tree. And they took care of each other until the end.

February Challenge Follow-Up: How did you do with the challenge on love? Were you able to share your own love with family, friends, and others?

Today's Joy: "The greatest thing you'll ever learn is just to love and be loved in return."—Nat King Cole[23]

BONUS DAY
JOY IS A UNIVERSAL LANGUAGE

I will share my joy.

When my son traveled to a foreign country with a group of fellow students, they decided that each person would learn a certain phrase in the foreign language. Between all of them, they would be able to ask or say anything important.

Even if you do not speak the same language as someone else, everyone understands and appreciates joy. It spans all ages and all cultures. Sometimes the language difference is simply a generational one. For instance, my granddaughter recently texted me, "ttyl." It sure sounded foreign to me.

A warm smile, a nod of your head, a helping hand; all these gestures tell the other person that you care. And, by reaching out in kindness, your joyful heart is obvious even when there is a language barrier

Speaking with love, living in grace and having a joyful heart is all you need no matter what the language you speak.

Leaning sign language to communicate with the deaf helps to build communication. How can you share with others who have a different language?

Today's Joy: Treat your joy like confetti and spread it all around you.

DISCOVER YOUR JOY

THE MONTH OF LOVE

Sharing Love and Joy

_____
_____
_____
_____
_____
_____
_____
_____
_____
_____
_____
_____
_____
_____
_____
_____
_____
_____
_____
_____
_____
_____
_____
_____

MARCH:
CHALLENGES, ENCOURAGEMENT, AND HOPE

*Spreading Hope
for Joy*

MARCH 1
A COMMON HOPE

I am hopeful and blessed.

This morning, I was reading the stories of several girlfriends who are battling breast cancer. A few days ago, I talked with the son of a girlfriend who has dementia. She no longer knows her family. On my heart are several friends who are struggling with various disabilities.

What ties all these friends together is their positive attitude and HOPE.

We know that hope is being positive under circumstances that are considered to be desperate. There is a proverb that says, "You reap what you sow,"[1] and these friends are experiencing miracles due to their hope. During the storms of our lives, we need to maintain our positive thoughts and turn our hope over to God through prayer.

Have you experienced desperate times where you relied on hope?

March Challenge: I challenge you to use hope to address your pain, issues, and problems this month. Is your hope in God's plan?

Today's Joy: "My hope is built on nothing less than Jesus' blood and righteousness."—Written by Edward Mote[2]

MARCH 2
ENCOURAGE OTHERS

*I spread joy by
encouraging others.*

Molly knew Fran was struggling with several things at home when she invited Fran to meet her for a cup of coffee. As Molly listened, Fran poured out her heart and tried to hold back tears. It was Molly's encouraging words that would carry Fran through the next week.

"How do you identify someone who needs encouragement? That person is breathing."—Truett Cathy[3]

What a true statement! Yes, we all need encouragement on a regular basis for everyday living.

Everyone you talk to is fighting their own struggles or battles. Offer each person a kind word, a smile, or a hug. Let people know that you care about them and are thankful to have them in your life.

Your spouse, kids, and family need encouragement, too. Sometimes, we tend to overlook those who are the closest to us.

Of course, the highest form of encouragement that you can offer to anyone is to pray with them and for them.

How can you encourage a friend or family member today?

Today's Joy: "Kindness is a language the deaf can hear and the blind can see."—Author Unknown[4]

MARCH 3
THE PAIN OF DIVORCE

*I am loved even as a
single woman.*

Lola was devastated. Her marriage was over, and she had no idea how to move forward. She couldn't even think straight enough to make a plan. She needed a friend, and she knew exactly who to call.

If you, or someone you are close to, has been through a divorce, you know how painful it can be. Even the most amicable divorce can leave you feeling sad, lost, empty, rejected, or like a failure. It is also hard on all the extended families involved and even your friends.

There is no simple solution. It's a long, difficult road and takes time to navigate. Hold steadfast to your faith. Forgive yourself and forgive your spouse. It really is the only way to move forward without bitterness.

Then it's time to dig deep to find your own personal joy. What will it take for you to move forward in joy? Where is your passion, your truth, your heart? There's no rush; take your time and be kind to yourself. You are stronger than you know.

Have you or someone you love been through a divorce? Were you able to get or give the encouragement needed to make the transition easier?

The message that got me through divorce: "Overcoming Fear with Faith" based on II Timothy 1:6-8. Twenty-two years later, this note still hangs on my mirror.

Today's Joy: Forgiveness frees your heart.

MARCH 4
YOUR HEALTHY BODY

I love and care for my body.

Marie has several health issues. She knows having a healthy body is important but it's so hard to find the time and motivation to do the exercises she can and to eat healthy.

The key to having a healthy body is having healthy habits. Marie is good about eating her veggies and drinking lots of water, but she loves her chocolate, too.

Our bodies function better when we get exercise. You don't have to run a marathon or be an Olympic swimmer. Just move your body some every day. Yoga is a great way to keep your body stretched.

Learn to meditate, even if it's only a few minutes a day. Meditation calms the chatter in your brain and can lower your stress level. Top it all with a good night's sleep, and your body will reward you for your efforts.

How do you take care of your body? Do you have an exercise routine or healthy recipes that keep you motivated?

Today's Joy: You'll notice results as you choose healthy habits.

MARCH 5
LET YOUR LIGHT SHINE

Be the light.

Fran, like many other women, is living a life of darkness. She is overwhelmed with her job, caring for her family, paying off debt and so much more.

Matthew 5:16 NIV tells us to, "…Let your light shine before others…." We can be the light for someone who can't see out because of their circumstances. We can offer a cheerful smile or encouraging word as we go through our day.

"This little light of mine, I'm gonna let it shine," is a popular gospel song. The lyrics talk about how the light comes from love and it shows what our light can do.[5]

Martin Luther King, Jr said, "Darkness cannot drive out darkness; only light can do that."[6]

What can you do today to encourage someone? How can you share your light? Let it shine for the whole world to see every day!

Today's Joy: "Your word is a lamp for my feet, a light on my path." Psalm 119:105 NIV

MARCH 6
HAVING IT ALL

I recognize my own potential.

Mary is a go-getter, and she wants to *have it all*. She wants to have a successful career, be a great wife and mom, and be involved with her church and community.

Can you really have it all? Like a lot of other questions, the answer depends. It depends on what *having it all* means to you.

There's always the possibility that you're not sure what it is that you want all of. I encourage you to take time to think, research and contemplate what it is you want from life.

Before it's too late, start the process of planning your life well lived. You can make a timeline with goals for each year. And one day, it will click. You'll realize how far you have come, and you'll be proud of all you've done.

What does "having it all" mean to you? Are there things you're willing to put on hold for now? How can you balance your responsibilities along with your dreams?

Today's Joy: "You can't go back and make a new start, but you can start right now and make a brand new ending."—James Sherman[7]

MARCH 7
FACE YOUR CHALLENGES

I have the courage to make this a great day.

Earlier this year, Ann faced the fact that her husband had been drinking and coming home late. After talking with a friend, she talked to her husband and she also joined AA. She was not going out without a fight. Ann's determination and courage were helping her to survive.

Courage isn't always loud and bold. Sometimes, it's your quiet self-saying, "I will not give up. I will try again tomorrow." However, having courage is what keeps you fighting the battle even when you don't have the strength.

Face your challenges with faith and gratitude. Be still. Pray for courage and strength. Isaiah 43:2 tells us, the Lord will carry you through the storm.

What kind of challenges have you faced recently in your own life? How did you find the courage to move forward?

Today's Joy: ". . .Be strong and courageous! Do not be afraid or discouraged. For the LORD your God is with you wherever you go." Joshua 1:9 NLT

MARCH 8
INTERNATIONAL WOMEN'S DAY

I am proud to be a woman.

Today, March 8th, is *International Women's Day*—a day to celebrate the accomplishments of all women. We are mothers, daughters, wives, sisters, and aunts to our families. However, we are also entrepreneurs, employers, and achievers who strive to make a difference in the world around us.

We have knowledge and have pursued opportunities to better ourselves and the lives of those we care about. We are nurturers and look after those in need. We are strong and we support other women in their causes.

Today, we celebrate women and their achievements—past, present and future!

What are your personal achievements that you are proud of? How have you assisted other women to celebrate their victories?

Today's Joy: "And one day, she discovered that she was fierce and strong and full of fire and that not even she could hold herself back, because her passion burned brighter than her fears."—Mark Anthony[8]

MARCH 9
FINDING MY WAY

I need to fly.

Windy Gail Boatright writes:

> It was never my plan to be a 50-year-old undergraduate student. Nor did I plan to suffer two failed marriages, to go through bankruptcy—not once, but twice—or to have a mass exodus from the business I dedicated more than two decades of my life to. It took me being stripped of everything to realize how truly miserable I was—how unfulfilled. I walked away from what I thought was my life to reinvent myself. I found I was never really living my life. Packaged tightly in a little box of misery, I was what everyone else needed and wanted me to be, all the while losing myself…more and more.
>
> Success, I believe, is all about rolling with the punches and remaining open. You must be open to see opportunities and embrace them. By allowing the potential for growth, I haven't reinvented myself, I have rediscovered myself, and every day provides a chance to get to know myself a little better. After a lifetime of feeling like a taut rubber band, ready to snap at any moment, I have embraced being highly elastic and wrapping myself around new opportunities. It is serving me well. I am finding my way to a peaceful life of fulfillment and purpose.[9]

Does the first paragraph sound like something you could have said about your own life? Can you try some of the advice from the second paragraph to enhance your life?

Today's Joy: "We never realize how much we believe what we believe just because what others around us believe, and their beliefs have been either silently instilled or pounded into our brains."—Windy Gail Boatright[*from same source]

I see the beauty in every child.

Ro Tamayo is a pediatric nurse who works with special needs children in their homes. She's there to work with these precious ones from a medical aspect, but she also tries to be a support system for the parents, as well.

Ro wrote to me saying,

> What I learn from my patients is that they just want to be loved. Most people might look at them as being different. It's easy for some to judge, stare or come up with these conclusions just because they may look or act differently. They're actually smart. These kids are very bright and intelligent, and they only know love. They don't know hate. Others who don't understand can sometimes take life for granted. I find that these kids are fighters and they're resilient, and the parents and families have a level of compassion, understanding, patience and love that is beyond measurable.[10]

Do you accept children just the way they are without judgment? How can you help to teach other children to be kind to special needs kids?

Today's Joy: "Embrace the unique way your child is blooming even if it's not in the garden you imagined."—Jenn Soehnlin[11]

MARCH 11
HOPE IN THE LORD

*I place my hope and
trust in the Lord.*

"But those who hope in the Lord will renew their strength. They will soar on wings like eagles; they will run and not grow weary; they will walk and not be faint." Isaiah 40:31 NIV.

The Bible gives us many opportunities to hope in the Lord, and God's promises give us the strength we need to face life's struggles. He watches over us just like a shepherd watches his sheep.

Romans 15:13 NIV offers us another view of hope. "May the God of hope fill you with all joy and peace as you trust in him, so that you may overflow with hope by the power of the Holy Spirit."

Let your prayer today be for strength and courage to place all your hope and trust in the Lord. You will be greatly rewarded.

What are your hopes that you are willing to turn over to the Lord today?

Today's Joy: "Be strong and take heart, all you who hope in the Lord." Psalm 31:24 NIV

MARCH 12
ENCOURAGE OTHERS

I will lift up those in need.

Molly is a deacon at her church. She spends many hours visiting the sick in hospitals, taking elderly members to doctor appointments, and delivering food to those in need. She definitely has a servant's heart and uses her strengths to encourage others in need.

"Anxiety weighs down the heart, but a kind word cheers it up." Proverbs 12:25 NIV

Caring and sharing, compassion and kindness are all about generosity. Use your time and talents to encourage those who are having a bad day or have a serious situation in their lives.

Give this person a call, send them a kind note, stop by to visit, take a meal. There are many ways to offer encouragement, and always pray for them.

Encouraging others also lifts our own spirits. We get a warm feeling just knowing our kindness gave someone else a ray of hope.

Who can you offer encouragement to today? What can you do or say to lift their spirits?

Today's Joy: "Therefore encourage one another and build each other up, just as in fact you are doing." 1 Thessalonians 5:11 NIV

MARCH 13
INVITE HAPPINESS INTO YOUR LIFE

I start my day by being happy.

My secret to a great day is to start with a morning routine. It's a game changer for happiness and success. A morning routine fuels you with focus, creativity and positivity. It's like getting a powerful vitamin shot that boosts you to last all day on a personal high note.

Also, affirmations are a fabulous addition to your morning routine.

Below are a few of my favorite affirmations. Say them aloud every morning.

> I am strong in mind, body and spirit.
> Today, I choose to be happy.
> I am positive and optimistic.
> My opportunities are endless.
> I believe in myself and my abilities.
> I am grateful for all that I have.

The secret of your success is found in your morning routine. And the success will invite happiness into your life.

Do you have a schedule in the mornings that gets you up, going, and motivated?

What could you add or change to bring more happiness to your regimen?

Today's Joy: My favorite affirmation—I am enough. All is well.

MARCH 14
UNLOCK YOUR COURAGE

I am strong and face my fears.

I have numerous girlfriends who have dealt with breast cancer. Even though they may be afraid in their hearts, they get up, put on a smile, and face the treatment for their disease. You may not really know your true strengths until you are tested.

Your strength and courage shine through as you deal with these everyday issues like health concerns, being a caregiver, or working a high stress job. However, the essence of real courage is due to your inner strength.

You strengthen your courage with every experience where you stop to look fear in the face. Courage gives us the opportunity to conquer our fears and make our hopes and dreams become a reality.

What fear are you facing or even avoiding facing? What dreams are being held back by fear?

Today's Joy: May the Lord grant you courage to face your battles.

MARCH 15
THERE WILL BE DAYS

I will follow my God.

There will be days in your life that are not all sunny and cheery. Even though I write a lot about happiness and joy, I am familiar with days of darkness.

Seven years ago, I was buried in work at the office during the busiest week of the year when I received a panicked phone call. My older brother had just passed away.

Within a day or so, a co-worker gave me a card with a verse that had gotten her through some tough times. Even though it is based on Isaiah 41:13, she wrote it in her own words, and it is those words that meant so much to me.

"That's right, because I, your God, have a firm grip on you and I'm not letting go. I'm telling you don't panic, I'm right here to help you."

I clung to that card and that promise. When times are tough and you feel like you're falling apart, read Isaiah 41:13. There you will find hope.

What are some words that have given you hope during tough times?

Today's Joy: "On Christ, the solid rock, I stand; All other ground is sinking sand." Taken from "My hope is built on nothing less."— Edward Mote.[12]

MARCH 16
SUCCESS THROUGH THE
EYES OF A CHILD

*I can see the world from
a different perspective.*

Wendy Bassett shares this story:

> My youngest son is a wonderful boy, but he has some
> challenges. He is on the autism spectrum, has anxiety,
> hand tremors, and other things that he refuses to let
> hold him back. My sweet boy has never felt entirely
> comfortable in the water.
>
> One day while swimming in the lake this summer, he
> made the sweeping declaration that he would be climbing
> up on the dock and jumping off. I watched him climb up
> the ladder, and I watched him standing there, just feeling
> the motion of the waves moving the dock. I watched his
> eyes scan the lake and look to his dad for reassurance.
> He kept saying how things looked so different from that
> perspective. He stood there for 30 minutes trying to get
> up the gumption to jump into the water. We encouraged
> him, but he ended up nervously climbing back down
> the ladder.
>
> I thought he would express feelings of disappointment
> because he didn't do what he set out to do. He did not
> feel embarrassed for not jumping. He was so excited that
> he tried something new and outside his comfort zone.
> He was blown away by how it felt to stand on the dock.
> He went on and on about how awesome it was, and how
> he can't wait to do it again.
>
> This adventure at the lake was an absolute success! He set
> out to jump off the dock and couldn't quite do it. But

what he found out was that he was brave and saw the world from a different view. Story submitted by Wendy Bassett at WednesdayMorningWhispers.com

Today's Joy: "That is not failure; that is success through the eyes of a child."—Wendy Bassett[13]

MARCH 17
JOY IS MY STRENGTH

I will sing joyful praises to my Lord.

When you're facing tough times, where do you look for strength to get you through?

I am reminded of the verse found at Nehemiah 8:10 NIV, "...The joy of the Lord is your strength."

This verse is both calming and uplifting. It tells us that the Lord was full of joy and that His joy is our strength. That is a powerful promise to us in our daily walk—even through tough times and struggles.

I encourage you to inscribe this verse upon your heart. It is encouragement for you to draw upon anytime you need strength.

The joy of the Lord is your strength.

Where do you turn when you need strength to face tough times?

Today's Joy: "The strongest people are not those who show strength in front of the world but those who fight and win battles that others do not know anything about."—Jonathan Harnisch[14]

MARCH 18
SHARE YOUR BOUNTY

I will share whatever I have with those in need.

What do you have to share in times of need?

Our area is in crisis mode. The worldwide illness has hit, and food and supplies are in extremely short supply. Schools are closed and children who are used to receiving free lunches are now stranded without their meals. Grocery store shelves are almost empty. Offices are closed and unemployment is high.

However, it is amazing that so many individuals and businesses have stepped up to help those in need. Both restaurants and individuals have offered to feed the children. Others are offering to share their groceries and supplies to whoever needs them. This is the true spirit of being kind and generous.

What will you share with someone else today? Love… kindness… wisdom… material goods. Bless others with some of the blessings you have received.

Today's Joy: "Sometimes miracles are just good people with kind hearts."—Author Unknown[15]

I am strong enough to navigate my journey.

Personally, I have learned that as long as I am on this earth, there will be valleys to pass through. But I also know that peaks always follow those valleys just like a rainbow follows a storm.

When things in life get you down, you have to hold on tight to the thought that this will pass. Keep your faith and talk to God. He already knows what's going on, but he wants to hear from you. As hard as it is, learn to be patient and wait for God's perfect timing.

As you climb out of the valley, be thankful for the protection. Your journey through the peaks will fill you with love and laughter. Enjoy the blissful days and be sure to share your joy.

Stay humble and kind. This is a time to reinforce your strengths and confidence.

Remember, in difficult times to trust God, and in good times to praise God.

What is your anchor as you navigate the valleys? Referring to the challenge question for March, do you put your hope in God's plan? How do you praise God when you're on the peaks?

Today's Joy: Even though our lives are a journey of peaks and valleys, God is always our constant companion.

I laugh because it is good for my soul.

Jacki was born with a physical disability yet has led an amazing life. She's a few years younger than I am and I've known her family most of my life.

Jacki lived alone most of her adult life and had a successful career. However, her disability caused her to often stumble, drop things, or spill her food. She soon learned that she could diffuse any tension or harsh comments with humor.

She laughs at herself when things happen. It puts everyone at ease around her. But we all are humbled by Jacki's laughter and good nature. She brings a smile to everyone's face and leaves joy in their heart.

Today, Jacki is battling cancer and with her strong Christian faith, she would appreciate your prayers. Even with her diagnosis, her trademark smiles and laughter fill her room.

Are you able to laugh at yourself when things go awry? How can you offer support to those who may need your concern?

Today's Joy: "Humor is mankind's greatest blessing." —Mark Twain[16]

MARCH 21
BEACON OF HOPE

I allow hope to sustain me.

I was totally lost in my own life. It was if God had refused every prayer I had. My dear friend, Patty, suggested we meet for lunch and I was glad to see her. I laid out all my issues and we prayed together. It was a year later when Patty said to me, "I remember the day you thought God had forgotten you and look at how happy you are now." Patty restored my hope and God took care of me.

As you find hope in the darkness, learn to become a beacon of hope for others who are struggling in their own darkness. Let your light shine to show others the way through their hardships. Your comfort and smile may be what pulls another person from the depths of their depression.

Hope heals the hurt deep inside of you. It allows you to see the light even on the darkest days. Believe there are better days ahead. Just follow your beacon of hope.

How can you be a beacon of hope for someone else? What can you say or do to be a comfort to them?

Today's Joy: "For what are we without hope in our hearts."—Bruce Springsteen[17]

MARCH 22
OVERCOMING CHALLENGES

I will lend a hand to help and an ear to listen.

I write a lot about joy and happiness and the good things in life. Today, I posted online that I was looking for stories of overcoming challenges for my blog—and my inbox blew up!

I have spent all day reading about everyday people who have overcome huge obstacles in their lives. They not only lived to share their stories, but they also have a positive attitude. They managed to overcome their personal challenges and continue forward.

This is often difficult to do. It requires a strong support system of family and friends. Many people will need therapy and it's always ok to ask for assistance.

The lesson is not everyone is in a place to choose joy. Be kind; be compassionate; be empathetic. You will be rewarded for the love you shared.

What challenges have you personally overcome? How can you share your story to help others?

Today's Joy: "Believe in yourself and all that you are. Know that there is something inside you that is greater than any obstacles."—Christian D Larson[18]

MARCH 23
ODE TO JOY

I sing praises every day.

You may be familiar with Beethoven's *Ode to Joy*.[19] It is a beautiful symphony that I had performed at my wedding.

Many years ago, I started a journal and titled it *Ode to Joy*. This journal is full of gratitude lists, quotes from books I've read, personal musings on a sundry of topics, affirmations, and so much more.

Writing in a journal is therapeutic. Actually, writing out words brings your focus specifically to those words. Even though there are some heartfelt discouraging moments in my journal, I try to always find a way to loop around and see the goodness or the blessing in the situation. Most of my journaling, though, is peaceful and joyful. Reading back over pages that were written some years ago brings new inspiration to my soul today.

What do you write about in your journal? It could be good things or unpleasant ones. It's your journal. Pour your heart out.

Today's Joy: If you're not journaling now, I encourage you to start. And, if you are already journaling, I encourage you to always look for the positive.

MARCH 24
RISE ABOVE

I will keep calm.

Fran knows there will be challenges; there will be obstacles; there will be hurdles in her life. She has already experienced so much of it. But she is stronger than all of it. She has decided to rise above all the chaos.

You, also, have the power and strength within yourself to rise above whatever is currently seeking to bring you down.

It may not be easy and some of your friends may question you. However, taking the high road and doing the right thing will always be the best thing to do.

Be confident in who you are. Be kind and gracious to the lives you touch. Let God fight your battles for you.

By leaving behind all the issues, the battles and the negativity, you will rise to a place in your life that is peaceful and calm.

What challenges do you need to rise above? How can you clear these obstacles?

Today's Joy: As you rise above the darkness, you will see the light.

MARCH 25
BE AN ENCOURAGER

*I will take time to
encourage others.*

How do you help a friend who is walking through stressful times?

Perhaps the best thing you can do is to offer them encouragement. Kind or supportive words are often what someone needs.

By being an encourager, you are giving them the courage, right from the middle of the word encouragement. This courage from you to someone else will boost them to new heights. It will provide them the strength to continue to fight their battle.

Today, talk to someone who needs encouragement. Your kindness will inspire both of you.

What words of love and encouragement can you share with a friend today?

Today's Joy: "Rise up; this matter is in your hands. We will support you, so take courage and do it." Ezra 10:4 NIV

COMPASSION CARES

I treat myself with compassion.

How does it make you feel when someone shows compassion towards you? Perhaps they sat with you during a tough time or maybe they shared their experience with you.

Compassion is letting go of yourself and completely feeling the emotions of another person. Just offering a word of encouragement to someone could make the difference for them between giving up or pressing on.

But we must start with self-compassion. Be kind to yourself and acknowledge your self-worth. Start a routine of self-care activities for yourself. As your compassion for yourself increases, you'll be more inclined to share compassion with others.

Are you kind and considerate to yourself? Today, how can you use your compassion to encourage someone else?

Today's Joy: "Love and compassion are necessities, not luxuries. Without them, humanity cannot survive."— Dalai Lama[20]

MARCH 27
THE PATH FROM PAIN TO JOY

*I move closer towards
happiness every day.*

I often struggle with back pain. After two operations and countless procedures, there are days I just want to stay in bed.

We all have days when pain takes over our life. It might be physical pain, or it might be emotional pain. However, it's there, and it's a struggle to get through the day.

I find that the best way to move forward is one baby step at a time. Find one thought that feels a tiny bit better than you are today and repeat that one thought to yourself over and over. As soon as you have accepted that thought, find a new one that again feels a little better. Repeat it to yourself and continue the process as you gradually build yourself up higher and higher.[21]

Here is an example of thoughts about your pain as you gradually feel better about it.

> I am confident my pain will feel better soon.
> I am grateful for doctors and medicine to help me cope with the pain.
> I will try to move around today to help my body adjust.
> I am thankful for the many prayers that help my healing process.

What new thought can you use today to move yourself closer to joy? Can you improve on that thought again tomorrow?

Today's Joy: Positive thoughts help you move away from pain.

MARCH 28
TIME OF CRISIS

I will pray without ceasing.

How do you react in a time of crises? Do you panic? Are you afraid?

Right now, our world is dealing with a crisis due to a world-wide illness. People are worried about the economy and are hoarding groceries and supplies.

I am reminded of the verse in 1 Thessalonians 5:17 KJV that tells us to, "Pray without ceasing."

Tough times require powerful prayers. Now is the time to be on your knees to praise God for all that he has done in your life. Then open your heart and tell him about your crisis. He hears your prayers and will always be by your side.

Throughout your day, continue to thank God even in short sentences. You will feel his presence and his blessings.

What crisis are you currently facing? Have you taken it to God in prayer?

Today's Joy: "Don't be afraid for I am with you. Don't be discouraged for I am your God. I will strengthen you and help you. I will hold you up with my victorious right hand." Isaiah 41:10 NLT

MARCH 29
OVERCOMING OBSTACLES

I will focus on turning my obstacle into a positive opportunity.

Have you ever travelled on a long road which zigzags its way up a mountain? Was the view from the top breathtakingly beautiful?

Well, life is like that winding road. It's full of obstacles and challenges that you must overcome in order to continue on this path of life.

Maybe you've suffered the loss of a loved one through death or divorce. Perhaps you lost your college scholarship, or your business collapsed.

Whatever your obstacle, it takes courage to tackle and overcome it. Some people focus on the trauma of the burden and overlook the positives of dealing with the challenge. Once you overcome your obstacle, things can be good again.[22]

What obstacles have you had to overcome in the past? How did you turn them into opportunities?

Today's Joy: "Sometimes adversity is what you need to face in order to become successful." —Zig Ziglar[23]

MARCH 30
RESET, READJUST, RESTART, REFOCUS

I'm a woman on a mission!

Did you make resolutions or goals at the beginning of the year? They are often discarded because things went awry. Instead of forgoing your goals this year, try to readjust or refocus your aim. Tweaking as you go along helps to narrow your plan to precisely what you are aiming for.

Reset, readjust, restart, or refocus as many times as needed. Just because you did something one way in the past does not mean it has to always be that way forever. As time moves forward, we learn and we grow. Through this process, we are in a position to make new decisions that require us to change the system.

Brainstorming, mind-mapping, and thinking outside the box are great methods to help you *reset, readjust, restart or refocus* on your goals!

As we wrap up the first 90 days of the year, it's a good time to evaluate your plans. How can you readjust your goals today? What can you change to make the rest of the year fabulous?

Today's Joy: "Where focus goes, energy follows." —Tony Robbins[24]

MARCH 31
HOPE ANCHORS YOUR SOUL

My ray of light is hope.

My Daddy lay in a hospital bed and his days to live were few. When Mom looked at him, she commented that his foot looked out of line. The doctors encouraged her to not focus on his foot because his life was almost over.

When I confided this statement to a girlfriend, she remarked that this was Mom's rope that was tied to her anchor of hope. Amidst the darkness surrounding the family, Mom chose to see a ray of light called hope.

Whatever your personal challenge may be, hope wraps you in a tender embrace when you are caught in the harsh storms of life.

Hope gives you the strength and courage to go forward. It makes your current problems less difficult to bear.

Christopher Reeve reminds us, "Once you choose hope, anything is possible."[25]

March Challenge Follow-Up: Where there is pain and difficulty, there is also hope. Did you find a way to lean on hope this month? Does hope bring you another step closer to feeling joyful?

Today's Joy: Never lose hope. Miracles happen every day.

DISCOVER YOUR JOY

CHALLENGES, ENCOURAGEMENT, & HOPE

Spreading Hope for Joy

APRIL:
SPRING, EASTER, AND NEW BEGINNINGS

Seeking New Beginnings and Joy

APRIL 1
WELCOME SPRING

*I know that all is well
with my soul.*

As nature crawls out of hibernation, and we transition from winter into spring, we witness the promise of new beginnings. Take a deep breath, smile, and feel the connection to the earth.

Spring seems to breathe new life into us. It cleanses our spirit and our hearts. There is the urge to make plans and start new projects. We feel a renewal of our own energies emerging. This is the time when we are called to flourish just like the blossoms on the cherry trees. There is an assurance that abundant blessings are coming.

Pure joy swells in my soul as I meander outside and ponder the beauty. It is healing to realize that spring comes after a long cold winter. Our lives are the same way. Joy comes onto our path after hard struggles and setbacks. Beauty is ahead if we patiently wait. There is the promise that new beginnings are on the way, and all is well with my soul.

April Challenge: How can you celebrate Spring, the season of new beginnings? Do you have new projects planned now that the weather is warmer?

Today's Joy: Let your joy burst forth like nature in the spring.

APRIL 2
A LIFE OF PURPOSE

My life is an adventure.

Lola and Jaclyn both felt called to write a book. Even though they are 50 years apart in age, writing bound their hearts together. Lola spent her days writing inspirational stories and Jaclyn was writing a dystopian novel. Even though they were different topics, the two women thrived in their time together. They were living their lives on purpose.

Joy comes from living your life with passion and purpose. Take a look at the things you are passionate about in your life. Your passions will lead you to your purpose.

There is a reason for you to be in the world today. By honoring what you feel called to accomplish, you can make a difference in people's lives.

By living your life purpose, you will thrive; you will share compassion; you will be intentional and mindful with your activities. These are all great things that our world needs more of.

Believe in yourself that you're meant to live a life that is oozing with passion and purpose. Appreciate where you've been, where you are now and where you're headed. Enjoy the journey!

What is your passion in life? Has it led you to discover your purpose?

Today's Joy: "The purpose of life is not to be happy. It is to be useful, to be honorable, to be compassionate, to have it make some difference that you have lived and lived well."—Ralph Waldo Emerson[1]

APRIL 3
ENJOY THE SUNSHINE

*I enjoy spending time
soaking up the sunshine.*

The sunshine warms my soul. Today, I am sitting on my porch; the trees and grass are green, the flowers are blooming, and there are white puffy clouds floating in the sky.

We have a neighborhood cat who floats between four houses; I am honored today as he sits here with me. Tiger found a warm spot to spend his winter and now he's enjoying the warm weather and sunshine as much as I am.

After being inside this morning, coming out here is truly a refreshing feeling. The sun seems to wash away all my cares and lifts my spirits. The air feels quiet even though there's a light breeze. I can hear birds chirping back and forth.

Daily walks outside, (for me, it's more of a stroll) are good for all of us. Fresh air warms us and engaging with nature helps soothe our soul and restores our inner peace. Also, try to stay close to people who feel like sunshine to you.

What's your favorite part of being outside in the warm weather?

Today's Joy: "I take brisk walks in the sunshine to invigorate my body and soul."—Louise Hay[2]

APRIL 4
FRIENDSHIP QUOTES

I cherish my friends.

Our friends are some of the strongest relationships in our lives. They are the ones who weep with us in the evening and sing praises with us in the morning. Molly has been by my side for over 40 years and she has always been there for me day or night. We regularly spend an hour or more hashing over things in both of our lives. Everything between us remain 100% confidential at all times.

"There is nothing on the earth more to be prized than true friendship."—Thomas Aquinas[3]

"Friends are like flowers. They fill the world with beauty." —Celeste Barnard[4]

"Friends are like the sun in spring, shining the light that makes our souls bloom."—Mary Davis[5]

"Friendship isn't a big thing; it's a million little things." — Author Unknown[6]

Angels often appear to us in the form of friends.

Joy is having forever friends who will always be by your side.

Good friends are good for your soul.

I cherish my close friends Sazzy, Molly, and Patty. Who are your dear friends? Do you take time to enjoy them and let them know you care?

Today's Joy: "A friend loves at all times." Proverbs 17:17 NIV

APRIL 5
YOUR NEXT BEST STEP

I focus on my goals.

What is your "next best step?" I credit my publisher, Author Academy Elite, with this question.[7] It was the theme of their recent author's conference.

I believe the question has many parts. What's my next best step for today? This week? This year? Or for my life? In order to accomplish my lifelong dream, what can I do next to be the most productive?

It's making a plan to achieve your goals. You could literally ask yourself this question at every junction in your day… week… month… year… life. Every answer would fill you with immense clarity.

After this question was posed to me, I did spend quite a bit of time pondering my response. I realized following through with completing this book and sending it out to the world was my "next best step." This decision gave me the clarity I needed to keep writing, working, and researching.[7]

What is your "next best step?" What can you do next to catapult your life in the direction you want to go?

Today's Joy: "Sometimes the smallest step in the right direction ends up being the biggest step of your life. Tiptoe if you must but take a step." —Naeem Callaway[8]

APRIL 6
YOUR SUPERPOWER

I live my truth.

Leslie recently asked me, "What is your superpower?" In the past, I've always felt like JOY was my superpower. But, after a lot of writing this year, my response was, "Joyful Inspiration." For many years, I was seeking joy for myself. Writing made me realize that I need to share the joy I have and inspire others to seek their own joy.

I believe *hope* and *gratitude* are your source for JOY. Believing that joy is possible in your life and supporting that hope with daily gratitude, you can experience overwhelming joy.

Even though, I've been a joy-fanatic for the last ten years, I am now trying to consciously share my own joy to inspire others.

We all have something that is unique about ourselves. This special characteristic is a steppingstone to build upon. It could lead you to be the best possible version of yourself.

So now, what is your own superpower? What is the one thing you do for yourself or others that makes you stand out from the crowd?

How can you use your superpower to show kindness or encourage others?

Today's Joy: Your superpower is just being yourself.

APRIL 7
OUT WITH THE CLUTTER

I clear my path.

Sazzy is selling her home and moving to be close to her son and his family. I've had several calls from her wanting to know if I would like various things that she will no longer have room for. She's cleaning out her clutter. There's a chair that came down through the family but it's extremely uncomfortable. There's a box of old family photos that we don't know who any of the people are. So much 'stuff' and we cannot keep everything.

What kind of clutter do you have in your life? It could be piles of *stuff* in the corner of a room. Or it could be mental clutter with an assortment of things, projects and to-do lists all rambling around in your brain.

No matter what your clutter looks like, it's holding you back from being the best you can be. Clutter tends to dull your focus in life. It's hard to see clearly when 'stuff' is in the way.

So, make an effort to clean out the treasures heaped along the path. Sort out the mind-boggling thoughts and lists.

Now you're fresh and clean. There's room for your heart and soul to expand. You're in a place to plant new seeds of goodness. Your life is now a light that will shine attracting all good things to you and your world.

What kind of clutter do you need to dispose of? Make a plan today to toss out all of life's clutter.

Today's Joy: "You can't reach for anything new if your hands are still full of yesterday's junk." — Louise Smith[9]

APRIL 8
CHANGE IS POSSIBLE

I am ready for a new beginning.

In the last three years, I have purchased a coastal cottage, sold my business, retired and remarried. It's been a lot of change and adjustments along with frayed nerves. Even though I've made these huge changes in my life, every one of them has brought me immense joy. I cherish every moment at the coast. Retirement has provided me time to spend with my new husband. Change is not only possible; lots of times, it's great!

Do you have something about you or in your life that you would like to change? Perhaps you would like to start a business or change the type of work you do. Maybe you want to run for an official office or go back to school. There are so many things in each of our lives that you could potentially want to change.

Fear often holds you back: fear of failure, fear of ridicule, and fear of losing money. To make the change you want, you must take a deep breath, face the fear, and step outside of your comfort zone.

Change is good but most people prefer to remain status quo. It's easier to stay with the known information then to drift into the waters of the unknown. However, there are huge opportunities waiting once you acknowledge that you are ready for change and you are willing to take that first step.

What changes would you like to make in your life? Make an outline today of how you can implement the changes. I encourage you to explore the possibilities

Today's Joy: "And suddenly you know: It's time to start something new and trust the magic of beginnings."—Meister Eckhart[10]

APRIL 9
SPECIAL MOMENTS

I will always remember.

Lola and Molly were sharing coffee and muffins during their weekly morning time. They reminisced over stories of the good times they've shared during the last 40 years. As Molly picked up her cup of coffee, she turned to Lola and asked, "Do you remember the week that I kept Auby for you so you could go on a cruise?" Lola definitely remembered and she recounted how the first thing Molly did was to wash her young son's shoes. What a wonderful kindness. Many years had passed since then, but the two women continued to spend special moments together regularly.

Life is our collection of moments. Every moment matters and they all add up. What does your collections of moments look like? Do you collect happy moments or not-so-happy moments? Your outlook on life is comprised of the moments you have stored in your brain and in your heart. Holding the happy moments in your heart will make you a happier person.

The things that you hold in your memories are the sum of your moments collected. It's never too late to replace your collection of moments with new and inspired memories of good days with family and close friends. Hold tight to these happy memories—they are the treasures of your heart.

What are the special moments that you have stored in your heart? You may want to write some of them in your journal.

Today's Joy: "Little moments become tomorrow's precious memories."— Sarah Langner[11]

APRIL 10
I AM

I am allowing joy to guide me.

Whenever you start a sentence with, *I am,* you create more of whatever follows in the rest of your sentence. "I am" are truly two of the most powerful words in the universe. These words give you the ability to attract into your life anything that you want more of.

However, the word of caution is it will also attract negativity into your life. Continual statements like *I am not smart enough. I am too tired. I am overweight* will attract more of all the things you do not want.

So, make a list of all the things that are important to you right now. Start each statement with *I am.* Hang the list where you will see it often and repeat your statements several times each day. See how these powerful words can bring you an uplifting day!

> I am good enough.
> I am worthy of my heart's desires.
> I am happy and enjoying my life.
> I am abundantly blessed.
> I am trusting the journey.
> I am at the right place at the right time.

What are your *I am* statements that you can repeat daily?

Today's Joy: Personally, I like to close my *I am* statements with, *all is well.*

APRIL 11
THE EASTER LILY

I will honor Easter in my heart.

Spring is here and it is time to celebrate Easter—both spring and Easter signify rebirth and new beginnings.

The Easter lily is the most common flower symbolizing the hope of Easter. It captures the sacred spirit of the holiday with its white trumpet shaped bloom. The lily is a joyful symbol of peace and purity. The flowers are stunning and meaningful to Christians during the Easter season.

I have two lilies that were given to me a few years ago. One was from my husband the year before we married. The other plant was from my Mom's neighbor. I planted both of them out in my garden and continue to enjoy them as they bloom each year. They bring sweet memories to mind and their flowers fill my heart with joy.

May you find the renewal of love, hope and faith on this Easter. I'm sending warm wishes to you and those you love on this blessed day.

Do you enjoy having a lily at Easter? Do you plant it outside?

Today's Joy: "The great gift of Easter is hope. . . "—Basil C Hume[12]

APRIL 12
THE EASTER NO ONE
WENT TO CHURCH

I can worship my God from anywhere.

It's Easter Sunday, April 12 and all the churches across the globe are closed due to a worldwide illness. In order to protect ourselves from the deadly virus, we are instructed not to gather together in groups.

Fortunately, technology has provided a way for ministers to livestream their glorious messages to their flocks. It seems odd and unfamiliar to "go to church" in whatever you happen to be wearing, maybe even your pajamas. Simply click your phone and you're at church.

The Easter service I am attending today is being held in Israel—virtually, of course.

Today, the churches are all empty but so is the tomb—Hallelujah!

Attending church virtually is not the same as being there in person. But it is better than not being able to attend at all. Are you attending a virtual church for Easter?

On April 1, we talked about celebrating Spring, the season of new beginnings. Easter is a perfect day to celebrate new beginnings. What are you doing today?

Today's Joy: "He is not here; he has risen, just as he said . . ." Matthew 28:6 NIV

APRIL 13
YOUR JOURNEY IS UNIQUE

I am the master of my fate.

A few weeks ago, I met a young couple with two small children and began to chat with them. They told me of their journey to leave Seattle and move to North Carolina. They had no jobs waiting for them and they left all their family behind in Seattle. They were following their dream. He said, "I am not the type of person who would undertake such an adventure." Would you be willing to leave everything you know and move 3,000 miles away to explore a new territory?

The path you follow, the road you travel, the journey you choose is unique to you.

Listen to your heart and soul. No one else is you and no one else has ever traveled the journey that you are on.

Embrace any detours you encounter along your way. The detours are there for a reason – to slow you down or to teach you something. This is your journey. You are independent and capable. You are strong enough to accomplish great things. Be bold and adventurous. Enjoy your unique journey!

People will try to influence the choices you make. Are you living someone else's dream? Or are you living your own life?

Today's Joy: "Do not follow where the path may lead. Go instead where there is no path and leave a trail."—Ralph Waldo Emerson[13]

APRIL 14
FAITH IN BRIDGES

I let love lead me across the bridges in life.

My sister and I, both, do not like to cross bridges. It is our fear of being suspended in air and nowhere to go but down. We have to rely on faith that the company that built the bridge did all the right things and it has been kept up to standards over the years.

What about our bridges in life? Building bridges is a way to connect with other people and other places. We leave where we are and cross over to a new experience.

Like many Scouts, my grandson participated in a Bridge Ceremony when he passed over from Cub Scouts to Boy Scouts. They leave the old behind and start anew.

We, also, can build bridges of understanding that reach out to others with patience, love, and even forgiveness. We can even cross these bridges to leave the old behind and start anew for ourselves.

Did you have bridges in your life that were difficult to cross? How did you handle the circumstances?

Today's Joy: "We build too many walls and not enough bridges."—Isaac Newton[14]

GIVE IT TIME

I will seek inspiration.

Lola was frustrated and generally feeling down. She was glad today was her usual coffee date with Molly. Her good friend seemed to always have the right words to get her back on track and in a good mood again. Today was no exception. Molly bounded in with a huge smile on her face and embraced Lola with a giant bear hug. "Hey girl! Where is your smile today? That frown is going to drag you down," quipped Molly. Lola's mood instantly brightened.

You've tried expressing gratitude, writing in a journal, and taking a walk outside. Nothing seems to be pulling you out of this slump you have been in for days.

Take a few moments to acknowledge this as a time when you need to rest your mind, your body, and your soul. We are so busy and often, overwhelmed, that we do not always take the necessary time to power down and just rest.

Give it time. There may be a reason for you to feel out of sorts. Perhaps you're feeling the emotions of a loved one. Maybe you need the time to sort things out. When the time is right, you'll know it's time to get going again.

Embrace the moment. You are enough just as you are. Whether you're flying high or creeping along, it's all ok just the way it is. Enjoy the ride.

How do you gain a new perspective when you've been out of sorts for a few days?

Today's Joy: "Only do what your heart tells you." —Princess Diana[15]

APRIL 16
ATTITUDE IS EVERYTHING

I choose positive thoughts.

I listened to Sharon, a passionate gal, on an online presentation today. She talked fast, flung her arms around, and wrestled in her seat. She knew her stuff and she knew that she knew it. Her attitude was, "I've got this figured out and if you want to know how to do it, hang with me."

Having a positive attitude can literally change your life. Your attitude, whether it's positive or negative, determines your direction for today, tomorrow, and into the future.

A positive attitude will open doors for you that you would never know existed before. People will feed off your positivity. They will want to work with you no matter whether it's planting flowers or arranging a mega corporate merger.

Think about the people you know. Do you avoid the ones with a negative attitude? Do you gravitate to the ones that are positive?

Are you a positive person or do you need an attitude adjustment? No judgment; just a question.

Today's Joy: "You can often change your circumstances by changing your attitude."—Eleanor Roosevelt[16]

APRIL 17
TODAY IS THE BEST DAY

This is a phenomenal day!

"Write it on your heart that every day is the best day in the year." —Ralph Waldo Emerson[17]

Just imagine how great life would be if you did tell yourself every day that it is the best day of the year! Every day you would be filled with awe. You would be excited to get up every morning just knowing how great your day will be.

On those days that are great, you are going to be ecstatic knowing that tomorrow is going to be the best day. I am smiling as I type this because I know every day is going to be better than the day before.

Having a positive mindset is the key to having a *best* day every day. Every morning, tell yourself, "Today is the best day this year." As you already know, my typical reminder is a sticky note on the mirror that refreshes my memory.

How would you feel if every day was the best day of your life? How can you make that happen?

Today's Joy: Make every day your best day.

APRIL 18
MEDITATIONS

I meditate on honor and trust.

I enjoy spending time on my porch overlooking the gardens. All I can hear is the breeze blowing and the birds singing. This is my favorite place for my morning meditation.

Meditations are thoughts you concentrate on or reflections in your mind. They can bring about a heightened sense of spiritual awareness. The best way to focus on your meditation is to be in a quiet place—even better is a place where you feel inspired.

The verse below reminds you that both your words and your meditations should be pleasing to your Lord. As you sit quietly and ponder your day, your family, your life, be sure that your thoughts are worthy of placing them before God. Weed out all of the negativity and replace with positivity.

And, as you go about your day, let your words pass the same test. Are they worthy of placing them before God?

Today's Joy: "May these words of my mouth and this meditation of my heart be pleasing in your sight, LORD, my Rock and my Redeemer." Psalm 19:14 NIV

I listen for clarity.

My husband is one of many people who loves to listen to music. As soon as my grandchildren Jaclyn and Clem jump in my car, their first words are, "Can you please turn on the music?" Everywhere, music lovers know the words to all the songs they grew up with.

Have you noticed that I do not write about music? I was born with a slight hearing loss and clarity is more the issue than volume. It has always been difficult for me to understand the words to songs.

Sometimes our lives also lack clarity. We are so busy and have long to-do lists and our calendar is a disaster. You may need clarity if the purpose of your day is to just get through it.

Clarity is removing unnecessary thoughts and focusing on the tasks you have deemed to be most important. Know what you want to achieve and make a plan. This clarity will transport you to success.

Where could you use some clarity in your life? What might you accomplish if you focused on the one important task or project?

Today's Joy: "Clarity is not found through intellect but experienced in stillness." —Buddha Groove[18]

APRIL 20
JOY IN THE GARDEN

I am blessed with a beautiful life.

One of my favorite places to spend time is outside in my flower gardens. It is there, amongst the birds, the flowers, the grass, and the trees that I find supreme joy!

I love the aroma of the wisteria and gardenias and the fresh cut grass. There is magnificent beauty in the tall palms, the hosta, the ferns and the multitude of containers brimming with colorful flowers.

In the garden, life is quiet and still. You can hear the gentle breeze, the birds singing and the water trickling over the rocks in the pond.

Take a stroll along the garden path. Sit a spell on a bench and watch the clouds. Breathe in the fresh air and just enjoy the nature that surrounds you.

Try to find a few moments to spend outside today. It is in the garden where you will find joy at its utmost beauty! Planting a garden warms your heart and soothes your soul.

Do you enjoy spending time in gardens? Where do you find your joy?

Today's Joy: "To plant a garden is to believe in tomorrow."—Audrey Hepburn[19]

APRIL 21
EVERY DAY IS A SECOND CHANCE.

I embrace the new day.

I love the quote by Ralph Waldo Emerson, "Finish each day and be done with it."[20]

What happened yesterday is now gone. That chapter is closed. But the good news is today is a new day. Today you have another opportunity to be all that you choose to be. It is your second chance at accomplishing your goals and moving forward with your plans. And whatever doesn't happen today, you will have another chance as dawn breaks again tomorrow.

Do not use your second chance to procrastinate. But instead, see it as an opportunity to be a better version of who you were yesterday. View it as a clean slate where you write all the things you missed on previous days. Enjoy this day to the fullest.

First thing each morning, take a few moments to consider your day. What are the possibilities? What are the opportunities? What will you do with these possibilities and opportunities?

Are you continuing to celebrate this season of new beginnings? Have you started any spring projects?

Today's Joy: "With the new day comes new strength and new thoughts."—Eleanor Roosevelt[21]

APRIL 22
START WHERE YOU ARE

I will cherish this new day.

We all have a few regrets for the days that we let slip by the things we didn't do, the things we did do. (Sigh.) I wanted to take my son to Tweetsie Railroad when he was a child, but we never made it there. I vowed to take his family with young children, but now they are teenagers, and we still haven't made it up the mountain to ride the train. It is a fun time for all as cowboys and Indians jump on the train. Now they've added an amusement park and picnic area. However, I have to let it go.

You cannot go back to the beginning. You cannot even go back a few moments in time. Your only option is to start where you are and go forward from here.

Do not waste your moments thinking or wondering about any "What ifs" from the past. Forgive yourself for any wrong doings and learn the lessons from the past. Don't dwell on what is already done. It is now history. Whatever you would have done differently can carry forward to your new experiences in this whirlwind called life.

Cherish this new day. It is a new opportunity to go forward. The time is now for you to start again with all the past lessons you have learned. Live in the present and savor the moments. Most of all, be grateful for the new day with all the glory it brings.

I hope I've made up for not going to Tweetsie Railroad with other special memories. What lessons have you learned from the past? How will you make today count?

Today's Joy: It's a fresh new day and a fresh new start.

APRIL 23
LIFE IN A BUBBLE

I expand my horizons.

I spent 30 years working long hours in a windowless office. It was my bubble. I craved the outdoors and sunshine. Once I retired, the one thing I wanted was to be outside in the sunshine.

If you're also living life in a bubble, it's time to get out—time to explore everything that life has to offer you.

Living the same day over and over again will stagnate your mind, heart and soul. Freshen your inspiration by taking a walk outside, spend time browsing a bookstore, or take a different route to work or school. Every time you expose yourself to a different environment, you're expanding your bubble and your world.

Our planet Earth is rapidly changing, and you can only stay tuned in by staying engaged. The old saying about learning something new every day still applies even if you are no longer in school.

New things, new places, even new tastes and smells will heighten your life. And your bubble becomes bigger and bigger.

What will you do to expand your horizons today? This week?

Today's Joy: "You don't always need a plan. Sometimes you just need to breathe, trust, let go and see what happens."—Mandy Hale[22]

APRIL 24
HAVE A GOD DAY

I am full of life.

Today, schools in my area teach kids to spell by using phonics. Students are encouraged to write words by sounding them out.

My granddaughter always loved playing school and she always wrote lots of notes when she was staying with me. One particular day while she visited my office, she made me a nametag that read, *Mis Mimi,* and I was honored.

But she also left a note on my desk that said, "Have a *god day.*" I do believe she meant the note to say, "Have a *good day.*" But phonics kicked in and *god day* came out.

She has no idea how much this note has meant to me. It continues to hang on my refrigerator and is a daily reminder for me to have a *God Day!*

Do you have a note or message from someone that meant a lot to you? Who can you leave a note for today to inspire them?

Today's Joy: A God day is always a good day!

APRIL 25
AN EMPTINESS INSIDE

I honor my calling.

"We're homesick for a place we've never been." —Kary Oberbrunner in *Your Secret Name*[23]

Do you sometimes feel empty inside? It feels like there's no life in your heart or your soul. There's a longing for something that you cannot explain.

It's time to examine your life closely. Think of everything you want to accomplish in life. Then for each statement, ask yourself, *Why*? You can actually keep asking, *Why*? for each answer you give. This is a way to reach deep in your heart and soul. Continue digging until you find your true passion. You will know it by the way you feel when you find it.

Don't rush the process and enjoy the adventure!

After a long career in the accounting and tax business, I found my calling as an author. What would fill the emptiness in your heart and soul? Can you take steps to follow your passion?

Today's Joy: "My mission in life is not merely to survive, but to thrive; and to do so with some passion, some compassion, some humor, and some style."—Maya Angelou[24]

I enjoy my quiet time.

I have a shelf full of books with meditations and devotions—in addition to the one you have in your hands. I love to choose one and simply open the book to any page. I feel that is the message I am meant to hear for that day. I usually note the day I read that page and add any other notes that come to mind as I read the passage.

Starting your day with a few quiet moments is sure to set the tone of your day to be fabulous!

Take time to read a few short meditations or devotionals. Study several verses of scripture. List ten things you are grateful for today. Take a walk outside to notice nature. And always, say a prayer.

These few quiet moments before you launch into the whirlwind of your day will calm your mind and bring peace to your heart. You will feel centered and grounded which will allow you to tackle the day with confidence.

Do you have a quiet time in the morning before the day rolls into full force? What are your favorite ways to spend that time?

Today's Joy: "My heart has heard you say, "Come and talk with me." And my heart responds, 'LORD, I am coming.'" Psalm 27:8 NLT

APRIL 27
SMILE AND SAY, "HELLO."

I will greet everyone with a smile.

Our office was working long days over several months. My co-worker decided to walk through our parking lot and over to a restaurant in the next building. She returned with a look of amazement and said, "You'll never believe what just happened."

Of course, I was curious and asked her to share with me. She replied, "I saw several people in the parking lot and they all spoke to me." I was still unsure of where this was going and asked her what these people said to her. "Hello." "Have a good day." "It's a nice day, isn't it?"

I kept waiting for an issue, but her point was that people were nice to her and she just wasn't used to it. Where she grew up, people rarely spoke to someone they did not know.

I'm a southern gal. We say hello to everyone, strike up a conversation and bless your heart.

Do you smile at people you pass? Do you chat with people while standing in line? Who will you say, *Hello* to today? Your kind greeting might just make someone's day.

Today's Joy: "I've learned that people will forget what you said; people will forget what you did, but people will never forget how you made them feel." — Maya Angelou[25]

APRIL 28
JUST A CARD

*I love to surprise friends
with a greeting.*

When I read online that the father of a girlfriend had passed away, I mailed her a card with a short note. Another week or so later, she thanked me for the card and said it was the only card she had received. It gave her something to hold onto, so she knew someone understood her pain.

In today's electronic age, so many people have given up sending actual paper cards. Instead, they are commenting on various forms of social media or perhaps sending an email. But there is still something heart-warming about opening your mailbox to find a card tucked inside.

Someone took the time to write you a note and send it your way. Electronic media just cannot replace the emotions that accompany a note or a card.

How do you feel when you receive a card from someone? Do you send cards or notes to those you care about? Go buy some postage stamps today. I hope you're going to need them.

Today's Joy: Let someone know you care; mail them a card today.

APRIL 29
RENEW YOURSELF

I will relax and rejuvenate.

I know it's easy somedays to stay in a rut. It's familiar and you just go through the motions. I feel the same way sometimes.

But, don't let yourself get caught up in just getting through one day to repeat it again the next day. Your mind and your life will become stagnant and lose meaning. Instead, make an effort to regularly renew yourself and re-energize your life.

Reading is a great activity to expand your horizons. Pick out a few books that are outside the genre you normally read. I recently read a true story about abuse. That opened a whole new world to me that I knew nothing about.

I try to see a live show at one of the local theatres a couple of times a year. Not only is it entertaining, but it allows my imagination to wander.

One of my favorites is to make new friends. As you learn about someone else's life, it opens up all kinds of possibilities that you didn't even know about.

How can you discover ways to renew your mind, your heart, and your soul?

Today's Joy: I am allowed to make changes in my life.

APRIL 30
NEW BEGINNINGS

I embrace each new day.

Many times, during my career in business, I dreamed of writing a book. I felt like it would never happen, and that dream sat in the top of my closet for years and more years. When my high school sweetheart came back into my life, I felt my new beginning taking shape. It was my time to leave the business world and take the creative delve.

Is there something hiding in your heart that you want to start over and take in a different direction? New beginnings are not just for New Year's resolutions.

Sometimes you just need to close the story and begin a new chapter. It's always ok to start over. You've grown in ways you never considered. You've learned a lot along the way. Now it's time to follow your heart and embrace the path.

Each morning brings a fresh start to a new day. Use this day with a new focus and a new mindset. Plan something totally out-of-the-box and go where it leads you.

As you set new intentions, you'll see exciting new results.

April Challenge Follow-Up: How did you celebrate April, a season of new beginnings? Did you start new projects or revamp old ones? Record your thoughts and ideas on the next page provided for your 'Notes.'

Today's Joy: New beginnings open up an amazing world to you!

DISCOVER YOUR JOY

SPRING, EASTER, & NEW BEGINNINGS

Seeking New Beginnings and Joy

_____
_____
_____
_____
_____
_____
_____
_____
_____
_____
_____
_____
_____
_____
_____
_____
_____
_____
_____
_____
_____
_____
_____
_____
_____

MAY:
MOTHER'S DAY AND
FAMILIES

Loving Joyful Families

MAY 1
LOVING OTHERS

I love my family.

How many times have you heard of families who do not get along or do not talk to each other? I spoke with a friend yesterday who said she had not seen her sister in many years. I'm learning this is not as uncommon as I once believed. These stories make me sad for the entire family.

God has commanded us to love others if we truly love him. 1 John 4:21 NIV tells us, "And he has given us this command: Anyone who loves God must also love their brother and sister."

The phrase "brother and sister" is not just a literal phrase. Brother and sister, for this purpose, includes all of our family, friends and neighbors. If you love God, you'll understand this, and you'll want to share your love.

There are some people that are not necessarily easy to love, but you can always be polite to them. Your kindness may eventually change their heart.

The love in your heart for God will fill your heart with love for others.

May Challenge: Spend extra time with your family this month. What events can you attend together? Do you share meals with your family?

Today's Joy: "In the same way, let your light shine before others, that they may see your good deeds and glorify your Father in heaven." Matthew 5:16 NIV

MAY 2
PRAY FOR YOUR FAMILY

I am thankful for my loved ones.

My friend, Daisy, shared her unique prayer plan with me and I want to pass it along to you.

She prays for each of her family members on a specific day every week. For example: Monday is Joey. Tuesday is Sally and so on. Sundays are a time she prays for the entire family.

This plan allows you to focus on one specific person's needs each day. It is a time to pray that the person chooses Godly friends, that they will treat others with kindness and set a good example. You can pray that this person will use their God given talents in a way to honor their Lord.

I encourage you to go to God each day in prayer. Praise his name, thank him for your blessings, and ask for his hand in your life. Set up your prayer schedule today. Post it in a prominent place to remind you to remember your family's needs.

Do you have a specific plan to pray for those you care about? Do you think it could be a good idea?

Today's Joy: I am a prayer warrior for my family.

MAY 3
FRESH FRUITS AND VEGETABLES

I nourish my body.

Today I bought a bushel of corn. After shucking it and cutting it off the cob, I bagged it for the freezer. Now I'm ready for our big family meals on Thanksgiving and Christmas. I just know how sweet and tasty the corn will be, and how much my family will enjoy it. This is one of the many traditions that I learned and maintained from my mother-in-law.

As a child, I remember picking blackberries with my Daddy in a field near our home. Then my Mom would make us a blackberry pie for dinner. It was always a special treat.

We always had big Sunday dinners when I was growing up. Everyone gathered around for a meal that always began with a blessing and ended with family visiting together through the afternoon hours. Today, everyone is so busy that family dinners are not as common as in the past. I miss those big meals together that nourished not only our body but also filled us with a sense of family, love, and connection.

Do you make time for family and loved ones? Take time to slow down and have a conversation about the daily events. Rest, relax and enjoy the connection.

Today's Joy: "Companionship is the secret ingredient."—Our State Magazine[1]

"People who love to eat are always the best people."—Julia Child[2]

MAY 4
NOURISH AND FLOURISH

*I nourish the relationships
in my life.*

The things that we nourish in our lives are the things that will flourish. Families, relationships, and homes are some of the things we all want to see flourish. Love, honor, truth, and respect are the nourishments we need to provide.

We also must nourish our own minds and bodies in order that we can flourish and bloom. It's easy to get caught up in taking care of everyone else and forget to nourish our own selves.

Becca Lee says, "The purpose of this glorious life is not simply to endure it, but to soar, stumble, and flourish as you learn to fall in love with existence. We were born to live, my dear, not to merely exist."[3]

What are the things or people that you want to see flourish? How do you nourish them?

Today's Joy: "May your life be like a wildflower, growing freely in the beauty and the joy of each day." —Native American Proverb[4]

MAY 5
BLENDED FAMILIES

We are blended and blessed.

Do you know someone who divorced and then remarried? Perhaps they had their own children or married someone who had children. It's not easy to merge families and make a new one.

In today's world, it is quite common for families to have *steps, halves, yours or mine.* But blended families are woven together by choice, not these titles. They are strengthened by love.

My friend, Melissa, married a man with two young children. With years of previous experience as a nanny, she was a great fit for a mom. She was also a creative person who planned awesome parties and made crafts a fun project for any day. The biological mom put up a struggle towards Melissa. However, Melissa knew the kids just wanted to be heard and loved no matter what part of the family they were with on a given day.

My friend's advice to other stepparents is don't overstep your boundaries, respect special events for the child, and set up a communication system. She also added that you and your spouse must present a unified front.

Are you part of a blended family? Do you know someone in a blended family? How can you be supportive in the situation?

Today's Joy: Every family has a story. Our family is defined by love, not blood.

"Blood doesn't make someone family. Love is what makes a family."—Nichole Chase[5]

MAY 6
A CHAT WITH JACLYN

I am capable of great things.

Armed with a list of 50 questions and an hour of spare time, I decided to have a chat with my 13-year-old-granddaughter. Like any teenager, she was not inspired by some of the questions. But I did get thoughtful and solid answers to many of the questions.

There was an obvious thread of thought I noticed in her responses. She is creative and loves to read and write. Writing makes her happy and she hopes to become a famous published author someday. If she could make one rule that everyone in the world had to follow, it would be that we all have to read a book once a month and join a book club. She has great ambitions!

The one answer I loved the most was to the question, "What is the most important decision you will ever make?" Jaclyn's response was "Choosing my college major."

Amongst games and fun, we will find that the younger generation is surely capable of great things. Support them every chance you have.

Do you make time to have thoughtful chats with your children and grandchildren? It's time well spent, and you are sure to learn something interesting.

Today's Joy: Life also has a lesson for us. Listen and learn.

MAY 7
ROAD TRIPS

*Happiness is planning a
trip with the one you love.*

Road trips are an opportunity to inspire us and enhance our
lives. We broaden our horizons by traveling. It is enlight-
ening to see the landscapes in different places, the cultures
and traditions in other cities, and how people live and work.

However, my favorite part of a road trip is the memories
I've made with my traveling buddies. The summer that my
family drove 2000 miles to see the Grand Canyon was my
favorite. My Daddy loved to camp, so our days were planned
around available campgrounds along the way.

Leaving from North Carolina, we took a southern route across
the Mississippi River and through Texas. Our return trip led
us on an adventure to outrun a tornado in Oklahoma. But
it was two weeks of being totally immersed in family that
stays in my heart many years later.

In recent years, my sister and I have traveled to a new location
together every year. Through these trips, we've learned a lot,
we've shared a lot of experience, and we've bonded.

Road trips are an opportunity to inspire us and enhance our
lives. We broaden our horizons by traveling. It is enlight-
ening to see the landscapes in different places, the cultures
and traditions in other cities, and how people live and work.

Do you enjoy traveling with your family and friends? What
is your most memorable trip? Where are you going next?

**Today's Joy: Sometimes all you need are good friends and
a great map.**

MAY 8
THIS DAY BELONGS TO YOU

It's a good day to be happy.

For over 30 years, I owned a business, and I was at the office most days by 7:00 am. Now that I am officially retired, I find it more difficult to get up early and kick start my day full of energy.

Every day is an opportunity for you to choose how to live it. Daily, you make thousands of decisions about everything from food and family to work and home. What choices will you make? How will your decisions affect your day?

You can choose what your day will look like. Even though you may have work or other commitments, you can choose to be happy and positive. You can be kind to the people you see today. You can offer everyone a smile.

Abundant enthusiasm and confidence will carry you far today and every day. It's a good day to be happy.

What is your motivation for the day? Will you honor yourself and take some time for self-care? You deserve the best.

Today's Joy: Today is your day! Choose happiness.

MAY 9
A KEY IN HIS POCKET

I am kind to everyone I meet.

Our mother had passed away on April 29th. My sister and I were still grieving when it was time for us to recognize Mother's Day. I decided an easy lunch on my patio would suffice for all of the family.

My ten-year-old nephew showed up with a clenched fist and announced he had something for me. As his fingers gently opened, there was a tiny little key. I asked him what the key opened, and his response was, with a big grin, "My heart."

Nothing else could have comforted my heart the way he did with this tiny key on this special Mother's Day. It really is the little things in life that mean so much.

Think about the little things that people have done for you. How can you pay them forward and brighten someone else's day? Little things like a phone call, a card, or a cup of coffee will mean the world to a friend or family member.

Today's Joy: Things that cost nothing have the most value. Thoughtful acts of kindness mean more than anything you can purchase for someone.

MAY 10
HONOR OUR MOTHERS

A mother is love.

This Mother's Day, I want to honor and celebrate all the mothers in our lives, not just our own mothers.

For me, I choose to **honor** the memory of my mother, both of my grandmothers, my former mother-in-law, my aunt, and especially my great-aunt. All of these women hold a special place in my heart for what they contributed to my life. From them, I learned spirituality, responsibility, grace, and love. I also have a huge file of yummy Southern recipes that were passed down to me from these special women.

Today, I **celebrate** my sister, my daughter-in-law, and my niece for all the things they continue to teach me and for their love and kindness.

Also, I have so many girlfriends, most of whom are mothers, and I **cherish** their love and support through the years.

All of these women have encouraged and inspired me in their own unique ways. I am eternally grateful for their wisdom and grace.

Who are the mothers that you will honor for Mother's Day? Let them know they are loved and appreciated.

Today's verse: "Do everything in love." 1 Corinthians 16:14 NIV

MAY 11
A MEMORY GARDEN

Meet me in the garden.

My Mom loved her yard and she tended to it regularly. When Mom claimed her seat in heaven and I sold her house, I knew I needed some memories of her yard.

I dug up some lilies and nandinas and spirea, and many other plants. Then, I created a small garden in the back corner of my property where I could watch over Mother's plants. Her neighbor gave her an Easter lily just before her death and that also became a piece of the garden.

With a chair where I could sit, I could contemplate all the cares of the world. For Mother's Day, my son added an arbor as an official entrance to the garden. Now my Memory Garden felt complete.

If you do not have plants from a loved one, you could choose plants that they loved or plants that remind you of your loved one. Even if you only have room for a few pots on the patio, plants are a wonderful reminder of someone special!

What will you plant in your own Memory Garden?

Today's Joy: "In the garden of memory, in the palace of dreams… that is where you and I shall meet." —The Hatter in Alice Through the Looking Glass by Lewis Caroll[6]

MAY 12
THE ULTIMATE GIFT

I will always love my children.

It was 1969 and times were different. Jill was 17 years old, a high school senior, single and pregnant. Her family sent her away, over a thousand miles, and she ended up living with her attorney until her baby was born.

She was all alone and a long way from home when she gave birth to a healthy baby boy. Two days later, her attorney picked her up at the hospital door and took her to the airport to return home. Back at home, the door was closed, and the baby was never to be mentioned. Jill thought of her son often especially on his birthday and holidays. She wondered if he was safe and happy.

Her ultimate gift came almost 44 years later when her son's wife called asking for medical info. There was hesitation to be sure it wasn't a prank call, then some shock and finally, lots of rejoicing. One of the first things Jill wanted to know was her son's name. His adoptive parents had named him Russell. Jill's family already had nine people named Russell. She believed that it was a sign that what is meant to be, will be.

Russell's grandmother had kept a scrapbook of his life to present to his birth mother if she was ever located. It was titled, *"You were chosen to be with us."* So many years later, Jill has a record of her son's life.

Today's Joy: Jill's message: "Things happen for a reason. Her son was not an accident. It was divine intervention."[7]

MAY 13
A MIRACLE BABY

I promise to love you.

Ruth had a little girl and now she hoped for a baby boy. She and her husband pursued adoption realizing it was potentially a long wait.

Some months later, a baby boy was born but he was on medical hold because he had crossed eyes. Ruth kept asking about the baby and finally, the agency agreed to go back and check on him.

The next phone call from the agency was an answer to prayer. There were no explanations, but this baby did not have crossed eyes. His medical hold was released and just before turning three months old, he was placed in the arms of Ruth and her husband.

Ruth does not know the circumstances surrounding his crossed eyes, but she truly believes God wanted her and her husband to have this baby, now named William, who is about to turn fifty years old.

Miracle babies are definitely a Mother's Day blessing. Do you or someone you know have a miracle baby?

Today's Joy: Ruth doesn't know how God did it, but once again, he performed a miracle!

MAY 14
HOSPITALITY

I share my blessings.

Have you ever been invited to someone's home and were treated with outstanding hospitality? If so, how did it make you feel? They likely went out of their way to make you feel comfortable and perhaps, to even serve you a delicious meal.

Romans 12:13 NIV instructs us to, "Share with the Lord's people who are in need. Practice hospitality." You may not have realized that the Bible tells us to practice hospitality. And as you see in this verse, it goes on to say to share with others who are in need. There are numerous opportunities to practice hospitality every day to those in need.

However, I also believe that service begins at home. Take time to entertain, share a meal, and spend time with your family and loved ones. They need to know that they are dear to you.

Invite someone to your home and share your hospitality. Cook a dinner or plan a game night with the family. Every day, share your hospitality with those around you.

How can you show hospitality to someone today?

Today's Joy: "Do not forget to show hospitality to strangers, for by so doing some people have shown hospitality to angels without knowing it." Hebrews 13:2 NIV

MAY 15
THE BENEFITS OF A SMILE

I will wear my smile today.

How do you feel when someone you're passing smiles at you? It usually makes us feel welcome to speak to them. Your happy face signifies gratitude, acceptance, and reassurance and it will brighten the day for those around you. Since smiling is contagious, you'll soon have everyone you meet beaming.

Smiling is a simple act that relieves stress and improves your mood. You just feel happier when you're wearing your smiley face.

Your smile also lifts your face and actually makes you look younger. Think about that the next time you are feeling all frowny faced. And besides, people would prefer to be around others who are happy and smiling.

So, light up the world every day with your smile.

Keep being happy, laugh often, and always, wear your smile! How many people can you smile at today?

Reflecting on our May Challenge, have you been able to spend extra time with your family this month?

Today's Joy: "When they were discouraged, I smiled at them. My look of approval was precious to them." Job 29:24 NLT

MAY 16
SERVICE

I will serve where needed.

How will you serve others today? What can you do to help someone in need?

"The best way to find yourself is to use yourself in the service of others." —Gandhi[8]

You may think of volunteering at a soup kitchen or an animal rescue shelter. Those are certainly worthy causes but even small deeds of service brighten the days of those in need. Maybe make a call to an elderly shut-in or take food to a sick neighbor. I have a friend who just needs someone to bring her trash can up from the road.

I remember the time my Daddy was cutting grass with a brace on his leg. A passerby stopped and finished cutting the large front yard for Daddy. It was definitely an act of service and greatly appreciated by my Daddy who could barely walk.

You won't have to look hard to find someone who could benefit from your time and service. How can you offer your time and talent to benefit others today? Who can you serve today?

Today's Joy: Your service makes a lasting impression on the hearts of others.

MAY 17
LONG TERM PLANS

I trust the journey.

When my son was in college, he planted a tree at the corner of my patio and said, "In 20 years, this tree will completely shade your patio." I laughed and never thought I'd see the shade. But today, that buckeye tree offers shade in my back yard.

Twenty years seemed a forever when the tree was planted but time goes by quickly. Planning 10, or even 20 years in the future makes good sense.

There are times when you need to think beyond this week, this month, or even this year. Think about where you want to be in five or ten years. You can start laying the groundwork now. Make steppingstone goals along the way to keep you moving in the direction of your dreams.

What are you planning to accomplish over the next few years? Have you made a plan to keep you moving forward?

Today's Joy: "For I know the plans I have for you," declares the Lord, 'plans to prosper you and not to harm you, plans to give you hope and a future.'" Jeremiah 29:11 NIV

MAY 18
TREASURED MOMENTS

I am making family memories.

What are some of your treasured moments that you remember about your family? Do you continue to make family memories or has life gotten too busy?

Our lives are distracted and involved. We all have many commitments, careers, and a whirlwind of activities. However, don't let this busy pace of your life diminish time with your precious family.

I remember how my heart overflowed with goodness when I saw that my son and his wife got down on the floor and played games with their young children every night after dinner. Those are memories the kids will never forget.

Also, take time for your parents and other family elders. Their days are limited, and I promise you will want to ask them one more question or have one more conversation with them after they claim their seat in heaven.

Spending time with family lets them know they are loved. How will you preserve precious times spent with those you love? What questions do you want to ask your elders while you still have them?

Today's Joy: Time is measured by moments and memories.

MAY 19
A THING OF BEAUTY

I see beauty everywhere I look.

What are the most beautiful things to you? Perhaps a sunset or a waterfall; both are lovely.

Whenever you observe and acknowledge a thing of beauty, your heart enters gratitude mode. Whether it be nature, food, a person or anything else; as you ponder something charming, you begin to feel gratitude. Expressing gratitude brings more divine and good things your way.

Remember to look for beauty in small things too, like a child holding a dandelion. Or a smile on the face of someone with an illness.

As you go about your day, look for things of beauty along your path. Take time to stop and appreciate them. Your heart will be warmed with gratitude and your soul will sing a happy song.

Where do you like to be to observe beauty? What lovely things inspire you the most?

Today's Joy: "I see and appreciate all the beauty that surrounds me. I am grateful for all things big or small that make my world beautiful."—Saratoga Ocean[9]

MAY 20
A BALANCED LIFE

I take time for my loved ones.

Balance is my word for this year. I've got a lot of balls in the air and the only way I can handle all of it is to consciously balance my activities.

Last night I was rearranging some books and out fell a page from a daily devotional magazine dated 13 years ago. You know what it was about… Balance! God knew the perfect time to unearth that tidbit.

The article talked about always being busy with multiple projects. That is exactly who I am and what I do. It goes on to say that God created us for relationships, not work. He wants us to have a relationship with him, our spouses and families, and others.

When we're so busy, our lives become out of balance and we don't nourish our relationships. It was a reminder I needed today. Perhaps you needed it, too.

Do you need more balance in your life to allow time for personal relationships? What do you need to do to obtain that balance?

Today's Joy: "Life is all about balance. You don't always need to be getting stuff done. Sometimes it's perfectly okay, and absolutely necessary, to shut down, kick back, and do nothing." —Lori Deschene[10]

MAY 21
SET A GOOD EXAMPLE

I do my best every day.

As Nancy's children were taking things off the store shelves and tossing them on the floor, she let out a string of indecent words. While Nancy continued to shop, her children then repeated these words to strangers in the store. The children were following the example set before them.

The Bible instructs us that in all that we do, every day and all the time, we need to set a good example. Speak with kindness and let our actions reflect goodness.

Other people, especially children, will follow your example before they follow your advice. Make your example worthy of being followed—both in words and actions.

No matter what your position in life is, someone is watching you; someone is trying to be like you. Be the person you would want to follow. Be the person who is honest, yet kind. Be the person who provides discipline with love. Be the person who is patient and offers encouraging words.

Let both your words and your actions be honorable.

If someone repeated what you said or what you did, would you be proud, or would you be embarrassed? Are you setting the example you want your children to follow?

Today's Joy: "And you yourself must be an example to them by doing good works of every kind. Let everything you do reflect the integrity and seriousness of your teaching." Titus 2:7 NLT

MAY 22
EMPATHY FOR OTHERS

I am here for you.

Lola sat beside Ann and listened as she poured out her heart. The two women had been friends for a long time and they always looked out for each other. Ann has had a lot of challenges in her life and Lola has a heart of empathy for her.

There is power in the statement, "I'm right beside you in this." It tells the other woman that you are in this situation with them; you are standing by them; you believe in them and they are not alone.

Empathy is seeing and feeling what someone else has going on in their life. It is listening to the other person and believing from their point of view. Empathy is your heart beating the same as the heart that is hurting.

You can show empathy to someone in need by practicing active listening and using encouraging words. Envision yourself in the other person's place. Sometimes the best thing we can offer is to simply be present.

Our kindness and empathy can help heal the heart and soul of someone who is troubled. Judith Orloff said, "Empathy is the sacred medicine the world needs."[11]

How do you empathize with women who are hurting?

Today's Joy: Share your light to heal another heart.

NO ONE IS YOU

You are one of a kind.

My sister and I have often been mistaken as twins. We look a lot alike; we buy the same purses, clothes, even cars; and if one of us likes something, the other one probably likes it too.

However, no one else is you and that is your superpower. No one else has your smile or your personality. No one else has your mind or your heart, and no one else has your fingerprint. You are a totally unique being.

Your kindness, generosity, and joy are yours alone. You can share your abilities and characteristics, but no one can duplicate who you are.

Use your unique talents wisely. Don't disregard your idea just because no one else is doing it. Your magnificent way of thoughts, ideas, and actions belong only to you.

Be proud of who you are. Put your personal trademark on everything you do. Your stamp of approval tells the world you are serious. You mean business. You have superpowers! No one is you.

What is your unique superpower? What traits are you known for?

Today's Joy: "I don't like to gamble, but if there's one thing I'm willing to bet on it's myself."—Beyonce[12]

FOLLOW YOUR HEART

I listen to my heart.

Does your brain often override your heart? And then, you find it hard to follow your heart? Yes—me too.

The heart is your innermost organ that has the important task of pumping blood throughout your body. Even though it has this important task, the heart symbolizes love and literally gives you life.

When you choose to follow your heart, you are making decisions based on love. Your mind wants you to think logically and determine all the pros and cons. It's a tough battle between mind and heart. Realistically, you should always listen to your mind, but following your heart will usually provide you with positive results.

And, following your heart is another way of finding and following your path in life. Your heart knows your passions, and those passions lead you to your purpose. Will you follow your heart; it knows the way?

Are you willing to follow your heart and your intuition?

Today's Joy: "Have the courage to follow your heart and intuition. They somehow know what you truly want to become. Everything else is secondary" —Steve Jobs[13]

MAY 25
BE KNOWN BY YOUR ACTIONS

I will practice being courteous and kind.

I'd like to introduce you to Mimi, my former mother-in-law. She was one of the most kind and gracious women you have ever met. She greeted everyone with a smile and usually even a hug. Her words were warm and gentle, and she immediately put you at ease. As a side note, Mimi was a fabulous cook, and she loved to share her meals with others.

There are people in your life that are like Mimi. They go out of their way to make you comfortable and shower you with their loving hospitality. However, there are also some people you know that no matter what, they are going to be cranky.

It is your actions that people will remember you by. They'll know how you made them feel. With this in mind, strive to be the friendly and pleasant women that we all look forward to interacting with.

Just like you know which group most people belong to, they also know which group you are in. Is that your group of choice? If not, there's still time to make changes in your actions.

Do you know someone like Mimi? Do you strive to be this type of person?

Today's Joy: Strive to be the kind of person that makes everyone feel special.

MAY 26
YOUR LEGACY

I am writing my legacy every day.

One of the people who had the biggest impact on my life was my great aunt. She lived her life with love and grace. Her legacy was based on her ***gifts of time.*** She took the time to listen, chat, visit and teach me.

The other person who greatly impacted my life was my Daddy. He had a ***thankful heart.*** Every time anyone did even the smallest thing for him, his response was, "I appreciate your kindness."

Both my great aunt and my Daddy left a great legacy, not just on my heart but with everyone who knew them.

Most people want to be remembered fondly and leave part of themselves behind. Think of your loved ones who have already passed on. What are your thoughts about the legacy they left behind?

How do you want to be remembered? What thoughts and feelings do you want to leave with your loved ones? What will your legacy be?

Today's Joy: Loved ones leave their fingerprints on your heart.

MAY 27
WELCOME HOME

I love my happy home.

Do you remember buying your first house? Can you recall walking in the empty rooms and hearing an echo? The house probably felt hollow and void.

Once you added curtains, and rugs and furniture, it started to feel a little better to you. It was when you added photographs and all your personal treasures that you felt like it was your home.

But, when the family gathered around the table or the fireplace and you listened to the laughter and love that was shared, you knew your house had become your home. This is where hopes and dreams are born.

"Home is where love resides, memories are created, friends and family belong, and laugher never ends."—Author Unknown[14]

I believe fresh flowers make a home complete. What do you do to make your house a home?

Today's Joy: It is with patience, kindness, laughter and love that we make a house our home. Personally, my home is my refuge where I renew, restore and refresh my soul.

MAY 28
BLAST OF APPRECIATION

*I appreciate the good
things in my life.*

Think of one thing you love and appreciate it to the fullest extent. This blast of appreciation will bring you to a positive mindset. Here is one of my blasts from my 2009 journal.

> I appreciate my beautiful yard,
> and my lovely pergola with the fabulous furniture,
> and my gardening cottage,
> and my memory garden,
> and the wicker furniture on my front porch,
> and my arbor,
> and the stone terrace,
> and the plants on my patio,
> and the big oak tree in the front yard,
> and the Japanese maples trees.
> Yes, it is this acre plot and all that is on it that I love so much!

By appreciating everything about my yard, I am now inspired about everything in my life, not just my yard.[15]

Re-reading your blast of appreciation on other days will also bring you back to this positive place. What can you appreciate to the fullest extent today?

Today's Joy: I am blessed to have an abundant life of family, friends, love, and joy!

MAY 29
THE JOY OF TEAMWORK

*I focus on the positives
in my marriage.*

You often think of teamwork with co-workers or sports. Today I want to talk about teamwork with your spouse.

I recognized the teamwork between my son and his wife when their first child was born. One was changing a diaper while the other was making a bottle. Today, they both contribute to making meals, taking care of the yard, and getting the kids to various activities.

This is the kind of teamwork that makes marriages strong and their children are learning the value of working as a team.

My husband and I plan our meals together and he does a lot of the cooking. We make the bed together and run errands together. Not only is this our form of teamwork, but it is also time that we're spending with each other.

What can you do to work in harmony with your spouse?

Today's Joy: A happy marriage is a daily choice.

MAY 30
GRANDMA AND MIMI

I cherish my family.

Extended family vacations are a special time of making memories. Last year, I was honored to spend several days with my son's family and the grandkids' maternal grandmother at the coast. She is known as Grandma and I am Mimi. Like most grandparents, we love spending time with the grandkids and watching them as they grow.

One afternoon, on this particular trip, our grandson asked Grandma and me to play cards with him. At first, I said I didn't know how to play. But Clem was insistent and said he would teach me. So for the next few hours, Clem engaged with his two grandmothers in a game of Rummy.

Clem was 14 years old at the time and there were many other things a teenage boy could have been doing. Instead, he entertained Grandma and Mimi with funny stories, a bowl of popcorn, and most of all, his time. Both Grandma and I will always treasure this memory.

How can you share your time with someone today? Will you give it willingly and without rushing?

Today's Joy: Never underestimate what giving of your time will mean to someone else.

MAY 31
A HUG A DAY

I offer hugs to my loved ones.

Some people offer quick little hugs when they see you. And others hold you in a long and tight hug. I prefer the long, tight hugs, and I know who to go to when I need that special hug.

My nephew has always offered me those enveloping hugs, and I always look forward to seeing him to get a hug. When he was young, he gave me a framed saying, "A hug is a perfect gift. One size fits all and nobody minds if you exchange it."

According to Virginia Satir,

> We need four hugs a day for survival.
> We need eight hugs a day for maintenance.
> We need twelve hugs a day for growth.[16]

During a long hug, you can feel your body releasing stress and tension. Hugs, also, increase our good hormones that come from feeling loved and appreciated, and hugging can soothe painful feelings in our bodies.

May Challenge Follow-Up: Were you able to spend extra time with your family and loved ones this month? Did you share conversations over a meal? Did the kids and adults bond with each other?

Today's Joy: Sometimes all you need is a hug to make you feel better.

DISCOVER YOUR JOY

MOTHER'S DAY & FAMILIES

Loving Joyful Families

JUNE:
SUMMER AND FATHER'S
DAY

Enjoying Summer Joy

JUNE 1
FINDING HAPPINESS IN A
FIELD OF DANDELIONS

I choose happiness.

As I pulled into a parking spot, I noticed the field beside me was uncut and full of weeds. I wondered why management hadn't taken care of this maintenance.

My sister and I had taken the grandkids to an old gold mine to explore the grounds and pan for gold. As my eight-year-old granddaughter climbed out of the back seat, she grabbed my hand and raced towards the field that I was just mentally complaining about.

"Look Mimi," she said. "Look at all the dandelion wishes. Mimi, what would you wish for if you had a thousand dandelion wishes?" Wow! This sweet little girl had just instantly upgraded my mood and changed my perspective.

As adults, we often tend to see the less-than-perfect side of things first. If we look a little harder or a little longer, we can find beauty even in the small things.

On that same trip, my grandson did strike gold that day. The geologist on duty confirmed his gold nugget and safely packed it for the trip home.

June Challenge: This month we celebrate the beginning of summer. Will you have more time to relax and enjoy your family and friends? How can you share your favorite summer activity with someone else?

Today's Joy: I am filled with happiness, laughter and joy.

JUNE 2
LOOK TO HEAVEN

I will follow Jesus.

I am one who loves to look at the moon in all its phases and my husband knows a lot of the star constellations. Summer nights are perfect for star gazing. So, we spend evenings looking up to heaven.

We know that we have many loved ones and friends now abiding in heaven. On evenings like this, I miss my own Daddy so much. I know he is ready to welcome me home when that day comes.

It is God's promise of heaven that provides all with hope for eternal life. We live each day with the peace that all is well. We know that every step and every day is ordained by God. He holds our hand and leads the way. We only need to believe and follow him.

Do you enjoy star gazing? Does it remind you of friends and family that are now in heaven?

Today's Joy: "Jesus answered, 'I am the way and the truth and the life. No one comes to the Father except through me.'" John 14:6 NIV

JUNE 3
SIMPLE TIMES

I enjoy a slower paced life.

Tiger, the neighborhood cat, is sitting on the front porch with me this morning. Porch sitting is a favorite past-time in the South during the warm months of the year.

"Back in the day" before air-conditioning, families sat on the porch or even under a tree just to enjoy a cool breeze. These gatherings were usually accompanied by a tall glass of sweet tea. The adults shared stories while the kids played games. Those were definitely simpler times.

The last three months have returned us to a simpler life. A worldwide illness has people staying home, preparing their own food and spending time with family. Even though I've missed seeing my son and my sister and their families, my new husband and I have enjoyed the return to a simple life. We've been sharing stories of our lives growing up. Dinner has become our favorite time of the day as we prepare and share our meal together. Life is good.

One day, everything will be busy and hectic again. For now, I'll listen to the song of the birds and love on this sweet kitty beside me. I know my husband will be joining us on the porch shortly.

How do you slow down and enjoy the quiet simple times in your life?

Today's Joy: Our lives are usually busy and hectic. Take time to enjoy the small and simple moments when they do come around.

JUNE 4
STOCK YOUR POND

I grow in the Fruit of the Spirit.

You know how fishermen try to keep the water of their ponds or lakes stocked to make for great fishing?

Today, I want to encourage you to stock your own pond with the Fruit of the Spirit as written in Galatians 5:22. Your pond will include love, joy, peace, patience, kindness, goodness, faithfulness, gentleness and self-control.

You can stock your pond by focusing on your relationship with God, spending time in prayer, and reading His Word. Believing in Christ and following Him are ways to grow in the Fruit of The Spirit.

As you invite joy into your heart and walk in peace, you will find yourself more loving and patient. Your actions will reflect the kindness, goodness and gentleness described in the scripture, and your faithfulness will guide you in self-control. All of these fruits that God provided for you work together in perfect harmony.

Having your pond abundantly stocked with these blessings will certainly guide you on your daily walk with God. Which characteristic mentioned here do you need to work on? How will you improve on that characteristic?

Today's Joy: "Create in me a clean heart, O God. Renew a loyal spirit within me." Psalm 51:10 NLT

JUNE 5
LIVE LIFE IN FULL BLOOM

I let flowers fill my life with joy.

Picture in your mind the bud of a rose. Then, choose your favorite color…. red, yellow, or perhaps pink. As the rose bud is exposed to the sunlight, day after day, it gradually opens a little more. One day, it is completely opened and in full bloom.

You can live your life in full bloom just like the rose. By exposing yourself to regular sunshine (kind people and positive situations), you too will open your mind and heart to the world beyond.

Just know, you are beautiful and adored just like the rose. Live each day with your petals open wide, your color glistening in the sun and your center open to gratitude and joy.

What can you do to live your life in full bloom? What changes do you need to make to your attitude? How can you be more aware of the world around you?

Today's Joy:

> **"Let happiness bloom**
> **In the freshness of your mind,**
> **In the gentle wind of your thoughts.**
> **On the ground of kindness and compassion."—**
> **Debasish Mridha**[1]

JUNE 6
A JOY STONE

I take joy with me.

I carry a small heart shaped stone in my pocket every day. There's a stone terrace just off my kitchen and it was there that I found this stone.

I quickly realized how joyful I felt every time I looked at the stone and it was an instant reminder of joy—so, in my pocket it went.

Now, every time I put my hand even near my pocket, I feel the stone and a little tingle travels through my body. I have appropriately name it my *Joy Stone*.

I encourage you to find a small stone or a flat rock, a marble, even a tiny seashell, anything that brings you happiness. Put it in your pocket or purse and keep it close at hand.

Now, you're bringing your joy with you wherever you go. You have a constant reminder to always smile, spread happiness, and be joyful.

What can you carry in your pocket, or keep close by, to remind you to have a great day?

Today's Joy: Paint a picture on your stone or write a quote on it. You are enhancing the joy!

JUNE 7
SIMPLE PLEASURES

I take time to enjoy the simple things in life.

In the year 2020, a worldwide illness changed all our lives. As we stayed quarantined and wore our masks, I became focused on the simple pleasures of life. Here are some things I enjoyed from home.

The smell of freshly mowed grass
Flowers in bloom
The feel of warm air outdoors
The sound of a friend's voice on the phone
A quiet dinner with my sweetie
Rocking on the porch and watching the squirrels play
Listening to the birds sing sweet songs
Reading a book start to finish
Trying new recipes. Thai Sweet Chili Chicken, anyone?
Livestreaming worship services
Waking up without an alarm clock
Lounging on the patio while my sweetie grills dinner
Texting with the grand kids

What's on your list of simple pleasures to cherish?

From our June challenge, have you been able to spend more time with your family? Have you found some great activities to share with those you love?

Today's Joy: "I am beginning to learn that it is the sweet, simple things of life which are the real ones after all."— Laura Ingalls Wilder[2]

JUNE 8
UNPLUG AND UNWIND

I will take time for a technology detox.

We have become wired up and plugged in all day, every day. Most of us own various electronics from phones to tablets and computers. Our televisions are no longer limited to what ten or so channels offer. There are thousands of options for shows and movies and binge-watching is common. Whew!

Try to take a weekend, or even a day, to unplug and unwind without all the gadgets. Instead of surfing social media, take a long walk outside. Invite your kids or grandkids to join you. Nature offers lots of opportunities for good conversation. Maybe you enjoy playing cards or a board game with your family. Chat with a neighbor over coffee or read a good book. There are so many options that don't involve an electrical plug.

Take time to observe and enjoy the world around you. Without all the stimuli from electronics, your brain has an opportunity to rest and become more creative. You may even sleep better by digitally disconnecting.

Take time to observe and enjoy the world around you.

I have set aside Sunday afternoons to read my way through the growing stack of books on my coffee table. Now that summer is here, what time can you block off to be unplugged? What will you do to unwind?

Today's Joy: Reconnect with yourself, your heart and your soul.

JUNE 9
DAYDREAMS

I take time to daydream.

My favorite place to daydream is soaking in the hot tub. It is there that my mind and body are totally relaxed. Creativity fills my mind. Many ideas have come to light during these peaceful moments.

Once you clear your mind of all the chatter of the day, you can then see and feel your dreams. New ideas burst forth. Solutions to your problems appear out of nowhere.

Find your quiet zone where you can be silent; where you can let your heart, your mind, and your soul explore new territories. Let your imagination go wild. Dreams give birth to change. Nothing is impossible in your daydreams.

In fact, dreams are a form of planning and one of your ideas may just change the world one day.

What do you daydream about? Do you have a special place where you go to daydream?

Today's Joy: "Laughter is timeless. Imagination has no age. And dreams are forever." —Walt Disney[3]

JUNE 10
STARVING FOR WISDOM

*I seek wisdom from my
daily experiences.*

I've always believed that knowledge is, in fact, power. The more you learn, study, and know, the farther you can go in life and the more you will enjoy living.

But wait. I just read this quote by E.O. Wilson, "We are drowning in information, while starving for wisdom."[4] That shook me in my flip flops.

We live in an information age. Almost anything you need to know; you can find online with just a few clicks. We are inundated with constant pieces of breaking news. Perhaps we *are* overloaded with information and now it's time to seek wisdom.

Experience combined with knowledge and good judgment is the source of our wisdom. It's not something you learn from reading a book or research online. It's taking time to think things through, learning from life experiences and applying your insights.

What can you do today to seek more wisdom in your life?

Today's Joy: "Wisdom and money can get you almost anything, but only wisdom can save your life." Ecclesiastes 7:12 NLT

JUNE 11
ABUNDANT LIFE

I am abundantly blessed.

Have you ever thought that a neighbor or co-worker was living an abundant life and you wanted to know their secret? First, don't confuse abundance with having material items.

An abundant life is driven by personal values such as generosity, kindness, and gratitude. Another major ingredient in the recipe is mindfulness.

Positive thoughts and gratitude are also pathways to living an abundant life. You can practice gratitude by giving thanks daily for all that you have.

Generosity is more than giving from your purse. It is also being generous with your time, your skills and in showing kindness to others. The more you give, the more you will receive in return.

Whatever you focus on is what you will attract more of into your life. By embracing an abundant mindset, you will reap the rewards of living an abundant life.[5]

How can you incorporate more generosity, kindness, and gratitude into your life? Do you believe it will reward you with a truly abundant life?

Today's Joy: "I came that they may have life and have it abundantly." John 10:10 ESV

JUNE 12
FINDING JOY AMIDST YOUR PAIN

I seek the good in each day.

I've had back pain for the last two months and it's getting me down. You may also be having pain. It might be emotional pain like grief or anxiety. Or it could be any kind of physical pain – acute or chronic.

You still want to feel joyful, but the pain is overwhelming.

The first step is to find a positive thought amidst the pain. Look for a thought that you can remind yourself of several times during the day. My personal thought is, "Even though I have this severe back pain, I know it will be better soon."

Another story comes from a friend of mine who is moving a thousand miles away to be closer to her family. She recently said to me, "I'm really sad about moving away and missing my friends." Then she immediately added, "But I'll get to see my grandchildren more often." How precious is that comment.

What kind of pain are you experiencing? What positive elements can you focus on today?

Today's Joy: The first step to get from pain to joy is to maintain a positive attitude.

JUNE 13
THE JOY OF CREATIVE LIVING

My life is filled with joy.

Elizabeth Gilbert defines creative living in her book *Big Magic* as "any life that is lived more by curiosity than by fear."[6]

So, creative living is more about your mindset than the home where you live. This is the time to use your imagination and think outside the box. Getting outside of your comfort zone is where you can experience and enjoy creative living.

Discover what brings you joy or what maintains your overall happiness. Therein lies your path to living a creative life. Perhaps you'd like to learn a new skill like cooking or writing. Maybe you'd like to take up snorkeling or sky diving.[7]

What are you curious about? Would you learn how to do it even if it scares you? How will you act and start living a creative life?

Today's Joy: Aim to experience something new regularly.

JUNE 14
FRIENDSHIP

My friends are inspiring and motivating.

I recently connected with a new group of friends through a meet-up. Meeting with this group helped me to discover that spending time by myself in coffee shops is a great way to meet new people and make new friends.

After the group met a few times, Becky and I struck out to explore a nearby labyrinth and spend an afternoon together. The labyrinth is somewhat of a spiritual experience so we each walked it quietly by ourselves. Then we sat down on a nearby rock wall to contemplate the experience and enjoy the beautiful garden surroundings. A new friendship blossomed from our time together.

True friends bring great joy to our lives. They give us a sense of belonging and purpose. Women, especially, enjoy having close friends to celebrate our successes with and to lend support during difficult times. We have lifelong friends who have been through everything with us. But we also make new friends while standing in the grocery line. How many times have you exchanged recipes with someone based on the contents of their grocery carts?

You may not even realize how dependent you are on the treasures and memories that come with having special friends. Hold them tight in your heart and make time to share, and always, let them know they are loved.

Who are your close and treasured friends? Do you reserve time to spend with them? What actions do you take to let them know how much their friendship means to you? During the summer, are you spending more time doing outside activities with your friends?

Today's Joy: "Truly great friends are hard to find, difficult to leave and impossible to forget."—G. Randolf[8]

JUNE 15
TAKE TEN

I take time for self-reflection.

It was probably twenty years ago when I started writing in a journal. I was living alone and after dinner every evening, I would sit down to write. Any and everything that came to mind was inscribed in my journals. The good, the bad, the happy, and the sad; it's all there. Today, I have stacks of journals that hold my deepest thoughts.

If you have ten minutes a day to devote to yourself, block it out so no one will disturb you. Use this time to write in your journal your innermost thoughts about anything that is on you mind or your heart.

Writing out your thoughts instead of using some type of electronics is good for you. The slower process of writing is therapeutic and can lower your internal stress. It allows you time to process your thoughts as you put pen to paper. If you write long enough, you will usually find clarity within your thoughts.

Do you write in a daily journal? If so, do you find peace within your thoughts? If not, consider giving it a try.

Today's Joy: "Who you are tomorrow begins with what you do today."—Tim Fargo[9]

JUNE 16
DESIGN YOUR DESTINY

I will follow my heart.

Have you ever wondered what is your destiny? Have you tried to affect your destiny?

Some people believe destiny is your fate and you cannot control it. I choose to believe that destiny happens when we make conscious decisions and allow God to determine our steps. Looking back over my life, I believe I am living my true destiny. I have gone down the path that God prepared for me.

I also believe that things work out the way they are supposed to in our lives. Having an open mind, staying positive, and praying for God's will in your life will likely lead you to the best possible life that you could ever imagine.

It is said that people cross our path for a reason. It could be something we need or can learn from them. Or, it could be something they need or can learn from us. Once I accepted this thought, it was easier to dismiss someone's crazy comment or not to wonder about someone who is no longer present in my life.

Pay attention to people or things that you feel drawn to. Likely, this is pulling you towards your passion, your purpose, your destiny.

Do you feel like you are living your destiny? What could you do differently to put yourself on the path that has been prepared for you?

**Today's Joy: "What is meant to be will always find a way."
—Trisha Yearwood**[10]

JUNE 17
SCATTER KINDNESS

I spread kindness everywhere I go.

I had no idea who was at my door but I scurried to answer the doorbell. My precious friend, Molly, stood there with a smile on her face and muffins in her hand. We made a pot of coffee and settled down for a chat. She filled my heart with kindness and I want to share some of those thoughts with you today.

- Treat everyone with kindness.
- Be especially kind to pets and young children. They need your love.
- Practice random acts of kindness regularly.
- Remember to be kind to yourself too.
- Be the reason someone smiles today.
- Unexpected kindness is powerful.
- You will never regret being kind.
- Kindness changes everything.
- Use your voice for kindness.
- Be known for your kindness and grace.
- Overwhelm someone with your kindness.
- Kindness is magic!

Who can you share your kindness with today? What random act of kindness will you offer?

Today's Joy: Kindness is free. Sprinkle it everywhere!

JUNE 18
YOUR STORY

I will share my story.

I can remember spending summer evenings sitting around a picnic table listening to my father-in-law tell stories of growing up on a farm during the 1930's. His stories were both elaborate and entertaining. You could envision exactly what he was saying.

We all have our own story. And your story could be just what someone else needs to hear. By sharing life's ups and downs, good things and not-so-good things, trials and triumphs, you can encourage others. Stories of inspiration, stories of encouragement, stories of overcoming challenges, all give hope to someone else in similar situations.

Your story might be a beacon of light to lead another person to their needed destination. Think about how you can share it with others.

What is the story inside of you? Have you shared it with others?

Today's Joy: "I now see how owning our story and loving ourselves through that process is the bravest thing we will ever do."—Brene` Brown[11]

JUNE 19
CHOOSING JOY WHEN YOU DON'T FEEL JOYFUL

I make joy my priority.

Over the past few years, Ann has faced one challenge after another. Her husband was gone a lot and she was having trouble adjusting to his new schedule. The kids were mostly interested in their friends and electronics. Her supervisor at work was constantly micromanaging. Life had beat her down and choosing joy does not come easy to her anymore.

We all have times when we're not feeling our best. So, how do you reclaim your joy when you're struggling with a tough day or situation?

Start by refusing to let negative thoughts take root in your mind. Choose a slightly better feeling thought. By being intentional about looking for positive thoughts, you'll save yourself from all the negative turmoil.

I've always believed that gratitude is the shortcut to joy. Take a few minutes to think of just three things you are thankful for. This thought gives you an immediate flip from negative to positive.

Take a walk outside. Chat with a friend, meditate, have a cup of coffee. Any type of self-care will help you to choose joy when you don't feel joyful.

What is your shortcut to joy when you're not feeling joyful?

Today's Joy: You can choose joy even if your life isn't perfect.

JUNE 20
GETTING IT RIGHT

*I've got the potential to
do anything I choose.*

One of the few guys that I interviewed for this book shared with me that he grew up with tough love and discipline.

The number one thing that was drilled into his brain as he entered the work force was, "Do it right, or don't do it at all."

That's good advice for all of us. I know I've taken a short cut on something, then had to go back and fix it later. In the end, it's usually not worth the effort to take the shortcut.

Here are some other tips for "getting it right."

> Learn to be the best version of you.
> Be focused and consistent in your actions.
> Don't be afraid of hard work and exercise patience.
> Good things will come your way at the appropriate time.

Did you experience tough love and discipline when you first started working? What impact did it have on your life?

Today's Joy: "Self-discipline begins with the mastery of your thoughts. If you don't control what you think, you can't control what you do. Simply, self-discipline enables you to think first and act afterward."—Napoleon Hill[12]

JUNE 21
INSPIRED TO REST

It's ok for me to rest.

It's the first full day of summer and time to talk about afternoon naps. Taking naps are good for us. (My adult son is thrilled to hear this.) It's a time for our bodies to rest which keeps us functioning properly. And, relaxation is nourishment for our souls.

My favorite "*rest*" time is soaking in the hot tub. All my cares seem to dissipate, and new ideas burst forth. It truly is my favorite "*thinking*" place.

Any change from your normal routine is a type of rest for your mind and body. It allows time for your creativity to surface.

Give yourself permission to slow down and rest. Let your mind and heart carelessly flow wherever it chooses to go. Breathe deeply and enjoy where you are.

Rest, relax, recharge, and refocus. You'll be a better mom, wife, friend, employee when you're not running on empty.

Do you make time to rest and recharge in the afternoons or on weekends? How can you add this into your routine?

Today's Joy: "The Lord replied, 'My presence will go with you, and I will give you rest.'" Exodus 33:14 NIV

JUNE 22
HONOR MY DADDY

Fathers are our guides.

It is on Father's Day every year that I choose to **honor** my Daddy who claimed his seat in heaven twenty-five years ago. He was my first and forever love. My sister and I try to do things on Father's Day that we know our Daddy would enjoy. Homemade ice cream is high on the list!

I believe we need to **celebrate** all the men in our lives who are fathers. For me, that includes my son, my husband, my former husband, and my nephew. These men have all been my rock at various stages of my life. They all loved and uplifted me in their own unique ways.

Today, I encourage you to honor all the fathers that have been a part of your life. Reach out to them with love and respect. **Cherish** the memories they left on your heart and soul. Their guiding hands will remain with us forever. They are our heroes!

How do you honor your father and other fathers who impacted your life?

Today's Joy: "Honor your father and mother" appears at least nine times in the Bible.

JUNE 23
INSPIRING STORIES ENRICH OUR LIVES

I will share my story.

My father was a man of very few words and telling stories was not something he did often.

However, my father-in-law loved to tell detailed stories of his life growing up in the country. His stories were about everyday life in a world our kids cannot even relate to. He opened our eyes and our minds to life in simpler times. He shared perspective that couldn't be found in books. He uplifted our hearts to know that life really is good.

Not only do these stories open our eyes to days gone by, it also opens our hearts to the people who share their stories with generations to come.

Do you have a storyteller in your family? If so, I encourage you to capture all the images and events in their minds. Commit them to paper or a tape recorder. This is part of your heritage that you won't find anywhere else.

Today's Joy: "There is no greater agony than bearing an untold story inside you."—Maya Angelou[13]

JUNE 24
A GIFT FROM GOD

I will nurture the
children in my life.

Do you have children? Perhaps you nurture nieces and nephews or the neighborhood kids.

My Daddy taught children in Sunday School for over forty years. I can still see him sitting in short little chairs with four-year-old boys and girls clamoring to sit on his lap. I can imagine this is how little children felt as Jesus welcomed them to sit with him.

Children are one of our greatest gifts from God. It is our privilege to lead and teach them in a way that they can grow and flourish. Our responsibility is to love and teach our children just as Jesus did during his time here on Earth.

Who are the children that are a part of your life? Take time to hug them today. Let them know that you love them.

Today's Joy: "But Jesus called the children to him and said, 'Let the little children come to me, and do not hinder them for the kingdom of God belongs to such as these.'" Luke 18:16 NIV

JUNE 25
LAUGHTER IS THE BEST MEDICINE

*I am filled with happiness
and laughter.*

"He has achieved success who has lived well, laughed often, and loved much," according to Bessie Anderson Stanley's 1904 poem.[14]

Laughter truly is good for the soul. Try to surround yourself with happy people who find joy in everyday activities and being around kids can provide a constant source of happiness and laughter.

A short burst of laughter brightens your mood immediately and is a great form of stress relief. So, take time to enjoy a TV sitcom or giggle at an online cartoon.

I'm a serious person and it has taken a conscious effort over the years for me to look for laughter every day. But now, I know who to call when I need my daily dose of laughter, and it usually starts with the grandkids.[15]

Do you find a reason to laugh every day? Who do you turn to in order to seek a good laugh?

Today's Joy: "Laughter is a sunbeam of the soul."—Thomas Mann[16]

JUNE 26
YOUR MASTERPIECE

I will be the best I can be.

A friend recently made the comment to me, "Make today your masterpiece."

His idea resonated with me and I began to think about what would make my day a masterpiece. Perhaps finish writing my book. Or maybe getting my yard in tip-top shape.

We all go along, day by day, doing the same things in the same ways. We mark things off a never-ending to-do list. There must be more in life. There is— it's your masterpiece!

What would be your masterpiece? What is the one thing you could do which would make you feel like you have accomplished your goal? Make plans now to move towards this accomplishment. Your masterpiece is closer than you realize.

After re-reading this during the editing phase of my book, I have decided that finishing my book, getting it out to the world and continuing to serve my tribe of women as they seek to discover their own joy is the masterpiece I want to attain. What is your masterpiece to achieve?

Today's Joy: "Make your life a masterpiece; imagine no limitations on what you can be, have, or do."—Brian Tracy[17]

JUNE 27
BE STILL

I give myself space.

"The answers you seek never come when your mind is busy. They come when the mind is still, when silence speaks loudest."—Leon Brown[18]

I find this statement so true in my everyday life. When I sit at my desk and try to think through a problem, I usually only frustrate myself. But, if I get up and walk outside and let my mind wander, a solution will often appear.

It is in the stillness of your mind, the stillness of your heart where answers and solutions lay waiting to be discovered. Our brains need some wiggle room in order to function with creativity. As we empty our minds of everyday tasks, we find new and extraordinary ideas.

Be still and listen. Don't think, just listen. The silence really is golden.

How do you silence your mind? Do you have a special place you go?

Today's Joy: "He says, 'Be still, and know that I am God; I will be exalted among the nations, I will be exalted in the earth.'" Psalm 46:10 NIV

JUNE 28
POWER OF MOTIVATION

I will slay my goals.

My favorite motivation comes from being around like-minded people. I have a business associate that I have lunch with occasionally. Every time he sits down, he has an in-depth, thought-provoking question for me. Barry has worked my brain more than almost any other stimuli. As a side note, I so wish I had kept a journal these last 20 years of all our conversations.

We often sit and wait for motivation to come to us. We wait for the moment of sudden inspiration. But that rarely happens. The best motivation comes from within us. We decide something needs to happen, and we do everything possible to make it happen.

Success in life is not always about how smart you are or what your career is like. The motivation to get up and do what needs to be done can be as successful as knowledge.

What are you waiting on motivation for before you take steps to begin? How can you find the motivation to move you forward?

Today's Joy: "Do something today that your future self will thank you for."—Sean Patrick Flanery[19]

JUNE 29
REFRESH YOUR INSPIRATION
WITH A MID-YEAR RESET

I am focused.

It's hard to believe that half of this year is almost gone. This is a good time to reflect on your goals, dreams, and opportunities for this year. Remember the plans you made back at New Years? It's time to refresh your inspiration with a mid-year reset.

What was your "word" that you chose for this year? My word for last year was "focus". I was making some major changes in my life and I needed to focus, or I would be more confused than a scrambled egg.

Take some time to revisit your goals and plans. Have things changed since the first of the year? If so, see how you can update your opportunities. You can add a different goal or tweak what you were planning back at the beginning of the year.

Look for new inspiration for completing this year's dream! Your dream can become a reality by renewing your spirit and recommitting yourself with a mid-year reset!

Have you revisited your plans for this year? Did you find inspiration to refresh your goals?

Today's Joy: This is your time to make your dream come true.

JUNE 30
THE PEACEFUL LIFE

I am whole.

Days at the coast are soothing, relaxing and good for the soul. Here, God's handiwork is evident every day. From sunrise till sunset, you'll see the waves roll in, feel the sand between your toes and watch the seagrass wave in the ocean breeze. Seagulls flying above, children building sandcastles and multi-colored umbrellas dot the beach. This is the peaceful life.

Beachcombers are out at daybreak to see what treasures the ocean left overnight. Fishermen have set up poles in the surf and on the pier waiting for the catch of the day. As the sun rises high in the sky, lunch is served on the deck. Then, afternoon naps or a good book are calming to our minds. This is the peaceful life.

It is here, at the coast that I walk in joy during the day and sleep in peace at night.

June Challenge Follow-Up: This month brought us the opportunity to enjoy many summer activities. What kind of summer fun did you share with loved ones?

Today's Joy: The ocean waves bring joy to my soul.

DISCOVER YOUR JOY

SUMMER & FATHERS DAY

Enjoying Summer Joy

JULY:
JOY AND HAPPINESS

Discovering Your Own Joy

JULY 1
FIND WHAT BRINGS YOU
JOY AND GO THERE

I am joyful every day.

What is it that makes your heart skip a beat? What makes your eyes light up? Therein lies the path to your own joy.

For me, I love to be at the coast. There, I find inner peace in the tranquility of listening to the waves as they gently roll in. The building roar of the waves and hearing them crash on the beach always brings delight to my heart. Walking barefoot in the surf, I feel the warm, damp morsels of sand between my toes. I let out a little squeal of happiness, and I especially enjoy watching sunrises to welcome the day and sunsets to close the day.

My other passion is being in my flower gardens. I love the feel of the sunshine on my face and the dirt on my hands. There is a feeling of accomplishment by planting, watering, and watching the flowers bloom. I am grateful to have my daughter-in-law help me choose the right plants for my mostly shady yard and the zone where I live. I believe planting a garden warms your heart and soothes your soul.

Make time for the things you love to do. These moments bring peace and joy to your heart and your life. Following your joy is one piece of taking care of yourself.

July Challenge: What brings joy and happiness to your heart? Make time each day to acknowledge your *moments of joy*. Give thanks to God who provides all of our joyful goodness. Gradually, your heart and your soul will become overflowing with joy and happiness.

Today's Joy: "The joy we feel has little to do with the circumstances of our lives and everything to do with the focus of our lives."—Russell M Nelson[1]

JULY 2
JOYFUL QUOTES

Today, I choose Joy!

As you already know, my life is inspired by joy, and I try to share joy everywhere I go. Here are a few of my own personal quotes on joy.

> A joyful life is a life well-lived.
> The ocean brings joy to my soul.
> Joy is a state of mind.
> Follow your joy.
> Inhale Gratitude, Exhale Joy.
> Gratitude is the foundation of living a joyous life.
> There is joy in my soul today.
> Joy will last when you make it a habit.
> Gratitude opens your heart to joy.
> Joy comes from a light deep within your soul.
> Joy resides in your heart.

You can use these quotes as affirmations or daily mantras. Continually reminding yourself of your joyful life will absolutely enhance the experience you are living.

Today's Joy: "We really are masters of our own joy. The journey starts with us."—Claire[2]

JULY 3
BREAST CANCER

I am joyful and hopeful.

What would be your reaction to a cancer diagnosis?

A dear friend, Emily, texted me this morning to say she just found out that she has breast cancer. She shared the details that she knew so far. Then she ended her text with, "I am joyful. And hopeful."

This is the heart of a Godly woman. Emily knows the Lord, and she knows he has his hand on her life. As she goes through the upcoming tests and follows the plan per her doctor, she will undoubtedly turn each day over to God for his comfort and guidance.

And through all of it, she chooses to be joyful and hopeful.

Through your own issues and storms of life, are you choosing to be joyful and hopeful?

Today's Joy: If Emily is willing to turn her cancer treatment over to God each day, are you willing to turn your challenges over to God?

JULY 4
UNLIMITED JOY

I sparkle with joy.

Happy Fourth of July! What are you and your family doing to celebrate today? As a kid, sparklers were always part of our entertainment on this patriotic day. We could hardly wait for dark when friends and neighbors would gather in the yard to light our sparklers. Cheers and laughter would close out our night.

Today is a great day to 'sparkle with joy.' There is no limit to the amount of joy you can have. Your heart and soul are made for joy, and there's always room for more.

And, just like a candle, your joy is not diminished by sharing it. Actually, your joy increases as you share it with others. When you bring a smile to someone, comfort them with kindness, or let them know they are loved, you will also enjoy a warm feeling.

Your joy is also contagious. People will notice how happy you are, how pleasant your personality is, and how willing you are to help. They start to crave the joy you have in your life. The more joy that is spread among friends and families, the better our world will be.

How will you *sparkle* today?

Today's Joy: My heart is filled with great joy!

JULY 5
A JOYFUL HOME

My home is my refuge.

Do you enjoy just being at home? Are you content there by yourself or with others?

You can look forward to coming home each day by creating your own joyful home. You may never want to leave again. Our personal joy comes from within ourselves and is possible even when living in a chaotic environment.

However, organizing things at home, controlling the noise volume, and filling your home with pleasant aromas, certainly inspires a more joyful home.

My husband brings fresh flowers home every week. Opening the door, the flowers are one of the first things I see. Immediately, I have a smile on my face.

Opening draperies, shutters and blinds is also a mood booster. Let the sunlight stream through your windows. A joyful home has a huge impact on your feelings, your emotions, and your mood.

What can you do to brighten your home and bring more joy inside?

Today's Joy: "The ultimate luxury is being able to relax and enjoy your home." — Jeff Lincoln[3]

JULY 6
EMBRACE THE RAIN

I will dance in the rain.

Where do you like to be during a rainstorm?

I enjoy rocking on the porch and listening to a light rain. It's been a hot summer here with very little rain. There was a fresh scent in the air after a recent rain and all the plants looked refreshed. The rain seemed to cleanse the earth. There is peace and stillness in a soft rain. It calms my soul.

Rainy days are great for reading a book or taking a nap. These are days to snuggle under a blanket with a cup of coffee and listen to the lullaby of raindrops on the window. My husband and I will often sit in the rocking chairs on the porch during a storm. It almost feels like sitting in the sanctuary with God. I can feel his presence in these quiet moments and enjoy his blessings of the rain.

Our reward comes with rainbows as they streak across the skies. They always bring a smile to my face. The plants and grass and trees have all been nurtured by the falling rain, and everything grows again.

Do you enjoy listening to the rain? What goes through your mind as you listen to the soft pitter-patter of the raindrops?

**Today's Joy: "The earth has music for those who listen."
William Shakespeare**[4]

JULY 7
JOY COMES FROM DEEP WITHIN

I am a light to all I meet.

Can you feel joy deep within yourself? I can vividly remember the day my minister spoke about always being joyful. Why did this particular message sink so deep within my heart? Now I know it was my time. I needed joy and Pastor Mike delivered it. Over the next ten years, I learned how to seek and embrace joy.

It's not something you can see or hold in your hands. Instead, joy is a feeling that you have possibly spent years building and nourishing. It comes from a light deep within your soul. It's not superficial or fleeting.

Once joy has well established roots in your heart and soul, it becomes easier to choose joy every day. You have made it a habit and now you have a deep well of JOY to draw on.

Sharing your joy with others will not diminish the shine of your light. So many people you meet today barely have a concept of true happiness. They certainly cannot grasp the fact that you are a joyful person with a joyful heart.

You can be the light for others who have not yet found joy! What can you do today to share your joy with someone who needs encouragement?

Today's Joy: "You may be the change and light needed by others, to shine on their path."—Sunday Adelaja[5]

JULY 8
START WITH A STRETCH

I stretch my body and mind.

Is stretching or working out a part of your daily routine? What kind of exercise do you prefer? How often do you exercise?

I've been starting my days early with a stretch program on public television. In thirty minutes a day, the coach manages to stretch every part of my body. With some recent back issues, I know these exercises are also helping me to heal. Stretching leaves me feeling energized, wide awake, and ready to face my day.

Stretching my body also opens up my mind. My thoughts are clearer, my mind is more creative, and I can focus on the details of my day.

This clarity also fills me with positive energy and thoughts. Because I feel good about myself after stretching, I also feel good about the world around me. I spread kindness and happiness everywhere I go.

What can you do in the mornings to ensure you have a positive day?

Today's Joy: "The body benefits from movement, and the mind benefits from stillness." —Sakyong Mipham[6]

JULY 9
EVERYDAY JOY TIPS

I share my joy.

By changing your focus, you can easily bring joy into your life every day. Here's the trick: Each time a negative thought comes to mind, stop and think of three positive ones. This has been a real game-changer for me.

Another tip that Sally shared with me is she changes her passwords to positive affirmations by using the first letter of each word. For example, if her positive affirmation is, 'I am happy and joyful every day,' her password would be 'Iahajed' plus any required numbers or punctuation. When she types her password, she is repeating the phrase as she types. It's a simple way to add everyday joy to her routine.

One of my favorite everyday joys are the fresh flowers from my husband. He keeps a vase of flowers for me on our dining table most of the time, and it's ok to buy flowers for yourself if they put a smile on your face.

Joy attracts Joy! What did you note on July 1 that brings you joy? What are your special ways to incorporate that everyday joy into your life?

Today's Joy: Look for joy in everyday places!

JULY 10
WORRY AND WORSHIP

I love to praise and worship my God.

Nadia had been feeling discouraged and I called to check on her. She said that, today, she was listening to praise music because you can't "worry and worship at the same time." Nadia had found a way to flip her worry through worship. Her comments and her happy mood inspired me to turn on my own praise music that day.

If you are busy praising God, reading his Word, and offering prayers, you're surely not worrying about anything at all.

This is exactly the way God wants us to be. Turn all of your worries over to him. Then spend your time in worship.

> Dear Lord, You are the Risen Christ, the Prince of Peace, the Mighty God, and the Everlasting Counselor. Grant us peace of mind and help our hearts to not be troubled during these difficult and uncertain times. Give us the strength and grace to trust you even when we cannot see the way. Remind us that you will never let us go and that you will always hold us in your everlasting arms of love. We ask all of this in the name of Jesus Christ our Lord. Amen. —Dr Winfield Bevins[7]

Today's Joy: In troubled times, I will seek God and trust God.

JULY 11
MOMENTS OF JOY

God is in every moment of joy that I experience.

Sometimes, we look for joy and we think it has to be a massive, earth-shattering experience. However, joy can be found in the smallest moments of the day.

Think about smiles and hugs and laughter. All of those are certainly joyous moments. Getting to your appointment on time, everyone in the house is well, and your sweetie is making dinner tonight are truly joy-filled moments.

For me, a cup of cappuccino and a couple of chocolates are pure and absolute moments of joy.

Abraham Hicks says, "Know that just one moment of joy is a sign of better things to come."[8]

This is so true. If you find just one little moment that brings you joy, you are on the path to find great joyful times ahead.

What are the little things that bring you 'moments of joy?'

Today's Joy: "Joy comes to us in moments—ordinary moments. We risk missing out on joy when we get too busy chasing down the extraordinary." —Brene` Brown[9]

JULY 12
MORNING ROUTINE

There is joy in my soul today.

What are the first things you do when you wake up in the morning?

Here's a schedule you might enjoy:

Wake up.
Feet on floor.
Grab caffeine.
Choose JOY!

By choosing joy first thing each morning, you will set the tone for your entire day. Make it a habit to be grateful for your blessings, say a few positive affirmations, and choose to have a joy-filled day.

When you make this a consistent start to each day, you will be amazed how well your day will be. You'll feel happy and confident. Your day will be productive, and your accomplishments will be amazing!

Today's Joy:

A beautiful day begins with a beautiful mindset. Every day you wake up, think about what a privilege it is to simply be alive and healthy. Stop focusing on the negatives and everything that could go wrong and start thinking about what could go right. Better yet, think of everything that already is right. Be thankful for nights that turned into mornings, friends who turned into family and past dreams and goals that turned into realities. Use this mindset of positivity to fuel an even brighter today and tomorrow. —John Geiger[10]

JULY 13
UNLOCK YOUR JOY

I am joyful!

Do you feel joyful every day? Our natural state of being is joyful. However, all the busyness, commitments and requirements of our lives sometimes robs us of that joyful feeling. Perhaps it is just locked away deep in your heart and only needs the lock to be released.

Unlocking your heart could be simple enough if you have a key. Otherwise, you'll need to dig down deep, discover why your heart is locked, and work towards releasing those barriers.

For myself, my heart became locked when my husband and I separated. For the first time in my life, I was all alone. I was sad and life was hard and difficult and overwhelming. You get the picture, I'm sure. Even though there were good days along the way, it was many years before I was able to unlock my joy. My key to the lock came through a message from my minister. It touched my heart and I was on my way to living a joyful life.

Is your heart blocked by shame or guilt? Is your heart reeling with jealousy? Do you feel unloved or unworthy? These and many other emotions could be blocking your joyful life.

Whatever you are feeling, just know, you are entitled to joy! You are worthy of joy! You deserve joy in your life!

Repeat those statements to yourself over and over. They will gradually ingrain into your heart, and you can return to your natural state of living joyfully!

Today's Joy: "I have told you these things so that you will be filled with my joy. Yes, your joy will overflow!" John 15:11 NLT

JULY 14
LIVE IN THIS MOMENT

I will pause for a moment.

Do you sometimes feel like hours, or even days, have passed you by and you have little recollection of what happened? I lived this life for a good number of years while I was single. I would work anywhere from 60 to 90 hours a week depending on the time of year. Then, one Saturday morning my young grandson called me at the office. Clem's words were, "Mimi, I know you're busy, but this is important." That was my moment of truth. That was the day that I realized my life was passing me by and I needed to take immediate action.

Our lives are fast-paced and it's easy to be too busy to notice the life we are living. But, once this moment passes, you cannot recapture it.

Yesterday is over and done. Tomorrow has not yet arrived. Your only opportunity is to live in this one precise moment. Make it be the best moment possible and be fully engaged in this precious moment.

Put down your phone and turn off social media for a while. Observe what is around you, particularly your spouse or children. They need your time and attention.

Take a walk and notice the stones along your path, the shape of trees, and the birds singing cheerfully. Remember, being a child, guessing what shape the clouds look like? It takes looking up engaging with nature, with others, and with God to connect to true joy.

Take time to smell the roses, pick the dandelions, and smell the fresh-cut grass.

How can you live in this moment to enjoy and remember it?

Today's Joy: "Learning to live in the present moment is part of the path to joy." —Sarah Ban Breathnach[11]

JULY 15
SHARED JOY IS DOUBLE JOY

There is joy in my soul today.

Joy is contagious, and it is meant to be shared. I believe that joy is my superpower, and I try to share it with everyone all the time. It was ten years ago when I truly discovered the joy in my life. I started collecting sayings about joy, reading about joy, and spreading joy with everyone I encountered. Over the next few years, I realized that I had the motivation and the ability to share joy with the world. It was then that I knew joy was my superpower.

The more people that each of us share our joy with, the wider the expanse of joy becomes across our universe. Carry your joy with you and scatter it everywhere! Here are a few ways to share your joy.

> Smile at everyone you meet.
> Compliment your spouse and kids.
> Use kind words.
> Hold the door for someone.
> Give someone a hug.
> Say "*please*" and "*thank you.*"

My favorite way to share joy is to leave a note on the mirror of a public restroom. I carry a pad of post-it notes and a marker in my purse. Most ladies' rooms that I visit, I leave a note with something like, "*Wishing you joy today*" or "*Hope you've having a joyful day.*"

How will you share your joy today?

Today's Joy: It's a good day to be joyful!

I will do the best I can every day.

After researching topics that are trending among women, I identified five areas that detail what women want or need in their lives.

#5 Success—Whether it be in a career, as a mom, or any other role, we want to feel accomplished.

#4 Relationships and Friendships—We draw strength, love and compassion from those closest to us.

#3 Encouragement and Strength—We crave inspiration and encouragement in our daily lives.

#2 Faith—Belief in a higher being gives us hope for our lives.

#1 Motivation and Positive Inspiration—The number one thing most women are seeking in their lives is motivation and positive inspiration. Our lives are a whirlwind and motivation keeps us focused.

All of these items are interconnected. As you score one item, the goodness flows to all the others. What is the most important area in your life? How can you encourage other women in some of these areas?

Today's Joy: Seek to encourage, uplift, and inspire other women along your way.

JULY 17
BLESSINGS OF JOY

I am blessed beyond measure.

My hope for you today is that you will be filled with blessings of joy. I hope you have moments where you will feel refreshed and encouraged. I hope you feel your spirits soar.

May your steps be a little lighter this day. May your smile be a whole lot wider, too. May you know that God has you in the palm of his hand, and you are safe there.

May you know the peace in your heart that only joy can bring. You are abundantly blessed and loved today and every day.

Pause long enough to absorb the bounty of goodness in this world. Remember to give thanks to our Maker. I wish you blessings of joy today!

What blessings are you particularly grateful for? Who can you share your blessing of joy with today?

Today's Joy: "You make known to me the path of life; in your presence there is fullness of joy; at your right hand are pleasures forevermore." Psalm 16:11 ESV

JULY 18
OFFER PRAISE AND RECEIVE JOY

I open my heart to joy.

By offering praise to God, our own hearts are filled with joy. This is a jubilant message that makes my heart sing and my soul dance.

There are so many ways to praise God: through song, reading scripture, prayer, and meditations. All these things bring glory to God, and in turn, we are filled with his joy.

Russell M Nelson captures the essence of joy in his quote,

> "Joy is powerful, and focusing on joy brings God's power into our lives."[12]

Do you offer praises to God? Have you been able to discover *moments of joy* in your days?

Today's Joy: "Until now, you have not asked for anything in my name. Ask and you will receive, and your joy will be complete." John 16:24 NIV

JULY 19
FINDING BEAUTY EVERYWHERE

My world is filled with beauty.

During a recent trip to Hawaii, I thought it was the most beautiful place I've ever seen. If you've been there, you might agree.

Returning to the US mainland, I was reminded there is beauty everywhere we go. I was thrilled to return home and find my flower gardens in full bloom. A quick trip to the NC coast proved the Atlantic Ocean never fails to be one of my favorite sights.

Try looking for beauty every time you go outside. There is also beauty in your friends, your family and your pets. Your favorite pieces of artwork provide beauty in your home. Even your favorite meal is a source of beauty.

Sometimes we have to consciously look for the beauty in every day. But with an open mind and a grateful heart, you're sure to find that every day is a beautiful day!

What are some of your favorite sights that remind you of the beauty of our world?

Today's Joy: "He has made everything beautiful in its time." Ecclesiastes 3:11 NIV

JULY 20
CREATE JOY

I create and share my joy.

You hear the phrase often to *Choose Joy*. Some days it's easy to choose joy and other days, it's an outright struggle. The day my Daddy entered heaven's gates was one of the saddest days of my life. He was my rock. He was my hero. I was his princess. What could possibly be joyful about that day or many days to follow? If you've lost someone dear to you to death, you know exactly how I felt the morning I received a call from his doctor.

On the tough days, you may need to create your own joy. If you've been writing in a journal or if you've kept a Joy Jar (See February 6), creating joy will be easier. Just go back through some of your writing and reread some of your positive remarks.

Otherwise, take a few minutes and scroll through your memory bank for some happy times. Relive those precious moments and you're sure to surface with a smile.

Feeling joyful is elusive to many people. But really, it's choosing to look for and embrace the positive aspects of your life on a daily basis.

How do you create your own joy? Can you recall happy times that encourage you through the day?

Today's Joy:

> **"'But,' Eva said, 'you can't just flip a switch and go from sad to happy.'**
>
> **'No, perhaps not,' Aunt Rose smiled gently, 'but God didn't design us to be sad. He created us to have joy!'"**– **President Dieter F. Uchtdorf**[13]

JULY 21
THE SECRET TO JOY

I choose joy every day.

For some people, joy seems to be this elusive happy emotion that they can never achieve. In reality, joy is always close by and ready to settle into your heart and mind. Some people look at me and ask how I manage to be happy and smiling most of the time. I know they have not truly experienced joy or they would not be asking. Perhaps they had a tough childhood or a rough life. And some people are happier just being unhappy. Whatever it is, these people have not discovered a life of joy.

Joyful living is accomplished by choosing positive thoughts over negative ones, spending time with other joyful people, and always looking for the good in people and situations.

Eventually, living in a joyful state will come naturally to you. In the meantime, do the things that help joy to become your default emotion. Use daily affirmations. Practice gratitude every day. Spread positivity with your smile.

Soon, you will become the *Joy Hotline* for all of your friends and family.

The real secret to joy is to wake up every morning and consciously choose to be joyful.

Do you have a secret way to choose joy? Do you share it with others?

Today's Joy: "Joy does not simply happen to us. We have to choose joy and keep choosing it every day." —Henri J. M. Nouwen[14]

JULY 22
FIRE OF JOY

I am thankful for this day.

The last couple of days, I've had one issue after another. Little things, but they all add up to feeling overwhelmed. Perhaps you can relate. The good news is I am filled with joy, and I chose to handle everything politely yet firmly. These are the kind of days that you want your soul to be on fire with joy. You have gracefully chosen joy every day and now your soul is ready to take on your struggles.

Choosing joy every day is not always easy to do. We get involved in our busy day-to-day activities and time gets away from us. That's why I recommend you set aside a few moments as soon as you wake up and think of three things you are thankful for that day. Or pull a few notes out of your JOY Jar and read them. (See February 6.) And my hope is that reading a page in this book, ***Discover Your Joy***, every day is filling you up with abundant joy. All of these things will become your storehouse of joy!

What does it mean to you to have a *fire of joy in your soul*? Could it be your soul is on fire to live a life of joy?

Today's Joy: "Gratitude is a powerful catalyst for happiness. It's the spark that lights a fire of joy in your soul." **—Amy Collette**[15]

JULY 23
POCKETS OF JOY

I find joy everywhere.

Even when life seems chaotic, look for pockets of joy during your day. Allow these little things to add up and fill your heart with joy. In recent days, I visited with my grandchildren, my husband made dinner and brought me flowers, and rain has watered my gardens for me. These are some of my pockets of joy.

In the midst of a stressful workday, someone compliments you. Put that in your pocket. Your child liked his lunch today. In the pocket, it goes. Traffic was light today. There were no bills in the mailbox. All these little things are pockets of joy.

Collect them; savor them; embrace them.

Our days may not always be joyful from beginning till end. However, these small things remind us that joy continues to thrive in our heart and soul.

What pockets of joy have you found in your days recently?

Today's Joy: I will always wear outfits with pockets, so I'll always have a place to carry my joy with me.

*I build reservoirs of
joy in my heart.*

We all know how things tend to go wrong, especially when we're in a hurry. Traffic is backed up for miles. Your boss is pacing while she waits for you to complete a project. You have a sick kid which means sitting in the doctor's waiting room with a lot of other sick children. You stop for a few essentials at the grocery store and the line is backed up down the aisles.

You want someone to acknowledge your pain, so you go home and rehash your day to your spouse or a friend. Complaining and rehashing the low points of your day will certainly sap your joy. My friend, Angie, suggested releasing your pain by writing about it in a journal. Give yourself grace for the bad day.

Then, remind yourself of all the goodness in your life. Make a mental list of all the good things that happened today.

Have you tried thinking three positive thoughts for every negative thought that went through your mind? (See July 9).

Today's Joy: "Radiate joy from the inside out." —Jenny Blake[16]

JULY 25
INCREASE YOUR JOY

My joy knows no bounds.

Joy is a state of mind! And there are so many ways to increase your own joy. Once you increase your joy, you can share it and spread it to everyone within your reach. And sharing your joy will not decrease your own joy. In fact, it helps to increase it.

Spirituality is probably my number one way to increase joy. Any time you spend worshipping or praising God will always increase your joyful heart. For many people, music is their joy of choice. I do love listening to the old hymns.

Being active in groups or physical activity also gives you all the good feelings inside.

Taking time to walk in nature and paying attention to the sights, sounds, and smells around you will provide you with a warm heart.

I want to say food will increase your joy, but perhaps, it's really the love and conversation that is shared with the meal that is most important.

What are some things that increase your joy? Can you share these activities with others to also increase their joy?

Today's Joy: "Never settle for anything less than pure joy."—Amy Atherton[17]

JULY 26
A WALKING MEDITATION

I will go wherever the path leads.

I have become fascinated with labyrinths and see them as a perfect walking meditation. After living in my home for over 40 years, I just discovered a labyrinth only two miles away. How did I not know this before? Perhaps I found it when I needed it. Life is like that sometimes.

And our lives are actually much like a labyrinth. We journey towards our own center seeking love, acceptance and wholeness along the way. There are many twists and turns but there are no wrong turns, just like our own lives. Things happen the way they are supposed to happen.

Once we reach the center of the labyrinth, it's time to follow the path back out and into the world. We return filled with new information and new inspiration. It is often considered a spiritual experience and many labyrinths are located on church grounds.

I have a friend who walks a labyrinth on a regular basis. It is her way of unwinding and finding peace within herself. I have a small circular area next to my patio that I dream of turning into a labyrinth.

Have you ever walked a labyrinth? Could you develop your own walking meditation?

Today's Joy: Find inspiration on your walking meditation. Commit the beauty to your soul.

OUTRAGEOUS JOY!

My life is filled with outrageous joy!

Do you know the feeling of bursting with excitement and enthusiasm most of the time? Have you ever experienced outrageous joy?

Most people would answer, "No." Outrageous joy is being totally filled with joy to the extent that you cannot even explain it. You feel so good that you can hardly contain yourself.

It is an incredible feeling, but it can be difficult to hold on to for a long time. Why is that? Life tends to get in the way.

The key to outrageous joy is to make a conscious decision every day to choose joy. Every morning thinks of things that you are thankful to have. Visualize a place that makes you feel happy and at peace. Make time for a few quiet moments throughout your day.

These types of activities, practiced on a daily basis, will reward you with outrageous joy!

How can you achieve outrageous joy in your life?

Today's Joy: "…[F]or the joy of the Lord is your strength."
Nehemiah 8:10 NIV

JULY 28
YOU CAN DO ANYTHING
BUT NOT EVERYTHING

I maintain balance in my life.

I love to garden, read, cook, and scrapbook; the list is endless. And my "to do" list is always a mile long. That's all OK, until I start feeling overwhelmed by all of my projects.

My dear friend, Linda, said to me, "Your problem is you want to do everything." Her comment took me by surprise, but I knew she was right.

You and I can really do almost anything we set our minds to do. However, we absolutely cannot do everything. There is not enough hours in the day for us to take care of our families, agree to all the volunteer positions we're asked to help with, take care of ourselves, and have time for every known hobby.

Self-care is an important part of your life. Always save time to relax and recharge. One of the hardest things for me is to decline requests from people when I know I would be overextending myself by accepting.

Are you also guilty of wanting to do more than you have time for? How do you decide which projects to accept and which to decline?

Today's Joy: Trust your heart. It knows what's best.

JULY 29
JOYFUL LIVING

I choose to be happy today.

Living a life of joy is choosing happiness in your everyday life. You learn to accept your challenges instead of allowing them to color your life.

There are things you can do to easily move into joyful living:

> Revamp your home or your personal space to make it your own oasis.
>
> Nourish your mind, soul, and body with a daily self-care ritual.
>
> Embrace meditation. If this is difficult for you, just use the quiet time to express love and gratitude. You'll gradually ease into meditation.
>
> Curate your own joyful playlist with music, podcasts, or poetry that will inspire your soul.
>
> And, start a joyful bucket list of all the happy experiences you want to have.[18]

What are your ideas for joyful living? Do you incorporate these things into your day?

Today's Joy: "Happiness is the best makeup!" —Drew Barrymore[19]

JULY 30
MY FAVORITE THINGS

I am joyful.

These are some of my favorite personal quotes about joy.

> Joy is a state of mind.
> There is joy in my soul today.
> Joy is my Superpower.
> Inhale Gratitude, Exhale joy.
> Joy is a feeling deep in my soul.
> My life is filled with outrageous joy.
> Joy will last when you make it a habit.
> Gratitude opens your heart to joy.
> Joy echoes through my soul.

And, here are some of my favorite affirmations about joy.

> I hold joy in my heart.
> I create joy for myself.
> Today, I choose joy.
> I am a fountain of joy.
> My life is filled with joy and abundance.
> I radiate love and joy.
> I am rich with joy.

Will you add some of these quotes and affirmations to your daily routine?

Today's Joy: I hope some of these quotes and affirmations resonate with you. Using them daily will increase the joy in your life.

JULY 31
EXPECT JOY

I know today will be a joyful day.

I've written many times about choosing joy. After you choose joy day after day, month after month, you start to expect joy.

Each morning, you know it's going to be a joyful day. Traffic makes you late for an appointment but you're not frantic. You accept there's a reason for the delay and continue on your journey.

As joy becomes a natural part of your mind and your soul, your heart feels a little lighter. Joy has become your default setting.

With joy as your default, you learn to celebrate even the small wins in life. You smile more often and share lots of hugs. You recognize that every day is a glorious day and you're thrilled to be alive.

July Challenge Follow Up: During July, were you able to discover what brings joy and happiness to your heart? Did you find time each day to acknowledge your *moments of joy*?

Today's Joy:

> **If joy is only tied to our external circumstances, we're all lost; very few of us ever experience joy. But when joy is turned around and has my definition of joy — it's the settled assurance that God is in control of all the details of my life the quiet confidence that ultimately everything is going to be alright and the determined choice to praise him in all things.—Kay Warren**[20]

DISCOVER YOUR JOY

JOY & HAPPINES

Discovering your own Joy

AUGUST:
PRAYER, BLESSINGS, AND GOD

Praying for Joyful Blessings

AUGUST 1
PRAYER WARRIORS

I am safe in God's love.

I have several girlfriends that I always know I can count on to be my prayer warriors. But today, I want to tell you about Linda. We met at church some 45 years ago and she is my number one go-to prayer warrior.

All these years, Linda has kept her current prayer list posted on her microwave. She keeps up with dates when friends have doctor's appointment or are going into the hospital. She calls to check in on everyone, offers prayers and encouragement along with a hint of medical wisdom.

If a situation is timely or critical, your name is moved from the microwave list to the daily list she carries in her pocket. I have always felt honored when I made her pocket list!

Linda is a good friend and a Godly woman. I truly pray that each of you have a committed prayer warrior in your life.

August Challenge: Do you have a prayer warrior in your life who regularly lifts you up to God? If not, take some time to find that person for your life.

Today's Joy: "Hear my prayer, Lord God Almighty; listen to me, God of Jacob." Psalms 84:8 NIV

AUGUST 2
BLESSINGS

I bless everyone I encounter.

How many times have you felt total despair? You know others have felt that same feeling, too. As a gift from your heart, you can give a short blessing to others when you see the need.

As a friend's name comes to your mind, you can say, "Bless this person's day."

If you see someone online asking for prayer, you can easily say, "O Lord, heal this person and bless them."

A neighbor is in financial hardship; your request could be, "Bless you with peace and abundance."

You know someone who is suffering from depression, "Bless you with peace and compassion."

There are so many times you have the opportunity to bless people that cross your path. Do not hesitate to offer a quick, silent prayer for them. It may be just the boost that their day needs.

Everyone you see is dealing with some issue or fighting their own battles. They all could benefit from your blessings. Even if you have no idea what they need, you can still say, "Blessings to you." God knows their needs, and he knows you have offered a blessing on their behalf.

Today's Joy: I usually sign short notes with "Blessings." It is my way of sending a blessing, love, and light to the person.

AUGUST 3
GOD HAS A PLAN

*I pray for guidance as
I travel this path.*

Some years ago, I found this saying, and I fastened it to my phone for safekeeping.

> All of your days have already been written in God's book. When you go through a disappointment, don't stop on that page. Stay the course. Keep believing. You may be tired, discouraged, and frustrated, but don't give up on your future. Our God is faithful. —Joel Osteen[1]

I was at a time and place in my life where I felt lost and just wandering through my days. It felt like I was missing something crucial, but I didn't know what it was. These words gave me comfort to face each day.

God has a plan. We need to listen to his will. Ask him to guide you down the right path for you at this time in your life. Know he will lead you exactly where you need to go. Ask his blessing on every step you take. God already ordains each step.

Are you willing to wait and listen for the plan God has for your life?

Today's Joy: "For I know the plans I have for you,' declares the LORD, 'plans to prosper you and not to harm you, plans to give you hope and a future.'" Jeremiah 29:11 NIV

AUGUST 4
A SCOOP OF HAPPINESS

I choose to be happy.

My sister and I always text each other every morning. Sometimes it's deep thought-provoking questions, but often it's a short cheery message. Those texts start my day out on a positive note.

Today, I'm having lunch with one of my favorite friends. And she always adds happiness to my day. Patty is a strong Christian woman and infuses our meetings with scoops of wisdom, dollops of Godliness, and sprinkles of laughter. Our conversations run deep with prayers for friends in need to the brightest moments in our lives.

We all can use an extra scoop of happiness. Today, try to intentionally choose things, people, or activities that would add enjoyment to your life.

But, it's also the little things that make a difference. Listen to your favorite songs. Have a conversation with your spouse. Spend time researching travel destinations. Enjoy food that you love. Sit outside or go for a walk.

Doing things every day that brings you happiness will help you develop into being a happier person. Happiness will become your default emotion.

What can you do to add a scoop of happiness to your day?

Today's Joy: Happiness blooms the more it is shared.

AUGUST 5
PERSISTENCE IN PRAYER

I will bow in prayer each day.

Have you ever just given up on a specific prayer request because it's been so long, and nothing has changed? For twenty years, I prayed for God to bring me my perfect mate. So many times, I felt alone and forgotten. When my husband did appear to me, I saw all the reasons I had to wait so long.

It's easy to become discouraged as you wait for an answer. However, don't let your discouragement win this battle. God is still in control, and he hears your every prayer. Just bow your head and stay on your knees in prayer. That is your job.

Ecclesiastes 3:1 KJV tells us, "To everything there is a season, and a time to every purpose under the heaven." We must patiently wait on God's perfect timing.

Continue to be persistent with your prayer. God hears each of your prayers, and he knows your persistence is drawing you closer to him. Continued prayers will strengthen your faith. God always answers, and he provides what is best for you.

What prayer of yours is still unanswered? Will you continue to exercise your faith through daily prayer?

Today's Joy: Continue to pray and continue to be patient.

SHOWERS OF MERCY AND GRACE

God is good to me every day.

Do you hear the words *mercy* and *grace* and wonder about their meaning? Both words are about love, but they are often confused.

Mercy is when God spares us from the punishment we deserve, and grace is where God provides us with good things that we don't deserve. Blessings are when the Lord is generous with both mercy and grace.

In our everyday lives, mercy is an act of kindness that makes you forgive someone. It is a feeling of compassion. Grace is known as giving love to those who are difficult to love.

We are all sinners and God offers us mercy for these short-comings. He also provides us with great and abundant things. For this grace, we give eternal thanks.

Is there someone in your life that you need to shower with either mercy or grace? Will you do that today?

Today's Joy: "The faithful love of the Lord never ends! His mercies never cease. Great is his faithfulness; his mercies begin afresh each morning." Lamentations 3:22-23 NLT

AUGUST 7
LET THE SUNSHINE IN!

I welcome the sunshine to my day.

As soon as day breaks each morning, I open my shutters and drapes to let the sunshine come inside my home. The light is fuel for my mind and body. As the sun warms my home, there is the promise of a bright new day.

Even when the weather is dreary outside, open your blinds or curtains, and be thankful for the new day of blessings that God has provided. Our earth needs the rain to nourish all the living things. And after rain, there is a fresh crispness in the air, and the sunshine will soon return.

So today, as you open your curtains, know it's going to be another glorious day filled with sunshine and blessings.

What were you thankful for when you looked outside this morning?

Today's Joy: "Wherever you go, no matter what the weather, always bring your own sunshine."—Anthony J D'Angelo[2]

AUGUST 8
FAVORITE BIBLE VERSES

*I memorize scripture and
store it in my heart.*

Tonight, I am reminded of a friend's life who was cut short. She had memorized hundreds of Bible verses and called on the scripture often as she battled her illness. Her battle encouraged me to ask several friends about their favorite verses. I want to share some of them with you.

"In the beginning was the Word, and the Word was with God, and the Word was God." John 1:1 NIV

"Trust in the Lord with all your heart and lean not on your own understanding; in all your ways submit to him, and he will make your paths straight." Proverbs 3:5-6 NIV

"Do everything in love." 1 Corinthians 16:14 NIV

"'For I know the plans I have for you,' declares the Lord, 'plans to prosper you and not to harm you, plans to give you hope and a future.'" Jeremiah 29:11 NIV

"When I am afraid, I put my trust in you." Psalm 56:3 NIV

"Come to me, all who labor and are heavy laden, and I will give you rest." Matthew 11:28 ESV

My favorite verse is, "Always be joyful." 1 Thessalonians 5:16 NLT

What is your own favorite verse?

Today's Joy: How many Bible verses are stored in your heart?

AUGUST 9
FAVORITE BIBLE VERSES – PART TWO

*I cherish the truth found
in these verses.*

When I asked friends for their favorite verses, I got quite a story from my friend, Linda. She indicated her verses had changed over the years as her needs and situations had changed.

In years gone by, Linda's favorite was John 11:35 NIV, which is very short, "Jesus wept."

Some other years, she said she would have chosen Proverbs 3:5-6 NIV. "Trust in the LORD with all your heart and lean not on your own understanding; in all your ways submit to him, and he will make your paths straight."

Linda went on to say, "However, the last five years have involved a lot of intense caregiving. Many days I got lost in the problem solving, decisions, and chores, etc. For these reasons, I find myself needing the verse from Psalm 46:10 NIV. "He says, 'Be still, and know that I am God; I will be exalted among the nations, I will be exalted in the earth.'"

Linda's closing comment was, "The 'know that I am God' part of this verse is much easier for me than the 'BE STILL' part!"

Today's Joy: Find a verse that brings joy to your heart and soul. Revisit your verse occasionally to determine if your circumstances have changed and, perhaps, your verse also needs to be changed.

I find joy by seeking God.

My son recently heard this meaning of joy in a morning devotional and shared it with me. Maybe you've already seen it.

J is for Jesus First,
O is for Others Second and,
Y is for Yourself Last.
    —Author Unknown[3]

This perfectly lays out for us how to live a meaningful, purposeful, and joyful life!

Jesus must always come first. Without our faith, we have nothing.

Next, we must love and serve others.

After Jesus and others, we seek to provide for our own needs and desires.

Having this easy-to-remember structure in your life will help you to align your daily priorities properly. Joy will be yours when you have first served God, then served others.

How can you serve God and other people today?

Today's Joy: "That at the name of Jesus every knee should bow, in heaven and on earth and under the earth." Philippians 2:10 NIV

AUGUST 11
PRAY BOLDLY

I offer my prayers to God.

I learned praying on your knees from my grandmother. When I stayed with her, I have vivid memories of her on her knees by her bed every single night in prayer, I know this was her nightly ritual, but she had no idea the impact she made on me as a young child watching her.

Sometimes our prayers are more recited than heartfelt. But, if you can get down on your knees and pour your heart out to God, you will see and feel the difference it will make in your life.

God loves for us to come to him with our prayers. Even though he knows our hearts and our circumstances, he wants us to talk to him.

Practice praying boldly and asking God to perform a miracle in your life. He knows your heart and He knows your needs, and we know he still performs miracles.

When was the last time you were actually on your knees in prayer? Have you contacted your prayer warrior (that was mentioned on August 1) with your prayer requests?

Today's Joy: "Remember the wonders he has done, his miracles, and the judgments he pronounced." 1 Chronicles 16:12 NIV

AUGUST 12
SUNDAY STILLNESS

I praise my God.

I enjoy having Sunday to relax and recharge my body, mind, and soul. Sunday mornings, in particular, seem to have a joyful stillness in the air.

Our Lord set aside the Sabbath as a day of rest. We can use this day for worship and praise, followed by relaxing activities. Take a walk and enjoy nature. Spend time with family and loved ones or read a book.

Always count your blessings. Listen to your heart. Breathe and say a prayer.

> Dear Lord,
> I praise your name above all others.
> Today I am grateful for my abundant blessings that you have provided.
> Keep my family safe and well in the coming week.
> Forgive my sins, O Lord, and give me to courage to forgive others.
> To God, be the glory!
> Amen

How do you like to spend your Sundays? Do you take time for worship and praise?

Today's Joy: "He restores my soul. He leads me in paths of righteousness for his name's sake." Psalm 23:3 ESV

AUGUST 13
STORMS OF LIFE

I pray through my storms.

Recently, a hurricane made landfall on the little island where we have a coastal cottage. I was reminded of the storms that have passed through my life.

No matter how great your life is, there will always be storms. Some will be like a mid-afternoon thunderstorm, and others will try to blow you away like some well-known hurricanes. Whatever the storm's intensity, you will need to hold steadfast to your faith and spend time on your knees before the Lord.

The Lord is on your side. Your prayers to him reveal the concerns of your heart. He hears your prayers. However, continue to pray and pray and pray. Try to pray specifically for what needs to happen or what needs to be healed.

Isaiah 43:2 NIV tells us, "When you pass through the waters, I will be with you; and when you pass through the rivers, they will not sweep over you. When you walk through the fire, you will not be burned; the flames will not set you ablaze."

Powerful prayers manifest mighty miracles!

Have you survived storms in your life by giving it to God in prayer? Be sure to thank him for all of your miracles, no matter how big or small.

Today's Joy: "When the storms of life come, the wicked are whirled away, but the godly have a lasting foundation." Proverbs 10:25 NLT

AUGUST 14
JUST BE THERE

I am here for you.

Ann was struggling with personal issues. She had not left her house in days, and she wouldn't answer her phone. Lola knew some of Ann's story and decided to stop by for a visit. She knew just being there beside Ann was the best thing she could offer.

There are times you want to help someone in need. They may be suffering through pain, loss, or confusion and you want to do something for them. You want to bring them food or take them out for an evening. If your friend is hurting inside, likely all they need is for you to be there.

Sitting by their side, you are saying that you are there for them. You are willing to listen if they want to talk. But they are not alone in coping with the situation.

Being alone when you are hurting or sick, often deepens the pain. And having someone to sit with you without any pressure to talk brings comfort to our hearts.

Use the quiet time as you sit with them to pray for the person and their needs. Even if you don't know the whole problem, God does.

Has someone sat with you when you were struggling with issues? How can you pay it forward to someone else?

Today's Joy: "Jesus said, 'Come to me, all you who are weary and burdened, and I will give you rest.'" Matthew 11:28 NIV

AUGUST 15
BELIEVE IN A HIGHER BEING

I am on the right path.

Most of us believe in some higher being. It is this belief in God (or whomever you believe in) that gives us hope. Knowing that God made the universe and all that is in it, and made you, too, is an awesome belief.

Realizing there is life for us after our days on this earth are complete is almost incomprehensible. However, that very thought gives us hope.

A lot of religions have the same fundamental beliefs, but procedures and protocols vary between denominations. Love is the one thing they all have in common. It spans all religions and cultures.

The underlying premise is to respect each other and their beliefs and trust that they will respect you and your beliefs.

Faith in God during the good times helps you build the strength that keeps you healthy through your life's storms.

Do you know other people in different religions? Have a conversation with them about their beliefs. It could be a real eye-opener.

Today's Joy: Believing leads to miracles!

AUGUST 16
PROTECT ME, O LORD

I am safe wherever I go.

If you watch the news, you know there is so much violence, and it seems to be worse every day.

Thinking about all that goes on around me, sometimes makes me afraid to leave my house. I've heard too much, and I worry too much.

Along with these concerns and anything else on my mind, the answer is always to take it to God in prayer. He knows what worries us, and he is still our shield and our protector.

Pray this simple prayer each time you go out the door.

> Dear Lord, protect my loved ones and me today on our travels. Keep us safe in traffic and on our errands. Send us a bank of your precious angels as our armor today. Praising your holy name. Amen.

Do you feel comforted and protected by your prayers as you leave your home?

Today's Joy: "Cast your cares on the LORD and he will sustain you; he will never let the righteous be shaken." Psalm 55:22 NIV

AUGUST 17
HEAVEN

I believe in heaven.

Have you heard stories about people who died and saw heaven, and then they were revived? For the stories that I have listened to, the accounts of what they saw is absolutely amazing!

Revelations tells us the streets are paved with gold, the gates are made of pearl and the walls are precious jewels. I have an idea that heaven will be much grander than we can possibly imagine.

We expect to see angels and our loved ones who have already gone to heaven. There will be choirs singing and people rejoicing. And of course, we will come face to face with God.

If you believe that Jesus is Christ your Savior, then heaven will be your eternal home. You will live in paradise forever.

Do you believe heaven will be your eternal home after you pass from life on earth? If you have questions about this, reach out to me or a trusted minister.

Today's Joy: "Jesus answered him, 'Truly I tell you, today you will be with me in paradise.'" Luke 23:43 NIV

AUGUST 18
PRAY FOR SOMEONE

I know that prayer works!

My church just finished a program where they asked you to choose someone and pray for them for 30 days. I'd like to suggest to you to do the same thing.

Choose someone whom you feel needs your prayers. Plan to lift them up to God every day for the next 30 days. My church said not to tell the person you are praying for them. But, make your own decision on that. I think it would be nice to know that someone cares enough to include me in their daily prayers.

Pay attention to see if you notice any difference in your prayer friend. Do they seem happier or more confident? Did they make a drastic life change or even small subtle ones?

Our church had a 96-year-old man accept Christ as his Savior because someone cared enough to pray for him. Will you care enough to lift someone else up in prayer for the next month?

Today's Joy: "Devote yourselves to prayer, being watchful and thankful." Colossians 4:2 NIV

AUGUST 19
LIFE IS A GIFT

I live my life to the fullest.

I am so guilty of beating myself up for not accomplishing massive projects every day. If you're the same way, keep reading.

Each day we have here on Planet Earth is a gift to us from our God above. Be thankful for each day and cherish the opportunities it provides.

Live today to the ultimate fullness you possibly can. Our days pass by quickly, and we function with duties, commitments, lists, and responsibilities. Treasure each moment. Be sure to take time each day to hug your loved ones a little longer. Tell them you love them every day.

Don't live by the *coulda, shoulda, wouldas*. That only fills your heart with regrets instead of precious memories. I am so guilty of this!

And remember, your life is a gift. Fill each moment with love, honor, and gratitude. Use your energy to find your passion and live your purpose.

Let's you and I make a pact to treat life as a gift. Will you dial down your to-do- list and dial up your moments to make memories?

Today's Joy: "My life is a gift. I will use this gift with confidence, joy and exuberance." —DevelopGoodHabits.com[4]

AUGUST 20
A PHONE CALL FROM GOD

I listen for God's call.

One night, as I struggled with a situation, my prayer was, "O Lord, just tell me what to do." And clear as day, I heard, "Get up and go call this person." And so, I did. Thinking about it later, I wish I had taken time to think through what I was going to say. But I was elated to have a clear and immediate response that I did not tarry.

Prayer is a conversation with God, and your heart is the phone to talk and listen with. Take time each day to offer praise and gratitude to God. Then talk to him about what is on your heart. Ask him to speak to you. Sometimes, you may feel an immediate answer. Other times, you may need to wait patiently.

Phone calls from God are not always as clear as mine was that night, but you'll know when he is calling you.

Have you called your prayer warrior this week to tell them what is on your mind and your heart?

Today's Joy: O Lord, speak to me and I will listen.

AUGUST 21
SUNDAY MORNING

I will praise the Lord today.

Good morning, my friends. Today is Sunday, and I'm going to worship in the house of the Lord. Attending church regularly is important in the life of a Christian. It is there that we sing praises to our Lord, worship with other like-minded people, and offer fervent prayers.

If you drift away from church, it's easier for your "fire for Jesus" to burn out. You gradually put away your Bible and devotionals. Prayer comes only when you need something. You lose the constant support of your Christian circle of friends.

Today is Sunday, and I'm going to worship in the house of the Lord. I'm eager to sing praises, read scripture, and hear what the minister has to share. I hope you're headed to worship our Lord today. He's our Savior!

Do you attend worship services regularly? If not, ask God to lead you back to your church.

Today's Joy: "Turn your worry into worship and watch God turn your battles into blessings." —Victoria Osteen[5]

I will always pray with joy.

Paul wrote in one of his letters, "In all my prayers for all of you, I always pray with joy." Philippians 1:4 NIV.

It is a sweet thought to imagine Paul praying with joy. Can you imagine him down on his knees, talking to God in joyful prayer?

Do you feel joyful when you go to God in prayer? Or when you have completed your chat with God? Perhaps if you've had a good day or have reasons to rejoice, you feel joyful. But Paul teaches us to pray for everyone and to pray with joy.

Joy is a warm and positive feeling. Try praying for your family, loved ones, neighbors, and co-workers with joy. You may be surprised how much joy will actually fill your own heart.

Sometimes, it may be more of a feeling of peace. You've spoken with God and given him all of your troubles. Yes, it is a peaceful feeling.

Will you practice praying with joy? Praise God for all of your blessings. Turn your cares over to him with joyful expectations.

Today's Joy: "I thank my God every time I remember you." Philippians 1:3 NIV

AUGUST 23
SLEEP, WHERE ARE YOU?

Prayer calms my mind.

I often do not sleep well, just like many of you, I suspect. There are good things on my mind, and sometimes, worries slip into my mind. I find myself mentally making a to-do list. However, I want to sleep.

Instead of surfing on my phone or watching television, I have learned to use the quiet hours to pray. Some people need our prayers: the sick, the lonely, those with hardships or struggles, kids at school, our ministers, and our country's leaders. The list goes on and on. I try to pray for specific people and circumstances when I know the details. Otherwise, God knows their needs.

I pray for you, my loyal readers. I pray you will rest in peace and comfort tonight and awaken to a joyful day in the morning light.

Do you sometimes find yourself awake during the night? Try using that time for sincere prayer.

Today's Joy: "When a soul knows peace, the heart can sleep."—Angie Weiland-Crosby[6]

AUGUST 24
DO NOT BE ANXIOUS

I rest in God's assurance.

Paul writes in Philippians 4:6 NIV, "Do not be anxious about anything, but in every situation, by prayer and petition, with thanksgiving, present your requests to God."

Do not be anxious. That is a powerful statement. We know it is hard to accept at certain times in our lives. How can we not be anxious? A family member is sick. The mortgage payment is due. The car broke down.

However, we are instructed to take "every situation" to God in prayer. It doesn't matter how small or how big our request is….. We are to take it to God in prayer.

Continue to pray about each situation every day. Some prayers will not be answered the way we requested, but they will be answered. We must accept God's perfect timing and the answers that he deems to be the best.

Make your first prayer to be for strength to not be anxious about your situation.

Today's Joy: "And which of you by being anxious can add a single hour to his span of life?" Matthew 6:27 ESV

AUGUST 25
AFFIRMATIONS FOR YOUR KIDS

I have many talents.

I've talked about affirmations to help us have a joyous day. But we also need to say positive affirmations to our children. This will instill a great attitude in them from an early age.

Here are some affirmations you can regularly say to your children, grandkids, or neighborhood kids. Also, post the affirmations on sticky notes to find around the house or put them in their lunch.

> You're a great kid!
> I'm always so proud of you.
> You are kind and thoughtful of others.
> I love you today and every day.
> You are a good brother/sister/friend.
> I am grateful you are my child.
> You spread happiness everywhere you go.
> I know you can do anything you want.
> You are unique and special.
> You are awesome!

Saying affirmations to a child will give them confidence for their day. It can help them to learn to follow their dreams and pursue the possibilities.

What are your favorite affirmations for kids? Where can you post the affirmations for kids to find?

Today's Joy: Today is a fabulous day! All is well!

AUGUST 26
WAIT FOR THE LORD

I ask God for guidance.

There are times when we do not know which of the two choices would be the best in a given situation.

Recently, I was in just this spot. I had friends hoping for one particular outcome, yet I had doubt that it was the best option for them. There was a looming situation that could make or break their dream. I didn't know how to pray for them so my prayer was simply, "God, I do not know what is best for this couple. You do. Take care of them and provide the best for them."

When you don't know what is best for you or anyone else, let God make the decision. Turn your problem over to the Lord in prayer. He will lead and guide you in the best way.

Have you ever been in a situation where you don't know what would work out for the best for you or your loved ones? What did you do?

Today's Joy: "But they who wait for the LORD shall renew their strength; they shall mount up with wings like eagles; they shall run and not be weary; they shall walk and not faint." Isaiah 40:31 ESV

He is my constant companion.

Walking with God is having a daily connection with him. It's talking to him through prayer and praising him through worship.

Studying the Bible is also a vital part of your walk with God. Hosea 4:6 NIV says, "My people are destroyed from lack of knowledge …" You want to read and study your Bible as if your life depends on it, and actually, your life does depend on the knowledge you will gain.

You can use one of the daily Bible reading plans that are available. Or choose a book of the Bible you would like to read. I especially love to read Psalms and Proverbs.

You can find daily devotionals and praise music online to start your morning each day. Choose a favorite verse and write it on a sticky note to keep it fresh on your mind.

Do you like to study the Bible by yourself, or would you rather join a Bible Study Group?

Today's Joy: "For we walk by faith, not by sight." 2 Corinthians 5:7 ESV

AUGUST 28
KEEP THE FAITH

I will continue moving forward.

Sometimes it feels more comfortable to just walk away from a project and try to convince ourselves that it didn't matter anyway. How many stories have you heard about people who did just that, and yet, their prize was just over the horizon?

> No matter where you are on your own journey, have faith and trust that you have the strength within to survive, thrive and reach the summit of whatever mountain you're climbing.—Denise Marek[7]

Have a self-talk with yourself and say, "Self, I believe in you. I believe you can absolutely succeed with your masterpiece. You should keep moving forward."

Then, pray for trust and strength as you forge ahead towards your goal.

And lastly, simply keep your faith.

Have you ever been close to completing a project and you just gave up? Later, did you wish you had finished what you had started?

Today's Joy: "The best way out is always through." — Robert Frost[8]

I spend time each day in prayer.

Do you have a special place where you go each morning to start your day off with God?

I recently relocated my prayer corner to a quiet nook at the edge of the dining room. Here, I can read the Bible and devotionals and spend time talking with God. From the window, I can see the birds and the squirrels, flowers blooming and the sun beginning to rise over the trees. This is where I come to fill my emotional tank full of all the goodness God provides for me.

Our lives are busy and it's easy to say we don't have time to spend with God each morning. I think you will find your quiet time with our Lord will provide more for you than the time you would spend thanking and praising him.

Do you have a prayer corner? If not, can you find a place of your own for your quiet time?

Today's Joy: Let prayer be your favorite time of day. You are talking to God who loves you dearly and will always take care of you.

AUGUST 30
MY TRANSFORMATION

I feel the presence of light.

I recently reunited with my high school sweetheart, and we were married in a lovely ceremony on the beach. I was still working full-time, but Daniel had already retired. He was eager for me to be more available. So, I retired!

For the last 33 years, I had worked incredibly long hours in an office with no outside windows. I would sometimes go days without ever seeing daylight.

Now that I am no longer in that office, I want to be outside. I want to enjoy the sunshine and listen to the birds. Even as I write this now, it's 95°, but I'm sitting on the porch. Peace and calmness are here. It's like I'm seeing things for the first time and in Technicolor!

My friend, Karletta Marie, the creator of Daily Inspired Life says,

> You may have struggles so dark and heavy that you're kept from being immersed in the light. But, remember, those who have walked through the darkness are the ones who see life in full-depth color, when they step back into the light.[9]

Have you ever felt like you were hidden in darkness? How did you find your way out?

Today's Joy: If you feel like you've been in darkness, take time to experience and enjoy the benefits of the light.

AUGUST 31
A TIME TO PRAY

It is an honor to pray to God.

My dear friend, Molly, regularly makes a three-hour car trip by herself. She told me that she uses this time to pray. She prays for anyone and everyone. She prays for situations and battles. But she prays, and she keeps on praying.

When she said this to me a few years ago, I knew this would be my new thing to do when driving alone. Now, anytime I'm traveling, I also use this time to pray for anyone or anything on my heart.

Many times, I do not know the whole situation, or I do not know what is best for someone. In these cases, my prayer is simply, "God, you know the needs. Take care of my friend. Give them your comfort."

God cherishes these little prayers that we share, and it keeps our eyes focused on him.

So, next time you're on the road, turn the music down and turn the prayers up.

August Challenge Follow Up: Are your prayer warriors regularly lifting you up to God? Could you be a prayer warrior for someone else?

Today's Joy: "When I think of all this, I fall to my knees and pray to the Father".—Ephesians 3:14 NLT

DISCOVER YOUR JOY

PRAYER, BLESSINGS & GOD

Praying for Joyful Blessings

SEPTEMBER:
INNER PEACE

Resting in Peace and Joy

SEPTEMBER 1
FINDING PEACE

Peace reassures me.

I was once told that "peace is joy at rest." That's such a soothing feeling to me.

But how do you find peace? My first suggestion would be to spend time reading devotionals and praying. Those two things always bring me into a state of calmness.

Journal writing, can bring peace by getting your innermost thoughts and concerns out onto the paper. This is fantastic self-care.

Here are some other self-care favorites. Whether it be a soak in warm water, reading a book, or having a cup of coffee, time alone is always peaceful. It's the time where we can collect our thoughts and realign our bodies.

Inner peace comes from letting go of the things that do not serve you and choosing all the goodness this world has to offer.

A peaceful mind produces a grateful heart.

September Challenge: How do you fill your heart with peace? This month look for ways to calm your mind and your heart. Slow down when you can and enjoy the moments.

Today's Joy: "I've got peace like a river in my soul." — Taken from the hymn, "I've got peace like a river." Author of the hymn is Unknown[1]

*My paradise brings
joy to my heart.*

Paradise is one of my favorite words. Just the sound of the word allows my mind to go to many places.

I have a stone on my patio with *paradise* etched into it. My nephew gave it to me when I declared that space was my paradise.

Where is your paradise? Just by imagining your place of peace and seeing yourself in that environment, you can bring calm and peace to your mind, your heart, and soul. Picturing yourself there, in vivid detail, allows you a moment of escape—a moment in your own place of paradise. It brings happiness and inner peace to you. The peace nurtures your soul with kindness and goodness.

Where is your place of paradise? Take a few moments now to claim it and allow your mind to visit there often.

Today's Joy: "Today I create a paradise in my own mind."— Louise Hay 2019 Calendar of Affirmations[2]

SEPTEMBER 3
INSPIRE OTHERS

We rise by lifting others.

To know that you have inspired someone is a good feeling. Maybe the other person will write a book or travel to a foreign country based on things you said or did. You could have inspired someone to finish school or be a better parent. We all have something inside of us that is worthwhile to share with others. Often, you say or do something without even realizing the impact your words would have on someone else.

You may believe that nothing you say is worthwhile to inspire someone else. But many times, others are inspired by seeing how you dealt with your own battles.

Instead of looking at someone who seems to have a perfect life and thinking you could never do that, let others see your imperfections. Hopefully, their response will be, "If she can do that, so can I."

How have you been inspired by the words or actions of someone else? Will you let them know the impact they made on your life?

Today's Joy: Don't be ashamed of your story. It's sure to inspire others.

SEPTEMBER 4
TRIBE OF JOY

I cherish my joyful friends.

Who is in your tribe? Are they joyful beings? Your joyful friends are the ones who seem to always be shining for others. They are kind and gracious; they wear a smile on both their face and in their heart; and they are always ready to serve where needed.

As women, we all need a tribe of friends and family to love and support us at every turn in our lives. The best tribes are there to help us celebrate all the good that comes our way. They are also close by to pick up the pieces when things seem to be falling apart on us.

Be sure your tribe is made up of ones who are joyful and are positive thinkers. We want to be with women who are uplifting and encouraging and avoid negativity. Yet, if you see someone who is negative, you can offer some light to them to see if they shine. If they are not yet ready to, pray for them. There is hope for all of us.

Who is in your Tribe of Joy? Choose them carefully and realize you may need to be the joy-maker in the group. Wear the title proudly and with a big smile!

Today's Joy: "The joy you give to others is the joy that comes back to you."—Margaret E. Sangster[3]

SEPTEMBER 5
OVERCOMING ANXIETY

I stay focused on positive things in my life.

Perhaps most of us have had some level of anxiety in our lives. Sometimes it is so overwhelming, that we don't know how we can cope. I've had anxiety attacks that have landed me in the emergency room, and you may have had a similar experience.

Lots of deep breathing and prayer is an immediate source of relief. Long term, we need to practice positive self-talk, yoga, meditating, and daily affirmations. Some affirmations that I use are:

> I am safe.
> I can cope.
> I am in control.
> I am calm.
> I am strong.

Look for affirmations that resonate with you. Write them on a note, hang on your mirror, and say them every day.

And a short prayer for anxiety by Rev David Adam.

> Calm me, O Lord, as you stilled the storm,
> Still me, O Lord, keep me from harm,
> Let all the tumult within me cease:
> Enfold me, Lord, in your peace.[4]

Have you found ways to cope with anxiety in your life?

Today's Joy: "Cast all your anxiety on him because he cares for you."—1 Peter 5:7 NIV

SEPTEMBER 6
CULTIVATE KINDNESS

I will do all things with kindness.

One place that I always observe kindness is at the Post Office in my small town. Nearly every single day, someone will hold open the door for you. If you hold the door open for the next person, they usually respond with, "Thank you."

Kindness is a virtue and one of the fruits of the spirit. It doesn't cost us anything to be kind to one another. Being friendly and considerate are acts of kindness. True kindness radiates from the joy in your heart. My mother-in-law was one of the kindest women I have ever known. She was always ready to help anyone with whatever they needed. She made and delivered great dinners if you were sick. She sent cards and made phone calls to check on friends. Her welcoming smile greeted all the churchgoers. My dream has always been to be just like her.

Be known for your kindness and grace. Aspire to be the person that comes to mind when the subject is kindness. It really is one of the best traits you can possess.

One of my favorite sayings is, "Kindness is free. Sprinkle it everywhere!" How will you cultivate kindness in your life?

Today's Joy: "Never let loyalty and kindness leave you! Tie them around your neck as a reminder. Write them deep within your heart." Proverbs 3:3 NLT

SEPTEMBER 7
YELLOW FLOWERS

I find happiness in fresh flowers.

For anyone who knows me personally, you already know that yellow roses are my most favorite flower. A year ago, I married my high-school sweetheart and for our one-year anniversary, he sent me a fabulous bouquet of yellow flowers. It was brimming with 2 dozen roses plus yellow lilies and daisies. I think my heart stood still when I saw this arrangement.

Yellow flowers are usually thought of to spread happiness and joy. What flower could spread more happiness than a yellow daisy? They just seem to smile at you.

But, yellow flowers also symbolize friendship. It is the perfect color of flower to give to anyone on almost any occasion. In addition to roses, other flowers that are also beautiful in yellow include lilies and tulips.

Yellow sunflowers are also highly popular this time of year. When you picture a field of yellow flowers, what comes to mind?

Today's Joy: Yellow flowers are little bursts of sunshine!

SEPTEMBER 8
A JAR OF SAND

I share my life with God and my husband.

My husband and I were married on the beach a year ago. We had a small ceremony with only family just before sunset. Daniel and I walked out on the sand together, hand-in-hand. My lavender dress blew gently in the breeze as we approached the tent covered in flowers. One of my best friends played his guitar and sang, *The Wedding Song*.

Our minister used a lovely *sand ceremony* that led me to some deep thoughts. He first added a handful of sand right from the beach to represent our foundation in God. Then each of us had a slightly different colored sand that we poured together into the jar.

Just as the grains of sand mixed together, so would our lives. It would be close to impossible to ever separate the sand again back into individual containers. Once we are married, our lives become intertwined and you can never really separate yourself from your spouse.

It was always God's plan that the "two would become one."

Is your life intertwined with another? Is the relationship built on the foundation of God?

Today's Joy: ". . . [A]nd the two will become one flesh.' So they are no longer two, but one flesh." Mark 10:8 NIV

SEPTEMBER 9
JOYFUL ENERGY

Your energy introduces you.

Having a joyful attitude is more than just feeling happy. True joy that comes from your heart can change the energy around you.

As you are filled with joy, the energy that you exude will touch other people around you. Even without you saying anything, people can sense your joy when they're around you.

Everyone is made up of energy. Some people have negative energy and you usually sense this quickly. The same goes for positive joyful energy. Energy usually attracts similar energy so by having a positive energy, you will attract other positive and joyful people into your sphere.

My friend, Nilakshi at MerakiMusings.org sent me a lovely comment that she has on her blog, "If I am peaceful with joy, then my whole world vibrates with joyful energy."[5]

Multiply your energy by bringing plants into your home or adding pops of color in your rooms. Uplifting music can also increase your positive energy.

Can you sense someone's energy when they walk into a room? What kind of energy do you give to other people?

Today's Joy: "The energy of the mind is the essence of life."—Aristotle[6]

SEPTEMBER 10
PRAY FOR PEACE

I have peace in my soul today.

"Peace is a rare commodity today."—Linda Outka[7]

There are times in our lives that things will not be the way we wish they could be. And, it is at times like this, we must go to the Lord in prayer, and simply ask for peace. Ask for peace that our hearts may be comforted. Peace that we may accept what is. Peace that we know God is always good.

Peace in knowing that God is in control can calm our aching being. Pray this short prayer and feel the calmness it can bring.

> Dear Lord, I ask you to come into my heart at this time. You know my struggles. Give me your peace to calm my aching soul. Let me feel your presence and know that you are near to me. Amen.

Do you feel calmer and more peaceful when you take your struggles to God through prayer? Have you found ways to fill your heart with peace since the beginning of this month?

Today's Joy: "Now may the Lord of peace himself give you peace at all times and in every way. The Lord be with all of you." 2 Thessalonians 3:16 NIV

SEPTEMBER 11
YOU'RE A WARRIOR

I am strong and confident.

Today, I want to remember the tragedy of September 11, 2001 when the Twin Towers were targeted and soon fell. There were many heroes that day from individuals to first responders. Take a moment today to say a special prayer for the survivors.

I just had a day when I felt like I was a failure. Everything seemed to be against me. In reality, it was only one bad hour of one day. We both know how even small things can tear us down.

As hard as it is to do, you must look beyond the current situation. Try to remember all the good things in your life. Think of all the people who complimented you in the past. I have a document on my computer where I write out things people say or I copy the things they wrote to me. This is my go-to manual when I need to reassure myself that I am okay.

Until you can start your own 'Compliment Manual,' try using these phrases to remind yourself of your courage, your strength, and your beauty.

> You are stronger than you realize.
> You are braver than you think you are.
> You are more beautiful than ever.
> You have unique talents.
> You are a warrior. And, warriors, do not give up.

How do you remind yourself of your own worth? Do you remind yourself often, so you won't forget?

Today's Joy: I graciously accept compliments.

SEPTEMBER 12
BE HAPPY

I wake up happy.

Can you become a *Happiness Seeker*? This is someone who continuously looks for happiness in their everyday lives. A *Happiness Seeker* knows it is possible to find the good in everything. You just have to be willing to seek it.

Even though happiness comes from within your heart and your soul, you can still seek happiness all day, every day. Look for the good in everything you do and everywhere you go.

By recognizing the happiness all around you on a regular basis, happiness becomes your default mode of operation. Your happiness is on autopilot.

Use these happy affirmations as you strive to become a Happiness Seeker.

> My life is full of happiness.
> Happiness comes easily to me.
> I choose to be happy today.
> I deserve to be happy.
> I am in charge of my happiness.
> I create my own happiness.

Where are you on the happy meter today? How can you bring more happiness into your life?

Today's Joy: "There is no key to happiness; the door is always open."—Mother Teresa[8]

SEPTEMBER 13
VALLEYS AND HILLTOPS

I pray in the valleys and rejoice on the hilltops.

It was 4:15 in the morning when my phone rang. I needed to get up anyway so I could get back to see my Daddy in ICU for the 6:00 am visiting time. My mind was groggy as I leaned over to answer the phone. It was the doctor saying Daddy had taken his last breath here on Earth.

I remember this morning well even though it happened 25 years ago. The death of my Daddy threw me deep into a valley. I cried my heart out for days. I trudged through the next few holidays feeling empty and sad. It was a long time before I could climb out of my valley and start the journey up to the hilltop again.

Experiencing the valleys of life gives us the appreciation to sing from the hilltops.

Once you have been through situations of sadness, loss, or despair, you will eventually find your way out of the darkness and back to the light. It is after these low times in life that you will understand and appreciate happiness and the fullness of joy!

Use this time to express gratitude for all that you have. Let your heart sing praises of love and joy. This is your day. You are blessed.

Have you ever found yourself in a valley only to discover a hilltop right ahead?

Today's Joy: "Difficult roads often lead to beautiful destinations. The best is yet to come." –Zig Ziglar[9]

SEPTEMBER 14
FOLLOW YOUR DREAM

I allow myself to dream.

Forty years ago, a dear friend suggested I should write a book. That thought was in the back of my mind for so many years. But I was busy with a family and a career and didn't actively pursue the possibilities. It was only after I retired that I had the opportunity to follow my own dream.

If you have a dream in your heart, I hope you will find the means to follow it. In fact, gather up all your dreams, make a plan to follow them, and use the plan to create a life that you will love.

Dream BIG and great things will be yours. Daydreams are inspirations that challenge us to make plans, focus on the journey, and move forward. Try to visualize the outcome of your dreams, think positive, and have faith in the process.

Large corporations and small shops are all the results of someone's dream. Someone imagined what it would be like to achieve their goal and they made it possible. You can do the same thing with your dreams! Take action and make it happen.

Eleanor Roosevelt said, "The future belongs to those who believe in the beauty of their dreams."[10]

What is your dream? Have you made steps towards accomplishing it? What can you do today to make it happen?

Today's Joy: "If you can dream it, you can do it." —Walt Disney[11]

SEPTEMBER 15
GETTING FROM OVERWHELMED
TO FOCUSED

I focus on my plan.

Autumn is upon us and my to-do list is full. Bible studies are registering, and I've been invited to multiple workshops. There's a long list of fall festivals and holiday markets that have piqued my interest. I'm sure you've got similar activities and plans on your agenda.

Just looking at everything on my planner overwhelms me. This week, I've got a dentist appointment, Bible Study lessons to complete and attend the class, and a final draft due to my editor. I have several friends that I check on every week due to their circumstances. Saturday brings soccer and basketball games with the grandkids. I try not to forget laundry, groceries and making dinner. The list never ends. And as soon as I finish this week, I start a similar schedule for next week. Our schedules often lead us from overwhelmed to stressed and that's the wrong direction for sure!

We can make a list of everything that is a possibility for our schedule. Take a deep breath. Then choose what's most important for you and your family. Some activities will need to be cut. I will need to follow my own advice on this.

Write it down in your planner. Once you commit to it, you have a plan. You'll have to tell everyone else that your schedule is full, and you won't be able to add any new commitments at this time. I know this is easier for me to say than it is for any of us to do. I feel like the Queen of Not Saying No.

How do you control becoming overwhelmed? Do you have a plan to stay focused?

Today's Joy: Make a plan and stick to it. Focus on your plan and enjoy the journey!

SEPTEMBER 16
YOU'LL KNOW

I will follow my heart.

Through the years, many of my girlfriends have confided in me with various issues. There always seems to be one question that continues to come up.

"Should I do this now?" The question is presented in various forms. It may be "Should I call them now?" or "When should I go?"

My response is always something along the lines of "You'll know." Once you've made any plans or preparations that are necessary, ask God to direct your steps and wait for his direction.

I do believe if you listen to your mind and follow your heart, you'll always know the best thing to do and the right time to do it.

We live in a rushed society today and don't want to wait for God's perfect timing. But, with a still heart and patient mind, you'll know when the time is right. You'll know the best thing to do. You'll just know.

Have you ever just had the feeling that the timing is right? Did you take action when you had that feeling?

Today's Joy: "Be still before the Lord and wait patiently for him..." Psalm 37:7 NIV

SEPTEMBER 17
NATIONAL WOMEN'S FRIENDSHIP DAY

I am a good friend.

National Women's Friendship Day is observed on the third Sunday in September. It was created by women and for women as a way to promote friendships among women. We are nourished by our relationships with other women.

Lola has shared friendships with Sazzy and Molly for 40 years. The trio of women meet every week for morning coffee or lunch. They attend church, go shopping and travel together. Most of all, they support each other in every possible way, but especially through prayer.

So today, take time for coffee or lunch with your girlfriends. Call the ones who live farther away. Send cards, tag friends in online posts, share your love and support.

There are really two types of women. One has loads of friends and the other prefers a few close friends. If you have lots of friends, gather a group of them to celebrate today. If you prefer fewer friends with deeper relationships, be sure to reach out to those in your inner circle.

Today is the day to let your girlfriends know you care! I know I've got a few phone calls to make now to my dear friends.

Who will you reach out to today? How can you encourage and inspire your girlfriends?

Today's Joy: Cheers to all women today as we celebrate our cherished friends!

SEPTEMBER 18
GET OUT OF YOUR COMFORT ZONE

I believe in myself.

Retirement gave me the opportunity to try new adventures in life. I've traveled to places I've never been and spent time with new friends. I've read more books and written more articles. I wish I had taken the time over the last 30 years to get out of my comfort zone.

Life seems simpler, maybe even easier, when we have a schedule, and we keep to it. Fix breakfast, get the family out the door, then off to work or take care of the kids, straighten the house, and make dinner. You know the routine.

Having a schedule does give stability to our busy lives. But our minds grow, and we are more creative by being curious and learning new things. You can start with simple things like reading books in a genre you don't normally read. Go to different stores or take a different route to work. You will see things you know nothing about.

And if you're brave, let go of your comfort zone and say hello to new possibilities, new beginnings and new opportunities. What would your life look like? What is your dream? What is the fear that is holding you back?

Embrace the change. Embrace your journey. There is a multitude of interesting places to go and things to do.

What new adventure awaits you today? Will you try something out of your comfort zone?

Today's Joy: I can do anything I desire. I am creative and courageous.

SEPTEMBER 21
WORLD GRATITUDE DAY

It's a good day to be thankful.

World Gratitude Day is celebrated each year on September 21. It is an opportunity for individuals and organizations to celebrate and spread gratitude around us. Expressing appreciation for all the amazing things in our lives provides a positive impact on our well-being.

Even though this day is specifically set aside to show, express, and accept gratitude, we know that daily gratitude is the path to being happier and more contented.

Today, take time to express your appreciation to everyone you encounter. Tell them how grateful you are for their love, support, and friendship. Today, I walked outside to speak to the guys in my landscape crew. A storm blew though yesterday and there were sticks and leaves covering the yard and gardens. I told the crew leader that everything looked great and I appreciated them taking care of all of it for me. He flashed me an award-winning smile as I made my way back indoors. I noticed they stayed a little longer and did a little more.

Make a list of all the things you are thankful for but, don't just list physical things. Include the love of family, your eyesight and hearing, and your faith.

How can you express gratitude today? Who are you grateful to have in your life?

Today's Joy: "As we express our gratitude, we must never forget that the highest appreciation is not to utter words but to live by them." —John F Kennedy[12]

SEPTEMBER 22
CHANGE YOUR STORY

I start my day with positive thoughts.

Nadia is one of my favorite people to spend time with. She grew up in a family that did not appreciate her. They offered her little encouragement or support. But Nadia discovered she could change her life by changing her story. As she began using positive self-talk, she noticed how her life was overflowing with goodness. Kind people made their way into her world. She knew she was finally on the right path.

What is the story you tell about yourself and your life? If you're saying negative things and you're not happy with the way things are, it's time to change your story.

Look for all the positive people and things in your life. Put your laser focus on these positives. Keep telling yourself and others how great these things are.

Next, surround yourself with positive minded people. You will soak up encouragement from them. Leave all the negative nay-sayers behind.

And, as you begin to speak with positivity, you will notice the change it makes in your life. Good things will start to come your way.

What would you like to change in your life? How can you change your story today?

Today's Joy: "A positive attitude causes a chain reaction of positive thoughts, events, and outcomes. It is a catalyst, and it sparks extraordinary results."—Wade Boggs[13]

SEPTEMBER 23
SMILE

I will start my day with a smile.

Last week, there was a hurricane looming close to our coastal home. Our place is tucked back away from where most hurricanes head up the East Coast. But Hurricane Isaias was headed straight for our piece of paradise. We had boarded up and evacuated the island. All we could now was to stay glued to the news, wait, and pray. The hurricane did make landfall right over us but we were spared any damage. Others on the island were not as fortunate. The stress of watching, waiting, and wondering had torn down my pillars of joy.

In order to bring a smile back to my face, I decided to make a list of some of the things I have to smile about.

> My husband, my son and his family, and my sister and her family all bring smiles to me.
> I am safe and alive.
> I hung a lovely wreath on my kitchen door today.
> I found a couple of awesome recipes.
> My kitty came by for a snuggle.

Other ideas could include dinner with friends, a great mani/pedi day, a phone call from someone special or anything chocolate!

What has happened in your life that left you struggling to smile at the day ahead of you?

Today's Joy: When you wear your smile, you are gorgeous!

SEPTEMBER 24
CALM YOUR ANXIETY

I will stop and pray today.

Anxiety can wreak havoc with our minds and our hearts. It doesn't matter whether you're worried about a sick family member, an upcoming bill, or anything else. My friend, Maria, had a sudden bout of severe headaches that she knew were not normal. Scans revealed several brain tumors that were likely malignant. She chose to use her illness as a testimony about Jesus as she asked everyone to stay on their knees in prayer for her healing.

When we are anxious, we become frantic which leads to saying the wrong things, doing the wrong things, and a general turmoil within our lives.

Today, I'm going to ask you to:

> Stop what you are doing
> Drop to your knees
> And Pray for a calm mind and body.

As you pour your heart out to God about your cares, you will feel the peace and calm overcome you that only God can provide. Ask him to provide you with the comfort that you need during this time of struggle.

Then, rest in your faith that God is in control. He will restore your joy.

What method do you use to calm your anxiety? Will you stop, drop, and pray?

Today's Joy: "When anxiety was great within me, your consolation brought me joy." Psalm 94:19 NIV

SEPTEMBER 25
ALWAYS FOCUS ON WHAT
COULD GO RIGHT

I am in control of my life.

I am one of the worst for worrying about every possibility that could happen. My husband often reminds me to not worry when I don't have all of the information. Our human nature causes us to often find ourselves stuck on all the things that could go wrong with an idea, an event, or a situation.

I sobbed as my ex-husband walked out the door for the last time. For the first time in my life, I was all alone. I had never lived alone. I had never been responsible for everything—a home, a yard, a car, the bills. What if I couldn't support myself? What if I couldn't pay the mortgage? A gazillion other questions and concerns flooded my mind. In my usual manner, I took to pen and paper and made a long list of everything that concerned me. With a lot of prayer and a lot of positive self-talk, I made it on my own for the next 21 years. If we can let go of the worry and focus on what could go right instead, our lives will turn from worry to inner peace.

Our minds are powerful, and we can change our lives by adjusting our thinking. When we find ourselves stressing over the details, try to change the thought pattern.

Make a list of all the positives aspects of the current dilemma. And, focus on all the things that could go right. Read the list several times during the day to instill the positivity. As you continue the process, look for your inner peace.

Are you a worrier? Will you try to look for the positive aspects in the future?

Today's Joy: I choose to feel peaceful. Write it on a sticky note and put it in a prominent place to remind you.

SEPTEMBER 26
WHEN YOU DON'T KNOW WHAT TO PRAY

Great is his faithfulness.

I have a friend who recently lost her child in an accident. The mother was in shock, stunned, and inconsolable. She wanted to pray but couldn't find the words. In the days and weeks that followed, she quietly opened her heart and said what was on her mind. These words became her prayers.

Life gets messy and complicated. Sometimes, there's too much going on in our minds. We want to pray but the words won't come.

Just close your eyes and bow your head. God knows your heart. He knows what you need even if you don't know.

He has promised to love and protect you, to provide for you, and to calm your mind and heart. Take your heavy heart to God and let him take control of the messy stuff. You may not even have the strength to say what's on your mind. It's a long story. And, that's ok. He already knows the details.

Bow your head, take deep breaths and sit quietly. You will feel the tension drain from your body. You may even feel an answer come to you.

Have you had times when you didn't have the words to pray?

Today's Joy: "The Lord is good, a refuge in times of trouble. He cares for those who trust in him." Nahum 1:7 NIV

SEPTEMBER 27
IS YOUR SOUL TIRED?

It is well with my soul.[14]

I believe if you are still tired after a good night's sleep, perhaps it is your soul that is tired. If you've been through a discouraging time and find yourself exhausted, emotional or have a foggy mind, it's time for some self-care. Your soul is the essence of your body and sometimes it screams at you for attention.

Try to rest and unplug from all your electronics. Play some music or take a walk. Personally, I find rest for my soul in the hot tub with bath salts or on the porch, rocking and reading.

Your soul knows how to heal itself. The struggle is to silence your mind and let your body take charge. Meditation is a great way to calm the chatter in your mind.

Breathe… Stay calm… Relax… Be still… Refresh your soul.

Is your soul tired? How will you refresh it?

Today's Joy: "Quiet the mind and the soul will speak."—Ma Jaya Sati Bhagavati[15]

SEPTEMBER 28
ADJUST YOUR SAILS

I am free to sail anywhere.

Some years ago, I spent a week on a sailboat off the coast of Maine. There was a small group of us traveling together and we eagerly asked the captain where we would be traveling to this week. His response was that he didn't know. We would hoist the sails and go wherever the wind took us.

Oh, what a lovely thought to be simply moved by the wind. But, as the week went on, we learned how we could adjust the sails and go in a desired direction.

I have a photo of me on that sailboat with the caption reading, "Always remember to adjust your sails."

That's the way our lives should be …. a little bit carefree in the wind but make adjustments as needed to our sails.

What adjustments do you need to make in your life? Do you adjust to life as needed?

Today's Joy: "I am not afraid of storms for I am learning how to sail my ship." —Louisa May Alcott[16]

SEPTEMBER 29
POSITIVE ATTITUDE

I am a positive person.

A positive attitude is your gateway to joy! For many years, I went through life by dealing with whatever the day threw at me. I had a good life, but I didn't consider myself joyful. My life was changed the day a particular verse of scripture sank into my heart. "Always be joyful." 1 Thessalonians 5:16 NLT spoke to me. I began my adventure to having a positive attitude and living a joyful life.

Being a positive person doesn't exclude you from facing tough moments or battles in life. But, with your positive attitude, you'll be able to draw on your strengths and rise above the challenges.

One powerful benefit of being a positive person is that you are making regular deposits of joy in your heart and in your soul. This vault, full of joy, will sustain you whenever you have to travel the roads of negativity in life.

Lift yourself up with affirmations and believe in yourself. One step at a time, keep moving forward.

Focus on the joy you have stored in your heart. You are stronger and wiser than you realize.

Have you stored up a vault of joy in your heart? It's not too late to start.

Today's Joy: Stay positive, and always be joyful!

SEPTEMBER 30
FIND YOUR INNER PEACE

I am peaceful.

The fast-paced life we live in today has enforced a disconnect between our minds and bodies. Our minds are in constant overdrive, so we need to find an avenue to let it rest.

Three pillars that will nurture your spirit are yoga, meditation and affirmations. Regular practice allows you to get the elusive mind-body balance.

> Yoga is a combination of breathing, exercise and meditation. It's the perfect recipe to free yourself of stress and overwhelm.

> Meditation is like decluttering. It is a state of mind that allows you to detach your mind from negative thoughts.

> Affirmations are a simple set of statements about a specific goal. You recite them daily to affect a realization of the goal.

These three pillars have the power to transform your life. They will open your mind, allow you to get in touch with your inner self, and find your inner peace.[17]

After all, peace is joy at rest!

September Challenge Follow Up: Did you find your inner peace this month? Were you able to calm your mind and heart? What surprised you about finding peace within yourself?

Today's Joy: I am relaxed and calm. Peace dwells within me.

DISCOVER YOUR JOY

INNER PEACE

Resting in Peace and Joy

OCTOBER:
EMBRACE FALL

Walking through Nature with Joy

OCTOBER 1
EMBRACE FALL WITH GRATITUDE, BLESSINGS, AND FAMILY GATHERINGS

I enjoy the changing color of the leaves.

As crisp air moves in, our thoughts turn to the beauty of the changing leaves, fresh pumpkin pies, and warm cozy sweaters. Picking apples, solving a corn maze, or choosing pumpkins are great fall activities for the whole family. I'm dreaming of a big bonfire and roasting marshmallows.

One of my favorite fall foods is an apple crisp made from my mother-in-law's recipe. Be sure to plan menus that include apples and pumpkins, and other fall foods.

I have a lovely Japanese maple tree that turns a brilliant red this time of year. It is my fall blessing.

This is the blessing my Daddy said before each of our family meals. "Bless this food and thank you for the many blessings we have received. Pardon our sins for Jesus' sake. Amen." If you don't have a special blessing, consider using Daddy's every day this month.

Make a point to start and end each day with gratitude. Write in your journal the blessings of your day. Pause and reflect. Smile, because life is great!

October Challenge: The harvest of fall fills me with gratitude. How will you spend this fall month enjoying nature and sharing it with family?

Today's Joy: "Give thanks to the Lord for he is good; his love endures forever." Psalm 107:1 NIV

OCTOBER 2
FINDING HAPPINESS

It's a good day to be happy.

Happiness comes from within your mind, your heart, and your soul. No one else can make you truly happy because lasting happiness is something you have to do yourself.

The magic trick is to change the way you think. Developing a positive attitude is one of the fastest tracks to happiness.

Fill your mind with positive thoughts. Read articles or listen to podcasts that promote positivity. And spend time with other positive-minded people. All of this goodness in your life will make you one of the happiest people on planet Earth.

You deserve a lifetime of happiness, and it's waiting for you at the door of positive thinking.

What is your magic way to fill up with happiness?

Today's Joy: Every day I have the power to choose, and today I choose happiness.

OCTOBER 3
SPARKLE EVERY DAY

I was born to sparkle!

Are you a sparkly person? You know, sparkle is not just about glitter. A sparkly person greets you with a warm smile and hug and they sincerely want to know how you are. They're happy, and positive and you feel comfortable in their presence.

Let your smile brighten your day. Let your inner light shine. And leave a little bit of your sparkle everywhere you go!

Just as the stars seem to shine and sparkle on a clear night, you can also sparkle with a happy face and warm gestures.

Your glitter trail can be one of kindness and goodness. And, everyone will be inspired by your sparkle!

There is Sparkle in My Soul Today!

As you go about doing good things on this sparkly day, others will notice and wonder what you have that they don't have. The secret is your loving heart!

How will you sparkle today? Who can you share your sparkle with?

Today's Joy: Lead a life of sparkle and shine!

OCTOBER 4
OUR SENIOR POPULATION

I share kindness with others.

According to The National Council on Aging, there are millions of seniors in the US who are alone and living near the poverty level. Little is being done to care for these individuals, but you can make a positive impact on their lives.[1]

In my years of working as an accountant and tax preparer, I saw many seniors who had spent their life savings on medical care. Others had given their money to their children. Many people in my parents' generation were not fortunate enough to have pension or retirement plans. It is sad to see how some of these seniors are living.

You and I can help by practicing kindness regularly. Engage in conversation and ask questions if you encounter someone who potentially needs assistance. Be sure to check on your senior neighbors, particularly if they live alone.

There are numerous organizations, assisted living centers, and hospitals where you can volunteer to sit with seniors who need a caring person. Phone calls and cards are always appreciated, and lets one know they are in your thoughts. Because of my personal love of flowers, I like to take bouquets to friends. There is no way to value how much your kindness, happiness, and joy are worth when shared with someone in need.

Do you know a senior who is struggling, either financially or with loneliness? What can you do to make their day brighter?

Today's Joy: "It is not how much we do, but how much love we put in the doing. It is not how much we give, but how much love is put in the giving."—Mother Teresa[2]

OCTOBER 5
A WAKE-UP CALL

I release the stressors in my life.

Sally was working a stressful job with a long commute. It meant long days with little time for anything else. One night, she noticed a lump on her upper side. After doctor visits and tests, the decision was made to remove the lump. The surgeon showed Sally the lymph node and said it looked like cancer.

After several days of worry and many prayers, the biopsy showed it was not cancer. Instead, it was found to be cat scratch disease. Prayers of rejoicing followed the diagnosis.

After all the concern and worry, the experience convinced Sally that it was time to leave her stressful job. She decided that life was too short to live under all the pressure.

What kind of stress in your life do you need to let go of? You'll be both happier and healthier with life changes that allow you downtime and peace of mind.

Today's Joy: "I will breathe. I will think of solutions. I will not let my worries control me. I will not let my stress break me. I. will. simply. breathe. And it will be okay… Because I don't quit."—Shayne McClendon[3]

OCTOBER 6
RANDOM ACTS OF KINDNESS

I am kind and gracious.

You've probably heard stories of people doing random acts of kindness, like paying for the person behind you in the drive-through lane. How wonderful it feels to pull up to the window and be told your order is already paid.

But it is also a rewarding feeling to be the one that performed that kind and thoughtful act. There is a satisfaction in knowing that you gave of yourself or your time or your money so that someone else could experience a moment of surprising joy in their day.

No matter how small, these gestures genuinely make a difference for both the person giving and the person receiving them.

Here are some other ideas for random acts of kindness.

Bring a snack to a co-worker.
Mail a card to someone unexpectedly.
Surprise a neighbor with flowers.

It's sure to brighten your day as much as it brightens the receiver's day.

What random act of kindness can you offer to someone today? How will you surprise them with your gesture?

Today's Joy: Kindness is spreading sunshine all around.

OCTOBER 7
QUESTION EVERYTHING

I am curious.

From a young age, most of us are taught not to question our parents, our teachers, or any adult, really.

As we grow into being an adult, we are still taught not to question employers, doctors, or anyone with authority.

However, it is through questions that we learn and grow. I once had a co-worker who would always ask why we did things a certain way. She wanted to know the outcome we were seeking and a zillion other questions. But she came to understand the process better than anyone else through her quizzing.

Probably the one authority highest on my list to try to get answers from is my doctor. We know our bodies better than anyone else and we know when something is not right. Take a stand for yourself and keep asking until you find out what you really need to know.

Start children out young by asking why they want a particular item or how it will change their life. They will learn at a young age how to think outside the box.

What are the questions you always seek answers for? Do you persist on your quest even when it's not easy or comfortable?

Today's Joy: Cultivate curiosity and learning.

OCTOBER 8
A JOYFUL LIFE

I am joyful.

What do you think represents a joyful life? I believe joyful lives are built on hope, faith, and love.

Living a joyful life begins with hope. Our hope gives us the courage to keep going. But we also need faith. We have to trust and believe that everything will work out for the best.

Faith is 'Hope Extraordinaire!'

Hope and faith are strong actions but are reinforced when handled with love.

Fill your heart with hope, faith, and love, and you are sure to be living a joyful life.

> I believe that joy is at the core of my being. I know the joy I seek is already within me. I commit to it with a lightness and ease that evaporates all barriers. I will create joyful moments with every heartbeat.—Adrienne Enns[4]

Are you living a joyful life? If not, how can you start to bring more joy into your world, even a little at a time?

Today's Joy: "And now these three remain: faith, hope and love. But the greatest of these is love." 1 Corinthians 13:13 NIV

OCTOBER 9
WEARY AND BURDENED

I turn my concerns over to God.

Matthews 11:28 NIV tells us, "Come to me, all you who are weary and burdened, and I will give you rest."

We all have days when we feel tired and overwhelmed. It takes every ounce of energy we have just to get up and do what has to be done that day.

At times like this, take your burdens to the Lord. Tell him how you feel and ask him to provide you the comfort and strength you need to keep going. Once you turn your concerns over to God, let him handle them. It is our nature to pray for an answer and then go back to solve the problem ourselves.

God has it covered. You can try to rest and prepare for a better day tomorrow.

What do you do when you are weary and burdened? Do you turn everything over to God, then rest, knowing he has it under control?

Today's Joy: "However weak we are, however poor; however little our faith, or however small our grace may be, our names are still written on his heart; nor shall we lose our share in Jesus' love."—Charles Spurgeon[5]

OCTOBER 10
NATURE WALK

I enjoy my time outdoors.

Fall is in the air and the temperatures have cooled down from the summer heat. Leaves are beginning to fall from the trees, and they add a slight crunch to your step.

The season beckons us to come outside for a long walk. Our minds welcome the freshness in the air. The exercise replenishes our bodies. Taking a walk and observing nature also lowers our stress levels and calms our soul. It is a time to clear our minds and refocus our energies.

Watch the squirrels as they start putting away acorns for the winter. Enjoy the trees' transformation as their leaves change from green to flaming red, then golden, and finally fall to the ground.

Take a few deep breaths and fill your lungs with the cool air. Sit on a nearby bench and absorb the flow from summer to autumn.

My nature walk reminds me that all is well with my soul.

Thinking back to our challenge question on October 1, have you been able to take time to get outside and enjoy nature? What is your favorite part about being out in the fall temperatures?

Today's Joy: "Study nature, love nature, stay close to nature. It will never fail you."—Frank Lloyd Wright[6]

OCTOBER 11
TRUST THE JOURNEY

*I trust even when I
don't understand.*

Do you believe things always work out, or do you fret and worry over everything?

Wherever your journey, be it nearby or far away, try to kick back and enjoy the trip. Trust that things will happen the way they are intended.

Many years ago, we were traveling home late at night when our new car totally stopped. After a few scary encounters, the local sheriff from the closest small town stopped to check on us. He piled us in his car and took us to his office. As we waited on my sister to drive the two hours to get us, I was upset that my constant prayer had not been answered. It was days later when I realized my prayer had been, "Keep us safe," and that our God did.

Let the detours offer opportunities for new adventures. Believe that delays protect you from problems. Being open-minded and trusting the process will bring you more joy than stressing over details and trying to control circumstances. Always remember, God is in control.

No matter whether your journey is to a vacation resort, up the corporate ladder, or through daily life, trust the process. The low-stress method makes it easier to maintain your balance and appreciate the little things.

Trust the journey. And let joy fill your days.

I am among the ones that tend to worry about almost everything. Just ask my husband! However, I am trying my best to trust the journey and enjoy the adventure. Are you a worrier?

Will you go with me as we learn to embrace the detours and seek God's path?

Today's Joy: "If you cannot find joy in the journey, there will be no delight in the destination."—Will Craig[7]

OCTOBER 12
HATE IS A STRONG WORD

I will remove 'hate' from my vocabulary.

I worked with a gal some years ago who owned a home design consulting business. In her office one day, I heard one of her clients complain that they hated a particular color of a pair of curtains. I vividly remember the owner's response when she said, "Hate is a strong word."

Her comment has stuck with me many years now. I've even repeated it numerous times when someone talks about hating a person or anything else. I have tried to remove the word from my vocabulary.

When you hear the word *hate*, does it make you feel tense or even angry? Do you feel your body tighten up? There's no need to bring this undue stress into your life. There are so many good things in life to waste time on any 'hateful' topics.

Do you use 'hate' in everyday language? Can you remove the word 'hate' from your vocabulary too?

Today's Joy: "Hatred stirs up conflict, but love covers over all wrong." Proverbs 10:12 NIV

OCTOBER 13
APPRECIATE YOURSELF

I create a life I love.

Take time every day to recognize all that you've accomplished, all the kindness you've shared, and all the love you've spread.

Women, especially, do not give themselves credit for their real worth. We are so busy nurturing everyone else that we forget to appreciate our own contributions to life.

Examine all the fabulous things that you have done and continue to do every day. Give yourself sincere compliments that remind you that you are beautiful, loved, and awesome.

First, you deserve the compliments and the appreciation. However, hearing the words will boost your confidence and instill positive thoughts in your heart.

Do you take time to appreciate yourself and your contributions you have made to the world around you? How do you encourage yourself to feel worthy of appreciation?

Today's Joy: "You are worthy. You are capable. You are beautiful. Book the ticket. Write the book. Create the dream. Celebrate yourself. Rule your queendom."—Elyse Santilli[8]

OCTOBER 14
SORROW AND GRIEF

I will see you again.

There comes the time in all of our lives when we lose someone whom we dearly loved. All of a sudden, our world is filled with deep sorrow and unrelenting grief. We feel like we'll never breathe again, or we'll never quit crying. Grief is the result of truly caring and loving someone.

For myself, my biggest heartbreak was losing my sweet Daddy. My sister and I sat with him in ICU for five long weeks. We were both Daddy's girls. We adored him, and he doted on us. Our hearts were broken when God took him home.

Grief is natural. Grief is tough. We all grieve at our own pace and for different lengths of time. And that's ok.

Do you know someone who is grieving? Will you lift them in prayer for strength and comfort?

Today's Joy: "Blessed are those who mourn, for they will be comforted." Matthew 5:4 NIV

OCTOBER 15
BECOME A JOY THINKER

My joy has no limits.

Often something happens that catapults us into becoming a Joy-Thinker.

For me, I heard a message that my pastor gave on joy, and it resonated with me. I know people who have hit rock bottom in their lives. It is there that they realized they need to change their thought process to a positive one. Gradually, they made their way to becoming a Joy-Thinker. Your story could be anywhere in between.

Choosing positive thoughts is your first step to becoming a Joy-Thinker. Use affirmations daily to deepen your commitment to joy. Try to associate with like-minded people. One negative person can bring down your joy in a moment. Limit contact with these people and seek out happy faces.

Are you a Joy-Thinker? If so, what brought you to this joyful mindset? If you're not a Joy-Thinker, how can you move in that direction?

Today's Joy: "You have made known to me the paths of life; you will fill me with joy in your presence." Acts 2:28 NIV

OCTOBER 16
IT'S OK TO MAKE A MISTAKE

Mistakes are proof that I am trying.

Who isn't afraid of making a mistake? Yikes, it's so hard to face the embarrassment.

If you are fearful of making a mistake, you will never try anything new or different. However, mistakes are how you learn.

You try something, and it doesn't work, so you tweak it. Again, it doesn't work, and you tweak it one more time. Through a series of tweaks, your masterpiece will finally come to fruition.

This is a hard lesson for kids, and even some adults, to learn. We all aim for perfection, but a lot of trial and error usually precedes perfection.

Try not to take your mistakes personally. Learn from the experience and move forward. Wisdom is the result of learning from your mistakes.

Next time something doesn't turn out as planned, pat yourself on the back and remind yourself you did your best. Then, you can try again.

How do you feel when you make a mistake? Are you able to accept it and keep moving forward?

Today's Joy: "Now go and make interesting mistakes, make amazing mistakes, make glorious and fantastic mistakes. Break rules. Leave the world more interesting for your being here."—Neil Gaiman[9]

All my thoughts are pure positive.

I have written other pages about the Law of Attraction without specifically referring to it. If you are not familiar with the Law of Attraction, basically it states that whatever you give your attention to, you draw more of the same into your life.

If you think positive thoughts, you draw more positive things into your life. If you are a negative thinker, you'll attract not-so-good things.

This is one reason that I continue to emphasize positive thinking to you. This is the reason to always look for the good in everything.

The Law of Attraction is not something you can ignore. Just like gravity, it's a law of the universe.

Now that you know the science behind positive thinking, I hope you'll be consistent in looking for good things and sharing your positive attitude.

Are you a positive thinker? Do you see how it attracts more positivity into your life?

Today's Joy: "Whatever you hold in your mind on a consistent basis is exactly what you will experience in your life."—Tony Robbins[10]

OCTOBER 18
IN THE FOG

Today is a good day.

In the wee hours of the morning, I love to gaze out the window to see twinkling stars. The moon was full just two days ago, and he should be hanging high in the sky this morning.

However, I do not see either the stars or the moon this morning. They were clouded by a dense fog from all the rain yesterday. Sometimes, our lives are like this. Sometimes we cannot see what is really in front of us because of the fog.

Fog in the air usually dissipates as the day goes forth. The sun helps to burn away the fog.

By being patient, we will once again see the glory of a beautiful day. Just like the fog of the earth, we will also find the glory of a beautiful day in our lives by being patient until things pass.

Do you sometimes feel like you're looking at your day through the fog? By pressing forward, do you see things more clearly?

Today's Joy: "Faith is like radar that sees through the fog – the reality of things at a distance that the human eye cannot see."—Corrie Ten Boom[11]

OCTOBER 19
PLANT A SEED

I nourish my harvest with patience.

I have a friend who always wanted to know what I had produced that day, and that was the only thing that was important to him.

Some days we may not have finished products to show for our day. But, if we've laid some foundation or planted seeds, there will be a product or a harvest in our future.

Similarly, you may be trying to help someone with a project, but it seems to be going nowhere. It may be this person isn't ready to receive or act on this information now.

Be comforted by knowing you planted a seed. Give it time to nourish and grow.

Once I stumbled upon this quote, I began to live by it. "Don't judge each day by the harvest you reap but by the seeds that you plant."—Robert Louis Stevenson[12]

Continue to enjoy our beautiful fall season. Be grateful for the opportunity to plant a seed. Are you excited knowing you'll have a harvest to reap?

Today's Joy: "The day you plant the seed is not the day you eat the fruit. Be patient and stay the course."—Fabienne Fredrickson[13]

OCTOBER 20
INTENTIONAL LIVING

I choose to live my life on purpose.

Are you living to fulfill your passion? What do you value most in life? For me, I want to live in a comfortable home with someone who loves sharing life with me. I want to be surrounded by family, friends, and plants! This is what I call intentional living.

Instead of existing on autopilot, take some time to think about what you truly want out of life. Perhaps you want to consciously make better choices or exercise regularly. Or maybe you're planning for retirement or a world tour. Again, this is intentional living.

Whatever your intentional life looks like, make plans and steps towards your goal. Let your plan be the light that motivates you to keep moving towards your dream.

Focus on the values that align with your idea of intentional living.

How can you work towards living an intentional life? What does that life look life for you?

Today's Joy: "The greatest thing in this world is not so much where we stand as in what direction we are moving."—Johann wolfgang von Goethe[14]

OCTOBER 21
CULTIVATE JOY

I will rejoice and be glad.

Joy does not just come to us. We have to seek joy, and we have to continue to seek joy hour after hour and day after day.

Our lives are busy, and we don't need one more thing to do. But we must consciously cultivate joy. Put down the electronics and read an encouraging book. Take time to pray or meditate. Walk in nature and notice the wonders around you. Practice gratitude every day. You are rewarded with a joyful heart.

Cultivating joy quiets your mind and brings peace to your heart. It renews your focus on life. Once you've experienced joy and become accustomed to the warm-hearted feeling, it will be easier for you to continue your routine of cultivating joy.

Now, it's time to share your joy with others! Smile! Be kind! Hug someone! And, let others know you love them!

How do you cultivate your joy on a regular basis? Do you make an effort to share your joy with others?

Today's Joy: "So with you: Now is your time of grief, but I will see you again and you will rejoice, and no one will take away your joy." John 16:22 NIV

OCTOBER 22
PRAISE THE LORD

I offer praises to God each day.

By offering our praises to God, our own hearts fill with joy. I think of singing hymns in church and how joyful I feel with the words and music filling my soul. My favorite hymns are the old ones that I grew up singing with my family. These are the one that I know all the words by heart.

Our Lord loves us to praise Him through messages, songs, and prayer. It shows Him how pure our heart is in our love for the Lord. However, praising God also brings us closer to Him in our own heart. Praises stir our soul and remind us of the love that God has for us.

It's easy to praise the Lord when times are good. However, we must continue to praise Him even in times of struggles or needs. Praising and glorifying God through our battles reminds us that He is always close to us and will not leave us.

How do you give praises to the Lord? Does it make you feel joyful when you praise God?

Today's Joy: "Let everything that has breath praise the LORD. Praise the LORD." Psalm 150:6 NIV

OCTOBER 23
CHOOSE WISELY

I choose to have a positive attitude.

Every day, we make thousands of choices. What am I going to wear today? What am I going to eat for breakfast, lunch, and dinner? And on and on, day after day.

Every single one of these choices also affects the path your life will take. By choosing to take a certain class, you will meet specific people. How will these people affect your life's path?

You choose to be kind and happy to other people instead of being rude and grumpy. Your positive attitude will attract other positive people and situations into your life.

Instead of studying accounting, you decide to study music. Your path will involve people you probably would not have met otherwise. You may physically relocate to a place you never thought you would live and have neighbors you never dreamed of meeting.

With a young child who was frequently ill, it had become difficult for me to continue to keep up with my job. I made the decision to start my own business where I could be available as needed to care for my child. That decision led me to a career I never imagined possible.

As you can see, every decision is important to your life's path. Choose wisely.

What decisions have you made that shaped the path of your life?

Today's Joy: "Where our thoughts dwell, so becomes our reality. Choose wisely!" — Nanette Mathews[15]

OCTOBER 24
DREAMS LEAD TO SUCCESS

I am dedicated to my dream.

Do you have a dream of something you want to accomplish? Have you made a commitment to yourself to pursue your dream?

My grandson has the dream of becoming an Eagle Scout. He has been in scouting since he was old enough to join. He has progressed through the ranks and spends many weekends working on Boy Scout projects. His dedication to his dream of being an Eagle Scout will surely lead him to success.

Dreams and dedication go hand-in-hand. The main ingredient to dedication is hard work. You can be dedicated to a dream, but your hard work is what fuels your dedication to achieve success.

Have you committed to pursuing a dream of yours? Are you putting in the hard work and determination that is needed?

Today's Joy: "Dare to live the life you have dreamed for yourself. Go forward and make your dreams come true."—Ralph Waldo Emerson[16]

OCTOBER 25
MAKE A DIFFERENCE DAY

I strive to help my neighbors.

Make a Difference Day was established to recognize community service and the volunteers that make a difference. It is recognized annually on the fourth Saturday of October.

As a teen, I volunteered in nursing homes to talk to residents or read to them. This became an outing close to my heart. Today, I have two nursing homes in my small town where I love to visit, chat, and surprise the residents with flowers or small seasonal gifts.

For almost 30 years, individuals and organizations have worked together to improve their communities. They've done everything from working with animal shelters to picking up litter off the highways.

It has developed into a day of neighbors coming together to help other neighbors. I posted a tribute to this day on social media last year. One woman replied that she was going door-to-door, talking to all her neighbors about a specific community project.

We can do unlimited things to make a difference both in our neighborhood and across our country. In addition to helping others with your services, you will also come away with a warm heart and a feeling of accomplishment.

How can you acknowledge Make a Difference Day? What can you do to serve your community?

Today's Joy: Making a difference in your community will also make a difference in your heart.

I am inspired by the people around me.

Jim Rohn said, "You are the average of the five people you spend the most time with."[17] So, think of the five people you spend most of your time with. It could be family, friends, neighbors, someone at the gym, wherever you go. You could exclude co-workers unless you have a friendship with them outside of work.

What are their traits? Do you also have the same traits or values? The answer is probably *yes*.

Going one step further, here are the types of people you may most want to surround yourself with: those who are invigorated and encouraging, eager and accepting, and of course, those who are grateful.

Yes, can you see that having a tribe of friends with those traits would be valuable to your life? Those are all positive values that would contribute an abundance of happiness, gratitude, and joy to your life.

Make it a point to seek out friends who are positive thinkers. These are people you want in your tribe!

What are the qualities of the people around you? Do they possess the qualities you desire for your own life?

Today's Joy: Strive to be the person you desire to be.

OCTOBER 27
FOCUS ON YOUR SOLUTION

All of my problems have solutions.

So many times, when we are trying to solve a problem, we tend to focus on the problem. We think about all the wrong things; how unfair it is for us to be in this situation, and we want to commiserate with anyone who will listen.

However, if we can flip our thoughts to focus on the solution instead, we will make better progress towards solving the issue. Make a conscious decision to evaluate all the possible solutions and decide what will work out for the best under the circumstances. This positive mindset allows us to be more realistic and calmer in seeking the best solution.

Being problem focused is a negative mindset that keeps us dragging along in negativity. Flip the thoughts to being solution focused and you're ready to solve the problem and move forward.

How do you focus on solutions? Are you able to use a positive mindset?

Today's Joy: "A positive attitude gives you power over your circumstances instead of your circumstances having power over you."—Joyce Meyer[18]

OCTOBER 28
PEOPLE ALONG YOUR PATH

I greet everyone with a smile and a kind word.

I do believe that God puts certain people on our path for a variety of reasons.

It could be that someone is placed along our path to teach us a lesson. Or perhaps someone else needs to learn something that we can share.

Maybe it's not a lesson, but a need. Do we need something like encouragement or information from someone we recently encountered? Or vice versa. Does someone need information we have to share?

Some people are on our path for only a short while. But others have walked for many years with us on our path. We don't know the reasons for all of this; we just have to believe that it is all part of God's master plan.

The lesson is to be kind, gracious, and generous to everyone you meet. We don't know their battles, and they may not know ours. Let's just do our part to make this world a better place and help each other as much as possible.

What do you have to offer to people you encounter along your path? Have you ever met someone that seemed to be just right for a situation in your life?

Today's Joy: "Some people come into our lives and leave footprints on our hearts and we are never ever the same."— Flavia Weedn[19]

OCTOBER 29
LIFE'S REFLECTION

I choose to have a loving heart.

The things we do and say every day reflect what's in our own hearts. If your heart is filled with love and kindness, you will treat other people with the same love and kindness. And, if you're filled with bitterness, that's what you reflect to others. No matter where your heart is right now, you can take steps to be the one who spreads goodness to everyone you meet.

My friend, Molly, has been by my side for many years. She is the perfect example of someone filled with love and kindness. She continually checks on me and her other friends to see what we need or how she can pray for us.

First, ask God to turn your heart to the right. Read uplifting and encouraging books or articles. Use positive affirmations every day. Start writing your thoughts in a journal. Make an effort to change any negative thoughts into positive statements.

Honor where you are in life and trust the path you're on. You have the strength and the courage to fill your heart with love and kindness.

What do your actions show about your heart?

Today's Joy: "As water reflects the face, so one's life reflects the heart." Proverbs 27:19 NIV

OCTOBER 30
GIVE IT TO GOD

God has my cares in his pocket.

Last night, I had something on my mind, and it was all I could think about. I turned it over to God in prayer. But it still was flying through my mind off and on. My tactic was every time I thought about it, I reminded myself that God had it and he didn't need my input. I told myself variations of that statement at least 50 times.

It's easy for us to say we turned it over to God, but then we take it back and try to solve the problem ourselves. This time, I was determined not to worry and let God handle it. It took my conscious effort to keep telling myself not to worry.

Thankfully, it hasn't crossed my mind today until I decided to write about it.

What happens when you turn your problems over to God? Are you able to let it go?

Today's Joy: Give all your cares to God. Remind yourself he'll see you through. Then get some rest.

OCTOBER 31
IN THE GARDEN

I admire God's handiwork around me.

It was windy in the garden today. There's a storm blowing in from the west. But I sat on my porch in the rocking chair until the rain drove me inside.

It is fall, and the trees are all lit up with their red and golden hues. Soon, I'll be crunching leaves and gumballs (it's a Southern thing) under my feet. Pumpkins line the steps of my porch, and I notice colorful mums throughout the gardens. Words actually cannot describe their beauty. It is a time to pause, take in the beauty, and reflect on the fact that only God could create this beautiful masterpiece. Sing praises to our God for His glorious handiwork.

As I gaze at the gardens' soothing serenity, I feel my internal peace and joy being refreshed. Even with the wind blowing, there is a certain calmness in the air. Breathing in the cooler air, I exhale all my worries.

Taking time to enjoy nature reminds me that life really is good.

October Challenge Follow Up: October is a month of beauty in nature. Did you have an opportunity to experience nature and to share time outdoors with family or friends?

Today's Joy: "He has made everything beautiful in its time." Ecclesiastes 3:11a NIV

DISCOVER YOUR JOY

EMBRACE FALL

Walking Through Nature with Joy

NOVEMBER:
GRATITUDE AND
THANKSGIVING

*Giving Thanks
with Joyous
Gratitude*

NOVEMBER 1
BEGIN EVERY DAY WITH GRATITUDE

I am abundantly blessed.

Would you like to have a great day every day? It sounds delightful, for sure. And it is certainly possible by starting every day with gratitude in your heart.

Upon awakening each morning, let one of your first thoughts be, *thank you,* and name a few things that you are grateful for that day. You can go one step further and write down your list in a gratitude journal. By writing it down, you are more engaged with your gratefulness, and rereading it later also heightens your gratitude.

Here are a few suggestions to get you started on your morning gratitude list.

> You are alive and breathing.
> The sun is shining.
> You are thankful for your family, your job, the food you'll eat today.

This daily practice of gratitude is one of the fastest and easiest paths to living a joyful life. The more grateful you are, the more things you will find to be thankful for.

November Challenge: What are you grateful for today? November is often known as The Month of Gratitude as we celebrate Thanksgiving in a few weeks. Can you find something to be grateful for every day this month?

Today's Joy: Gratitude is the foundation of living a joyous life.

I am thankful for small blessings.

Sometimes our prayers are *big*, and we're looking for *big* answers from God. However, don't lose sight of the mini-miracles that happen along the path.

If you're praying for healing for someone with a severe illness, the mini-miracles could occur every few days as this person gradually, one step at a time, heals various portions of their body.

Always be thankful for these mini-miracles. Praise God for them. Share the mini-miracles with others and adjust your prayers to specifically pray for what else needs to happen to restore this person to health.

Mini-miracles probably occur regularly in our lives if we take the time to examine the details. Little things like avoiding a major accident could be God's hand at work to save you. Be sure to say, "Thank you."

Everything holds the possibility of a miracle! Have you been aware of mini-miracles in your life?

Today's Joy: "He performs wonders that cannot be fathomed, miracles that cannot be counted." Job 5:9 NIV

NOVEMBER 3
SHOWERS OF BLESSINGS

I am blessed beyond measure.

Each of us is so abundantly blessed. I want to share a few thoughts with you today to remind both of us of our bountiful blessings.

> Every new day brings new blessings.
> Gratitude multiplies my blessings.
> I am blessed with so much more than I deserve.
> Etch your blessings deep in your heart.
> I am grateful for my abundant blessings.
> Family is one of our greatest blessings.
> Count your blessings every day.

Do you feel abundantly blessed? How many blessings can you count today?

Today's Joy: "From his abundance we have all received one gracious blessing after another." John 1:16 NLT

NOVEMBER 4
3 WAYS TO FIND JOY IN EVERYTHING

I've got joy in my soul today.

I'm a joy-fanatic, and I like to tell people that joy is my superpower.

But, joy does not always magically appear in our lives. It needs to become a habit that you seek joy every day. Therein, you will build a reservoir to sustain you when life gets you down.

Here are my three, somewhat magical, ways to find joy every day in everything.

1. **Be thankful.** If it is raining, I am thankful my yard is being watered. If traffic is backed up, I am thankful I am safe.

2. **Blessings.** I bless my family, friends, neighbors, and co-workers. I also bless people I see at the store or the doctor's office. It's quick and easy to say, "Bless this person for what they need today."

3. **Quiet time.** Every day, I take time to read devotionals, scripture, or anything inspirational. It sets the course for me to have a great day.

What are your magical ways to find joy in your day?

Today's Joy: "…The joy of the Lord is your strength."
Nehemiah 8:10 NIV

NOVEMBER 5
FORGIVENESS

I forgive myself.

Forgiveness is a difficult topic to discuss sometimes. We are taught to forgive others for any harm they caused us. We do this out of kindness, respect, and generosity, even though it is often hard to do.

Without sincere forgiveness, we hold a grudge, and anger destroys our well-being. However, forgiving others helps us to recover, learn, and move forward from the mistake.

Forgiveness typically focuses on others, but we must also learn to forgive ourselves. If you said or did something that you know was not right, make amends as soon as possible and ask forgiveness from the wronged person. Don't allow it to build within yourself.

Forgiving yourself is not something that is talked about regularly. But try to forgive yourself as you would forgive someone else. You need this peace of mind to continue your life with a clean heart.

Do you forgive others with grace? Have you tried forgiving yourself when appropriate?

**Today's Joy: "… Forgive as the Lord forgave you."
Colossians 3:13 NIV**

NOVEMBER 6
YOUR BUCKET LIST

I am inspired.

What's on your bucket list? Perhaps you'd like to visit a foreign country or drive a fancy car. Maybe you want to swim with the dolphins or see the Northern Lights.

Oscar De La Renta once said, "Things never happen on accident. They happen because you have a vision, you have a commitment, you have a dream."[1]

I challenge you to make a reverse bucket list. This would shift your mind from a traditional list of dreams to an exercise in love and gratitude.

How many of these things can you add to your bucket list?

> Be kind to everyone you meet.
> Practice gratitude daily.
> Spread happiness and joy.
> Be a calm and peaceful person.
> Love your family, friends, and neighbors.

Choose to be a strong woman and embrace a magnificent life!

What is on your reverse bucket list?

Today's Joy: "The important thing to you is not how many years in your life but how much life in your years!"— Edward J Stieglitz[2]

NOVEMBER 7
READ A GOOD BOOK

I enjoy reading and learning.

When I would pick up my grandkids to spend the weekend with me, the first thing they wanted to know would be, "Can we go to the bookstore?" They loved looking through all the books they had heard about and new ones, too. The two of them would agonize over which final books they would ultimately purchase.

A good book offers us a temporary escape from our busy lives. It's a way to discover worlds beyond our immediate reach. There are so many possibilities to explore. How about a novel set by the sea, or a historical fiction from World War II? You might enjoy a non-fiction or self-help book. Try to mix it up and read a variety of genres of books.

Find out what your friends or kids are reading and read the same book to discuss it. If you crave companionship, consider joining a book club. You will enjoy both the book and the company of like-minded people.

With the electronic age upon us, so many people are on their phones, or watching videos, surfing YouTube or playing games. However, books are a source of learning and understanding. Reading is a vacation for our minds. It's our passport to unlimited possibilities.

The time you spend reading stretches your mind and expands your horizons. What are you reading right now? How did you choose this particular book?

Today's Joy: "I do believe something very magical can happen when you read a good book."—J K Rowling[3]

NOVEMBER 8
KICK COMPARISON

I am good enough just the way I am.

Recently, I was in a meeting with a group of successful entrepreneurs. Everyone was dressed in their business attire and looked great, except for one lady. She was dressed like she might be homeless. Most people kept their distance and surely didn't speak to her. Comparison was rampant in the room that day. Since we never know someone else's needs, I approached her to see if she would share her story. The rest of the attendees glared at us as the woman and I shared a hearty laugh. She was experimenting to see how people would treat her differently based on her dress.

Can you kick comparison out of your life altogether? It is a natural tendency to compare grades, wealth, talents, and even hairstyles to others. However, comparison pulls you down. It brings out feelings of ineptitude, inadequacy, and discontentment.

No one else is at the same place as you are. No one else is working with the same skills or tools that you have. No one else is focusing on the same things.

Continue to be true to yourself, your passion, and your purpose. Continue to remind yourself of your goals and your talents.

Your only competition is yourself. Have you ever felt left out of a situation because you were being compared to others? How did you react?

Today's Joy: "Comparison is the thief of joy."—Theodore Roosevelt[4]

NOVEMBER 9
YOU ARE BLESSED

I am thankful and blessed.

You and I, and all of us, are blessed because of God's grace and favor.

Jeremiah 17:7-8 NIV tells us, "Blessed is the man who trusts in the Lord and whose trust is the Lord. For he will be like a tree planted by the water, that extends its roots by a stream and will not fear when the heat comes; but its leaves will be green, and it will not be anxious in a year of drought nor cease to yield fruit."

God cares about you as much as he cares about the tree. He will always be there for you in times of drought. You need not worry. God has it all under control if you trust in him and put your confidence in him.

How do you feel blessed by God? Have you been expressing gratitude for your blessings this month?

Today's Joy: "The Lord bless you and keep you; the Lord makes his face shine on you, and be gracious to you." Numbers 6:24-25 NIV

I am filled with positive energy.

One day as I headed into the gym, several women were standing around talking negatively about their husbands. Frankly, it was embarrassing that a woman would publicly share some of these stories. Finally, one woman spoke up to say how great her husband was and how proud she was of him. She successfully flipped the conversation to positivity.

Have you heard someone talk about how bad their life is? Then, everyone else has their own stories to share. Each story is worse than the one before.

It is easy to get caught up in the negativity, especially on social media. All of the negative emotions are not good for you.

It may be challenging to break away from a negative conversation. But try to find a positive element and turn the conversation around. If you share an inspiring story, perhaps others will also change to sharing positive stories.

Choose positive thoughts every day and it will lead you to a healthier and more satisfied life.

Have you experienced conversations flooded with negativity? Were you able to find a moment to inject a breath of positivity?

Today's Joy: I release any negativity and embrace positivity.

NOVEMBER 11
BE A FRIEND

I am friendly to everyone I meet.

Attending a business function for state legislators, everyone seemed to be working in pairs. My partner was unavailable to attend at the last minute, so I was participating alone and feeling out of place. Let's just say it was a long evening.

At some point, most of us have been in a gathering of people where we felt totally left out. Everyone else was chatting and having a great time while you were wandering around wishing you could hide in the coat closet.

We all want to spend time with our friends when we attend events. But, somewhere in that group, someone needs a friend. There is someone who is new to the group or who is shy and doesn't do well in groups.

Make it your mission to find a new friend when you attend events. Seek out the people who look like they need a friend. Speak to them and introduce them to others. Everyone has a story; spend some time and learn their story. Not only will your new friend be appreciative, but you will feel overjoyed because of the kindness you shared.

Have you been the person at an event feeling left out? Does it make you realize how important it is to include others?

Today's Joy: "Be kind and compassionate to one another, forgiving each other, just as in Christ God forgave you." Ephesians 4:32 NIV

NOVEMBER 12
YOUR ACCOMPLISHMENTS

I have an attitude of gratitude.

You're familiar with a vision board where you add pictures, quotes, or articles to focus on something you want to manifest in your life.

Instead, try making an accomplishments board or even a list. Think of your family, children, education, and career. Post pictures of you receiving any recognition or awards. And, remember the little things too. If that camping trip by a stream was important, post it on your board.

Having a poster or a list of your accomplishments and the good things in your life will fill you with gratitude. Hanging it up where you see it regularly will keep you in that state of gratitude.

The more grateful you are for the things you have now will attract more of the same things into your life.

What will you put on your accomplishments board? How will you express gratitude for your blessings?

Today's Joy: A life of gratitude is the pathway to joy.

NOVEMBER 13
WORLD KINDNESS DAY

*I will perform random
acts of kindness today.*

Many countries across the globe are celebrating *World Kindness Day* today. It is the perfect day to be kind to others, be kind to yourself, and perform random acts of kindness.

"Let no one ever come to you without leaving better and happier. Be the living expression of God's kindness: kindness in your face, kindness in your eyes, kindness in your smile."—Mother Teresa.[5]

One kind word or act from you can entirely change someone else's day. It costs you nothing to share kindness with others, and it's always a blessing to receive.

At first, you would have to make a conscious effort to leave kindness everywhere you go. Over time, it will become a habit, and you will be the *kindness* that everyone seeks.

How will you celebrate World Kindness Day? Who can you be kind to today?

Today's Joy: Kindness is free. Sprinkle it everywhere!

NOVEMBER 14
FINDING THE JOY YOU LOST

Gratitude is my pathway to joy.

When a friend wrote and said she was struggling to find joy, I knew she needed help. Bobbie had family issues and financial issues. She was overwhelmed with worry and guilt. She needed guidance and encouragement. Many of us have felt this in our own lives.

Remember, there are seasons in your life, and sometimes life is a drudgery. At those times, you need a reservoir of joy and continue to do the things that bring you joy. Don't let this time in your life sap your self-care journey. Self-care is necessary to plow through the darkness and into the light.

Take a walk. Notice the small things. Live in the moment. Savor the small stuff. Do something that gives you short bursts of childlike joy.

The best path to joy is challenging but powerful. Be grateful for everything. Make it a habit to mentally list or write in a journal several things that you are thankful for each day. You'll find your joy in the process.

How do you reclaim your lost joy? What do you do when you're overwhelmed with worry or guilt?

Today's Joy: There is always something to be thankful for.

NOVEMBER 15
GRATITUDE

I am filled with gratitude and happiness.

Gratitude is a great way to jump-start the process of training your body to be happy. But ultimately, it is one stepping-stone of many.

Take the first step and write down five things you are grateful for each day. Not every day is going to be a great day. However, if you can stick with your daily gratitude list, you will find yourself feeling happy about the way things are going. You will begin to feel more positive.

Your other steppingstones might include expressing gratitude out loud or sitting in gratitude and feeling the moment.

Daily gratitude can give you the positive mindset you need to get you where you want to go in life.[6]

Do you express gratitude daily? Can you feel the difference when you are more grateful?

Today's Joy: Gratitude opens your heart to joy!

NOVEMBER 16
THE POWER OF YES

I allow myself to say, "Yes."

It always feels good to respond with *yes* and the person we're responding to always loves to hear *yes* as an answer.

Something about *yes* gives you confidence and fills you with positivity. You can use the power of *yes* to jumpstart your morning or kick start a gloomy afternoon.

Just ask yourself questions that your answer will automatically be *yes*.

Is your name Louise? Yes. Are you a beautiful soul? Yes. Do you love to read? Yes. After responding *yes* a few times, you'll feel confident enough to conquer the world.

What questions can you ask yourself that will provide you with an automatic "yes?"

Today's Joy: Say yes to adventures. Say yes to yourself. Say yes to life. Say yes to joy!

NOVEMBER 17
PRACTICE GRATITUDE

I practice gratitude every day.

Sometimes we say we *have* gratitude, or we *give* gratitude. Perhaps what we're really doing is *practicing* gratitude.

Practicing gratitude is regularly repeating various forms of gratitude. It could be saying, *thank you*. Or making a gratitude list or writing in a gratitude journal.

Gratitude is not something we can do one time or even once a week and say we have or give gratitude. It is a lifetime of regularly being grateful for everything and everyone in your life.

You build up your gratitude muscle by saying *thank you* to God, to your family, to the person who holds the door for you and everyone else you encounter on any given day. After even a few days of practicing gratitude, you will feel more optimistic about life.

No matter what term you use for gratitude, the important thing is that gratitude is part of your daily routine.

How will you practice gratitude today? What are you thankful for?

Today's Joy: Smile. Be kind and gracious. Practice Gratitude.

NOVEMBER 18
CELEBRATE TODAY!

*I will celebrate every
day that I am alive!*

What can you celebrate today? It doesn't have to be a birthday or a holiday. You can find something every day to celebrate.

You completed a project at home or the office. Your child made good grades on some tests. The family is all home for a weekend together. Your best friend invited you to lunch. All of these occasions and every tiny victory calls for a celebration.

It's a new day with new possibilities, and you are alive! That is a celebration you can recognize every day.

Celebrating today is another form of gratitude. You are looking for the best things in your day every single day. You recognize all the positive people around you and their contribution to your life. The things that you celebrate in life will multiply.

What will you celebrate today? How will you celebrate?

Today's Joy: "The more you praise and celebrate your life, the more there is in life to celebrate."—Oprah Winfrey[7]

NOVEMBER 19
WELCOMING A NEW BABY

A Story Shared by Andrea

In 2005, my baby sister (age thirty-seven) shared the happy news that she was going to have her first child. Both sides of the family were delighted. It had been a long time since a baby had been born on our side: the first offspring of an only child for the other.

Let's jump forward four months to the gender reveal date! The ultrasound wand scanned her belly, fresh smiles and anticipation filled the room when suddenly they heard, "I think we have a problem." Down Syndrome was suspected and later confirmed. My sister's joy turned to fear, to anger, to someone who did not want to even mention the word *baby*. I regret to tell you, I felt devastated too. My sister was told that most people didn't keep those babies, and abortion was actually encouraged. Thankfully, my sister chose to fight for Jeremy's life.

Jeremy was light and we were the ones who were in the dark. The verse "…I am fearfully and wonderfully made…," Psalms 139:14 NIV brought us comfort and joy. By the time my nephew was born, our love for him exploded, and he didn't disappoint when he arrived looking just like his Dad. After only two months, his breathing became labored. He was taken to the hospital where he spent a month and underwent surgery on his lungs. I remember seeing his Dad come out of the NICU with tears in his eyes. Funny how a baby they weren't sure about became their world.

Jeremy survived and thrived! In 2019 I was able to mentor him for confirmation at his church. What a joy! This boy loves Jesus! And he loves girls, and they shower him with attention. He is an awesome swimmer and competes in the Special Olympics each year. With an infectious smile, generous hugs and kisses he loves everyone with unconditional joy!

Today's Joy: "I shudder to think we could have missed the joy my nephew brings." —Andrea

NOVEMBER 20
DOUBLE YOUR GRATITUDE

*I pause in my thoughts
of gratitude.*

I want to chat with you today about increasing the benefit of gratitude in your life. And I have one *over the moon* tip to double, or even triple, your wellspring of appreciation—talk about super charged gratitude!

I've always believed that gratitude builds a wellspring of joy in your heart. Imagine a bucket that you are filling up as you express, *thank you.* When you experience sadness, worry, overwhelm, or other similar emotions, you draw on your wellspring. Your bucket is depleted based on the amount you need to overcome your challenge. This is why I always encourage you to use gratitude daily and build up your wellspring bucket of joy!

Now, about that *over the moon* tip, as you list all the things you are grateful for, or writing them in your journal, take an extra few minutes to think about each item.

Why are you grateful?
How did this item, person, event make you feel?

By settling into the actual feeling of gratitude, your heart will receive more of the benefit. You are spending more time in a state of gratitude, which will pay huge rewards into your wellspring of joy.

Have you experienced more abundance due to your faithful gratitude practices?

Today's Joy: Double your gratitude with a pause for reflection.

NOVEMBER 21
EACH DAY IS A BLESSING

I count my blessings every day.

Every morning that you open your eyes, you have been blessed. Each day offers you a new blessing of twenty-four hours, which you can use at your own discretion. My hope is for you to use your day to share love and kindness with everyone around you.

Share your blessings so that others may also be blessed. Be thankful for another day to enjoy God's beauty. Another day to let your family know you love them. Another day to sprinkle joy everywhere you go.

Give thanks for all the little things in your life. You may realize that these are the things that your mind cherishes. The small things add up to epic blessings in your life.

Let your heart sing out for God. Let your soul be filled with love.

November is the month to celebrate gratitude. What are you grateful for today? How are you sharing your blessings with others?

Today's Joy: May your day be blessed with peace, love, and joy!

NOVEMBER 22
A THANKSGIVING BLESSING

Bless us, O Lord.

Thanksgiving is a day set aside to gather together with the people we love and give thanks for our abundant blessings. We celebrate with all kinds of amazing foods, and time spent with family and friends.

It is a reminder to count our blessings and realize just how blessed our lives really are. Take time to reflect on this year and all the things you have to be grateful for.

And now, let us give thanks.

> Our precious Lord and Savior,
> We come to you on this special day of Thanksgiving to
>   praise you and thank you for our bounty of blessings.
> We are grateful to gather together in your name.
> We are thankful for the food as it nourishes our bodies.
> We are thankful for this family as they nourish our souls.
> To God be the glory!
> Amen

One more thing - enjoy your sweet potato casserole today. It was my Daddy's favorite!

Today's Joy: "Enter his gates with thanksgiving and his courts with praise; give thanks to him and praise his name." Psalms 100:4 NIV

NOVEMBER 23
GIVE THANKS

I am thankful and blessed.

The electrical system in my car died and the radio/DVD/GPS all had to be replaced. It was different from before, and I was not happy. I told a friend how displeased I was, and I was making a list of everything I didn't like about it. His response was, "Try making a list of everything you do like about it." As his comment washed over me, I knew he was right.

Do you take time every day to be thankful?

This verse comes to my mind. "Give thanks in all circumstances; for this is God's will for you in Christ Jesus." 1 Thessalonians 5:18 NIV

It is God's will for us to give thanks. It is also our privilege and our honor to be thankful for all the things God has blessed us with. Life is not always easy, but giving thanks brings abundance to our lives.

We can give thanks to God through praise, prayer, and worship. Return thanks, through a blessing before your meals. Always give thanks with a grateful heart today, tomorrow, and forever.

It is gratitude that makes our lives joyful! Will you write down five things that you are thankful for today?

Today's Joy: "Give thanks to the LORD, for he is good; his love endures forever." Psalm 118:29 NIV

NOVEMBER 24
COUNT YOUR BLESSINGS

I count my blessings every day.

In Johnson Oatman, Jr.'s hymn he repeats,

> Count your many blessings, name them one by one.
> Count your many blessings, see what God has done![8]

You likely are familiar with this hymn of gratitude. It is so true that by counting our blessing and naming them one by one, we become vividly aware of all that God has provided for us.

Make it a daily habit of counting your blessings. As you drive to work, observe everything along your way and thank God for all of it. Count your family members and bless each one as your name them one by one. Include things like your five senses: for everything you taste, smell, see, hear, and feel. Thank God for our teachers and public service workers.

You absolutely cannot count high enough to run out of blessings!

How many blessings did you count today? Does your heart soar as you start recognizing the multitude of blessings you have?

Today's Joy: "I will make them and the places surrounding my hill a blessing. I will send down showers in season; there will be showers of blessing." Ezekiel 34:26 NIV

NOVEMBER 25
BENEFITS OF GRATITUDE

*I will start each day with
a grateful heart.*

Grateful people are likely to be much happier and healthier than their pessimistic counterparts. For example, expressing gratitude enhances your energy levels and reduces stress. Plus, recognizing and appreciating life's many blessings is one of the most powerful ways I know of to enhance your immune system, balance your hormones, and promote heart health.—Christiane Northrup[9]

As you can tell from Dr. Northrup's comment, gratitude is not only good for your attitude, but it also helps your physical body.

Our lives are so busy that we don't always slow down enough to express appreciation for all that we have. Actually, it only takes a moment to say, "thank you." As you are brushing your teeth, walking the dog, or driving to work, use a few moments to be thankful for everything around you. This could be your home, your neighbors, your job, and even your coffee.

Did you realize how healthy it is to practice gratitude? Will you increase your gratitude to live a happier and healthier life?

Today's Joy: "A thankful heart enjoys blessings twice—when they're received and when they're remembered."—Author Unknown[10]

3 THINGS TO BE THANKFUL FOR

My blessings are overflowing.

The month of November is often known as the month of Thankfulness. There are numerous challenges that go around naming something you are thankful for each day this month.

Actually, there are zillions of things to be thankful for, and I've got years of gratitude journals to back that up.

However, I believe if you are thankful for just these three things, your life will be abundantly blessed.

1. **Family** – Our families are our bloodlines. They are the ones who will stick by us during famine or feast.

2. **Faith** – Belief in God will get you through more struggles than anything or anyone else. Here, you find hope everlasting.

3. **Health** – We may have health issues, but we are alive today. Be thankful for the opportunity to take care of yourself.

What three things are you most thankful for? Do you thank God for these blessings?

Today's Joy: "Enter his gates with thanksgiving and his courts with praise; give thanks to him and praise his name." Psalm 100:4 NIV

NOVEMBER 27
SPREAD JOY

I can share my joy with others.

As my sister got out of her car in my driveway, she said, "Everybody on your street waved to me just now. What's up?" I laughed, knowing everybody thought it was probably me driving down the street. My sister and I drive the same car, and we look alike. All my neighbors know that I wave and often stop for a chat.

I try to spread joy every day, and I'm always looking for new ways to share my joy.

Here are a few of my favorites:

> Wave at my neighbors as I pass them on the street.
> Send cards to friends that I don't often see.
> Take flowers to someone who lives alone.
> Buy a favorite book online and have it delivered to a sick friend.
> Send happy text messages.
> Smile. Always.

As you spread joy to others, your joy will multiply exponentially.

What are your favorite ways to spread joy in your corner of the world?

Today's Joy: "Since you get more joy out of giving joy to others, you should put a good deal of thought into the happiness that you are able to give."—Eleanor Roosevelt[11]

NOVEMBER 28
A GRATITUDE WALK

I am grateful for all of nature.

Today, let's take a gratitude walk together. As we go through the door outside, the sun immediately warms my body, and I am thankful for the sun.

A stroll through the garden leads me down by the pond and reminds me that I am grateful for all of nature that God has provided. The trees and grass, the flowers and the rocks, the pond and the fish, the rabbits and the squirrels are all God's creations.

I am thankful for the bench to stop along our way and rest. As we sit here, we continue to see more of God's blessings. The blue sky above with white puffy clouds, my friend on the bench beside me, eyes to see the blessings and ears to hear all the sounds, I am grateful.

What did you find to be grateful for on your nature walk?

Today's Joy: "All things bright and beautiful,
    All creatures great and small,
    All things wise and wonderful,
    The Lord God made them all."—Cecil Frances
    Alexander[12]

NOVEMBER 29
LIGHT YOUR CANDLE

*I let my light shine for
all the world to see.*

Lunch with my friend, Patty, always brings lovely surprises. Today, she handed me a mini tea light. The smile on her face told me this was going to be good. I was intently listening as she switched the light on. She said, "Let this candle be your reminder to let your light shine so everyone can see Christ through you."

I sat quietly and thought about what she had said. It's such a simple thing, but it's a powerful reminder to sprinkle love and kindness, happiness and joy along your path every day.

I have now included in my daily prayer, "Let my light shine every day for others to see Christ through me."

As you light your own internal candle, think about your light, and is it spreading love and kindness out into the world. What can you do to let your light shine all the time?

Today's Joy: "Nothing can dim the light which shines from within."—Maya Angelou[13]

NOVEMBER 30
ORDINARY BLESSINGS

I am thankful.

There are so many tiny little things to be thankful for every day. You have the gift of another day. The car started when you left for work, and you arrived safely. All of the family is well, and the sun is shining bright.

Sometimes, when you try to list the things you are thankful for, you can only think of life's big blessings.

These blessings are indeed to be praised, but it is the ordinary blessings in our everyday lives that we want to be especially grateful.

We live in glorious times, and routine days bring calm to our lives. Look for the goodness in each day. There is always something to be thankful for. Gratitude will turn ordinary days into ordinary blessings.

November Challenge Follow Up: I know I overloaded you with gratitude inspirations this month, but I hope all of it resonated with you. As we wrap up November, what are the things or people you found yourself being grateful for this month?

Today's Joy: Ordinary blessings are like manna from heaven.

DISCOVER YOUR JOY

GRATITUDE & THANKSGIVING

Giving Thanks with Joyous Gratitude

_____
_____
_____
_____
_____
_____
_____
_____
_____
_____
_____
_____
_____
_____
_____
_____
_____
_____
_____
_____
_____
_____
_____
_____

DECEMBER:
WINTER SOLSTICE AND CHRISTMAS

Rejoicing with Christmas Joy

DECEMBER 1
MASTER OF JOY

Joy is my default setting.

You are your own master of joy. You get to choose every day, whether you are joyful or not. Also, you decide how much joy to carry with you on any day.

> Some days you choose joy.
> Other days, you create joy!

But always, there is joy around you. Smile at people you see. A smile has an immediate effect on the way you feel. It's sure to lift you to a positive realm. As you go about your day and smile at other people, you're also sharing your abundance of joy with them.

Being a master of joy is a role not to be taken lightly. Use your power to turn a joyful moment into a joyful day. Turn a joyful day into a joyful life!

December Challenge: During this blessed Christmas month, we hear the word *joy* many times. But joy is not just for December or Christmas. How can you build up your wealth of joy this month so that it carries you throughout the coming year?

Today's Joy: In all things, seek joy!

DECEMBER 2
FIND JOY IN THE SMALL THINGS

My joy comes from within.

Last December, there was a massive ice storm in our area. Thousands of people were without power, including everyone on our street.

To make matters worse, three trees across our street were hanging on power lines and blocking the only road out of our neighborhood.

There was a hurricane headed our way just three months before, and my husband had purchased a generator. So now, he got it out and filled it with propane. We were able to keep our refrigerator and freezer going. We also had one lamp, a small space heater, and a plug to charge our phones.

The outside temperature was in the 20's, and it was cold in the house, but we were safe, and we had the necessities. We stayed together and huddled by the little heater. For four days, we used the time to talk and read.

We discovered being together that week was our joy. When have you found joy in small things?

Today's Joy: Cultivate a life of simple joys.

DECEMBER 3
GIFTS OF JOY

Joyful gifts come from the heart.

The holiday season is upon us, and the shopping malls are packed. Black Friday and Cyber Monday have come and gone. Everyone is searching for the perfect gift for all the names on their list.

I want to challenge you this year to buy *gifts of joy* instead of a leaf blower for Dad and a mixer for Mom. As you consider each gift, think about it for a few minutes before you hit 'purchase.' Will it bring joy into the recipient's life? Does it represent joy in any way?

I'm into giving *foodie* goodies this year. I have spent hours making a Christmas Jam from cranberries and strawberries and a Carrot Cake Jam. Along with homemade toffee, spiced nuts, and loaves of banana bread, I think my family will enjoy all the love and goodness poured into their gifts.

What *gifts of joy* will you give to loved ones this year?

Today's Joy: The joy of Christmas is spending time with family!

DECEMBER 4
FULL OF GRACE

I've got grace in my soul today.

"Monday's child is fair of face. Tuesday's child is full of grace."[1] Do you remember this old nursery rhyme? It was supposed to describe you based on the day of the week you were born.

Even though I'm a Tuesday's child, I feel like I'm just now learning to be graceful. The dictionary describes grace as simple elegance or courteous goodwill. Perhaps grace is something associated with women as we age. As my life slows down, I'm more aware of people and events. I'm more conscious of sharing goodwill with the people I encounter.

When I reflect on graceful women whom I've known, two particular women come to mind. First, is my great Aunt Eleanor. She was beautiful, proper, and always immaculately dressed. *AuAu,* as she was fondly called, taught me kindness, generosity, and how to properly share a meal with loved ones. She loved to cook and never steered away from using the good china.

The other woman was my mother-in-law. Mimi was lovely, kind, and generous. She was well known and loved throughout her town for being there to help anyone through their needs or to celebrate their accomplishments. Mimi was also a fabulous cook who shared her goodies far and wide. Obviously, both of these women made an impact on my life.

What women in your life impressed you with their grace? What did you learn from these women?

Today's Joy: Grace is a beautiful quality that that comes naturally to some women and can be learned by others.

DECEMBER 5
A JOY JAR

I find joy everywhere I go.

Crank up your joy-meter with a *Joy Jar*. Find an attractive jar or vase and assemble colorful markers and note pads.

When good things happen in your life, jot it down and place the note in your *Joy Jar*. Simple and ordinary things that make you smile are perfect examples.

When your spirits are low, or just need a little boost, you can pull out a few notes to read. These reminders of all the good things in your life are sure to lift your mood.

My Joy Jar is a green-tinted Mason jar that sits on my desk beside me. The highlight of my day is adding a sweet note.

Even on tough days when you are struggling, you can find your own joy. Reading your special notes will bring gratitude to your heart and love to your soul. *Your life doesn't have to be exactly perfect for you to be joyful!*

What will you use for your Joy Jar? Will you add your first note today?

Today's Joy: Make Joy Jars for your friends and family for the holidays.

DECEMBER 6
THE LIGHT

I keep my light aglow.

Let me be the light that brings darkness into day. Let me be the light that warms hearts that have forgotten how to love. Let my light shine so that others can see and feel the goodness I have inside to share.

Your light is similar to a candle. The glow gives off warmth to those close to you. And you can light many other candles without dimming your own light.

Your smile, kind words, and compassion are all part of your light. Approach each day with light and love. Spread your goodness out into the world.

How do you let your light shine for others to see and feel? Are you honored to be able to share something so special as light for those who may need encouragement in their darkness?

Today's Joy: "In the same way, let your light shine before others, that they may see your good deeds and glorify your Father in heaven." Matthew 5:16 NIV

DECEMBER 7
BEAT HOLIDAY STRESS

I look forward to sharing Christmas with my loved ones.

All the madness seems to settle in by early December. Preparing a big meal, setting a lovely table, and having all the family over is just the beginning.

There's holiday shopping, all kinds of Christmas events, wrapping, cooking, decorating, entertaining, and so the list goes on. Many people will come to dread the holidays because all of this is so overwhelming.

Step back and simplify has become my key to beat holiday stress.

I've gradually pared down my gift-giving list and my Christmas card list. I usually make coffee cakes, jams, and other goodies as gifts, so I start this early and freeze them. Get everyone involved in helping prepare food for events, parties, and meals.

I love to attend Christmas plays, musicals, and other festive events. Many years ago, I decided to choose only one of these artful events to attend each year. This year, we have tickets to *The Nutcracker*.[2] Last year, we saw *It's a Wonderful Life*[3] at our local theatre; and the year before, we attended a holiday orchestra event.

What ideas do you have to beat holiday stress? Will you take time to enjoy the beauty of the season?

Today's Joy: Take time to enjoy the holidays!

DECEMBER 8
JOY OR HAPPINESS

My heart radiates joy.

Do you wonder what the difference between joy and happiness is? Joy and happiness are quite similar, but there is a powerful difference.

Happiness is a moment in time when something or someone makes you feel good. It could be an ice cream cone or a hug from someone special.

But joy is a feeling deep within your heart that all is well. Good things happen, and not-so-good things happen, but your heart is still filled with joy.

Continue to enjoy all of your happy times. Express gratitude for all of your blessings. These are the things that fill your well full of joy.

What can you do today to increase your joy?

Today's Joy: "May the God of hope fill you with all joy and peace as you trust in him, so that you may overflow with hope by the power of the Holy Spirit." Romans 15:13 NIV

DECEMBER 9
A JOYOUS ADVENTURE

I seek adventures.

What would be a joyous adventure for you? Anytime I'm with my family, it is bound to be joyful. I also like to explore out-of-the-way shops along the coast. My kids might say their adventure is finding new places to snow ski or ice skate.

We all might have different ideas of what an adventure means to us. However, the common thread is to make it a joyous event. Time spent doing things that make our hearts soar is good mental therapy for each of us. It revives the child in us, brings a smile to our faces, and fills our hearts with lovely memories.

Pictures are a fabulous way to keep these adventures alive in our minds. I have a gadget that provides an on-going slide-show of favorite images in my den. The constant reminder of joyous adventures restores joy to my soul every single day.

What are your joyful family adventures? How do you keep the memories alive?

Today's Joy: Allow life to be a joyous adventure.

DECEMBER 10
THE SEASON TO SPARKLE

*I will spread sparkle
all season long.*

The Christmas season has finally arrived, and everything seems to sparkle! Lights on trees and houses twinkle. Glitter covers my stack of cards. Wrapping paper shines as I prepare ribbons to attach. But more importantly, all the people I see seem to show sparkle on their faces and in their actions.

I got a head start this year. In August, I texted my son that I just bought Christmas cards and planned our Christmas Eve dinner. It is an exciting time for sure. And now, Christmas magic is in the air! You feel it. You believe it.

We are reminded by Charles Dickens in *A Christmas Carol*, "I will honor Christmas in my heart, and try to keep it all the year."[4]

Have you been working towards building up your storehouse of joy? Make a list of things that have brought you joy this month.

Today's Joy: Daniel and I send you a flurry of warm Christmas wishes!

DECEMBER 11
DADDY'S VILLAGE

I cherish my heirlooms.

Sazzy and I were telling Christmas stories over our hot chocolate when she shared this story of her father's Christmas dream.

"Daddy always wanted a beautiful ceramic village to enjoy under his Christmas tree. He had a few pieces passed down from his mother and now it was time for him to finish the scene.

Over the next ten years, he and I spent time in the ceramic workshop while he carefully constructed homes and a community of businesses. People, animals, and decorations all became part of the village.

Daddy loved his masterpiece and loved sharing it with family and friends. Every year, he meticulously arranged the pieces under the tree. His Christmas dream had become a reality.

My favorite piece has always been the beautiful white church. That piece was important to Daddy and it represents his faith and how important being involved in church was to him."

Sazzy is proud of her father's creation and knows her son and granddaughter will love it as much as she does.

What Christmas heirlooms do you cherish? Do they bring precious memories to mind?

Today's Joy: Sazzy was reminded of her favorite Christmas hymn, *Joy to the World*.[5]

DECEMBER 12
MAKE A JOYFUL NOISE

I sing praises to my Lord.

We can all make a joyful noise by singing, talking, sharing, playing an instrument, and even praying. Especially during the Christmas season, I love to hear the music at my church. Between the choir, the piano and guitars, and the orchestra, they definitely share a joyful noise. The congregation gets involved by singing, clapping, and swaying to the songs.

There are dozens of places in the Bible that we are instructed to "Make a joyful noise." We usually think of songs and music but speaking to others and praying are other ways we can make a joyful noise. I like to think there is nothing more joyful to God than to hear us pray.

The next time someone asks you to sing in the choir, you can tell them you are already making a joyful noise!

What are your favorite verses about making a joyful noise? A few of mine are below.

Today's Joy: "A Psalm of praise. Make a joyful noise unto the LORD, all ye lands." Psalm 100:1 KJV

"Shout for joy to the LORD, all the earth, burst into jubilant song with music." Psalm 98:4 NIV

"With trumpets and the sound of cornet make a joyful noise before the LORD, the King." Psalm 98:6 KJV

DECEMBER 13
POSITIVE THOUGHTS

I will focus on good things today.

When life gets you down, and you need a few uplifting thoughts, here are some favorites that I'd like to share with you.

Start every day with a positive thought such as, "I am OK today."
Take life one step or one day at a time.
Slow down and breathe.
Believe that you can handle anything that happens.
It's OK to ask for help.
Make yourself a priority.
It's quite possible that things could turn out far better than you expect.
I am enough just the way I am.
All is well in my world.

Did a quick read through these positive thoughts bring a smile to your face? Did you suddenly realize that everything is going to be ok today?

Today's Joy: "Always say 'yes' to the present moment."— Eckhart Tolle[6]

DECEMBER 14
YOUR JOYFUL HOME

My home is my refuge.

My new housekeeper walked into my home, stopped, and took a deep breath. As she gazed around my den, her words were, "Your home is a refuge of peace and calm." Of course, I felt that way, but I was surprised she sensed that feeling the first time she was there. I had lived by myself a long time, and home is where I renew, refresh, and restore my soul.

Are you searching for joy in your life? A good place to start is in your own home.

Gradually revamp your home, so it becomes your own personal oasis. Start by using calming colors to invoke peace. Then add splashes of bright colors to spark your joy. Bring the outdoors inside by using natural fabrics and keeping flowers in a vase close by.

Create a playlist of your favorite songs. It would be like a tidal wave of happiness flooding your soul daily. Be sure to have your own personal space where you can retreat to refresh your soul.[7]

What ways do you use to bring peace, calm, and joy to your home?

Today's Joy: "Find joy in everything you choose to do. Every job, relationship, home. It's your responsibility to love it or change it."—Chuck Palahniuk[8]

DECEMBER 15
A CHRISTMAS DREAM

I'm dreaming of a joyful season.

My dream this Christmas is for you to have the honor to sit outside on a bench overlooking a beautifully decorated tree. Who would you choose to sit with you? What would you say?

I would definitely choose my Daddy to sit and chat with. He loved Christmas and he always decorated a tall outdoor tree at our home. He also went out into the woods on our property and chopped down a tree to put inside our home. Daddy spent years making a ceramic Christmas village that he carefully spread beneath the tree.

I would tell Daddy all the things that have been happening, all the family gatherings he missed and how his grandson also loves to decorate outdoor trees. He would be thrilled to know that my sister and I still have an ornament that was on his first tree. We pass it back and forth each year. We also continue to use the ceramic village that was his gift of joy to us.

Daddy was taken from us much too soon and I still miss him tremendously.

Don't miss the opportunity this Christmas to spend time with those you love. Who would you choose to sit on the bench beside you?

Today's Joy: "Christmas is a season not only of rejoicing but of reflection."—Winston Churchill[9]

DECEMBER 16
BOXES OF MEMORIES

I cherish photos of my loved ones.

Do you have a stash of old photos stored away for another day?

My grandmother was a scrapbooker long before scrapbooking was popular. And I inherited all of her books dating back to the early 1900's. I also acquired boxes of photos from my parents in no order and with almost no information.

My sister and I quickly realized how our whole family tree would quickly disappear from future generations if we did not step up and organize these boxes of memories. Our children and grandchildren would not know the faces, the lives, or the stories of their ancestors.

Organizing all of this information is a time-consuming and pains-taking process. We have gradually started to work through the boxes in order to provide a legacy for our heirs.

I encourage you to share the photos and stories of your family with the younger generations. Help them to know the foundation of their lives.

How will you preserve the memories stored in photos of your loved ones?

Today's Joy: Cherish your memories always. Hold them in your heart forever.

DECEMBER 17
MORE PRAISE TO OUR GOD

I sing praises and worship my God.

There are numerous verses about praising God and reading them makes my heart leap with joy. I want to share some of these verses with you today.

"A psalm. A song. For the Sabbath day. It is good to praise the LORD and make music to your name, O Most High." Psalm 92:1 NIV

"Let all that I am praise the LORD; may I never forget the good things he does for me." Psalm 103:2 NLT

"Praise the LORD. Give thanks to the LORD, for he is good; his love endures forever." Psalm 106:1 NIV

"From the rising of the sun to the place where it sets, the name of the LORD is to be praised." Psalm 113:3 NIV

"For great is his love toward us, and the faithfulness of the LORD endures forever. Praise the LORD." Psalm 117:2 NIV

"I give you thanks, O LORD, with all my heart; I will sing your praises before the gods." Psalm 138:1 NLT

What is your favorite verse for praising God? Do you have the verse memorized and stored in your heart?

Today's Joy: "Praise the LORD. Praise the name of the LORD; praise him, you servants of the LORD." Psalm 135:1 NIV

DECEMBER 18
HOME FOR CHRISTMAS

I'll be home for Christmas.

Marjorie Holmes said, "At Christmas, all roads lead home."[10] And, Bing Crosby sang, "I'll be home for Christmas, if only in my dreams."[11]

In our hearts, I believe we all want to be at home and with our families for the Christmas holiday. It is there that we fill our hearts and soul with warmth and love. We take time to reflect on our traditions and the timeless memories of our Christmas' past.

Traditions vary among cultures, religions, families, and even households. I encourage you to embrace and cherish your family traditions and pass them down to the next generation.

Food is also a big part of our traditions. I tried for a few years to introduce new recipes for our Christmas dinners. My family was adamant about having the same menu that we've used for many years. It is a tradition!

Celebrate with those you love! What are the traditions that your family loves and shares?

Today's Joy: May your Christmas sparkle with moments of love, laughter and joy!

DECEMBER 19
YOUR GUARDIAN ANGEL

I am protected.

I believe we all have guardian angels, and yours is with you all day, every day, to watch over you and protect you. Imagine your angel riding on your shoulder and guiding you when you need a little assistance.

If you sense someone around you or feel a tug to do something you had not planned, there's a good chance it is your guardian angel trying to relay a message.

Guardian angels also protect you from harm and can intervene to save you from trouble.

Use this short prayer when you want to call upon your angel.

> Angel of God, my guardian dear,
> To whom God's love commits me here,
> Ever this day be at my side,
> To light and guard, to rule and guide.
> —Roman Catholic Traditional Prayer[12]

Do you believe you have a guardian angel? Can you feel their presence at certain times?

Today's Joy: "For he will command his angels concerning you to guard you in all your ways." Psalm 91:11 NIV

DECEMBER 20
O CHRISTMAS TREE

How lovely are thy branches? [13]

Some years ago, my Mom sat admiring my freshly decorated tree when she said, "Your tree is as beautiful as the most elaborate tree anywhere." Her words touched my heart and inspired me to take pride in decorating the tree every year.

By the mid-1800s, Christmas trees were gaining momentum in the United States. And, in 1923, the first National Christmas Tree was lit in Washington, DC.

Today, elaborately decorated trees are in most malls, shops, offices, and even in our homes. The debate over live trees versus artificial trees will continue forever. I've had both at different times in my life.

We love to choose themes and colors to decorate our tree. Are you a white-light or colored-light person? I love to add ribbons and beads to my tree before decorating with ornaments. Many trees are topped with either an angel or a star as a reminder of the birth of Jesus.

No matter what your choices for a Christmas tree are, just take time to enjoy the process of choosing and decorating it. Sit quietly and admire the lights. Reflect on what Christmas means to you in your heart. Share the moments with those you love.

Do you find joy in decorating your tree? Are all of the Christmas traditions building up your wealth of joy?

Today's Joy: Wishing for you joy, love, and peace this Christmas season!

DECEMBER 21
GIVING JOY

I share my joy with others.

Do you like giving gifts to others, especially if they're not expecting anything?

Joy is one thing that you can give away all day, every day, and never diminish your own joy. Sharing your joy with others will increase your own joy. The act of sharing your love, kindness, and compassion with others fills your own heart full of so much joy. You're then ready to share it again and again.

The hope is that the people receiving joy from you will continue to spread it also. One person at a time, joy can spread far and wide.

With all that is going on in our world today, joy is what we need to be sharing with everyone.

> Choose joy every day.
> Share joy with everyone.

Do you make an effort to share your joy and happiness with others? What is your favorite way to share?

Today's Joy: "Since you get more joy out of giving joy to others, you should put a good deal of thought into the happiness that you are able to give."—Eleanor Roosevelt[14]

DECEMBER 22
CHOCOLATE COVERED CHERRIES

I love to share.

Each Christmas, I purchase chocolate-covered cherries by the caseload. I take them to nursing homes, help centers, churches—anywhere that has a group of men to enjoy them.

You see, this man in my life thought chocolate covered cherries were the greatest joy known to mankind. I bought them for him every year at Christmas. And, when he claimed his seat in heaven, the boxes in the stores brought tears streaming down my face every holiday season.

The first year, I bought one box just like all the years before. It didn't take long before I would buy all the boxes on the shelf. Twenty-six years later, you never know where I will show up with a case of chocolate-covered cherries.

But first, before I set out on my journey to deliver them, here's a box just for you this Christmas. My Daddy would want you to have them. Enjoy! Merry Christmas!

Do you have a special Christmas memory that influences you every year?

Today's Joy: May the spirit of Christmas fill your heart with love, peace and joy!

DECEMBER 23
CHANGE THE WORLD WITH KINDNESS

Today, I choose kindness.

Kindness is so powerful that a single act can inspire similar acts of kindness. The feel-good factor is passed on and on. In this way, the world can be supercharged with the joyous current of selfless service.

Some of the most gifted musicians of our time gave their time and skills to create *We are the World*.[15] They raised over $63 million for humanitarian aid in Africa. That was genuine kindness in action.

There are also thousands of non-profit and charitable organizations motivated purely by the generosity of spirit that is the bedrock of kindness. Some international examples include Habitat for Humanity and Doctors without Borders.

In addition, local communities have organizations that serve the needy, homeless, and hungry. There are winter coat and blanket drives and soup kitchens.[16]

Kindness can definitely change the world. Are you involved with a charitable cause this holiday season?

Today's Joy: Be known for your kindness and generosity.

DECEMBER 24
JOYFUL CHRISTMAS

*Merry Christmas to you
and those you love!*

It's the most wonderful time of the year! Magic is in the air!

The joyful Christmas season is upon us, and I'm dreaming of an old-fashioned Christmas.

There are so many reasons that Christmas is the happiest season of the year. It is a time to connect with family and friends and a time to remember that Christmas is a celebration of Jesus' birthday.

Like many of you, my Christmas spirit soars as soon as the last plate of Thanksgiving has been washed. My Daddy was always ready to grab his ax, and off to the woods, we would head to chop down the best Christmas tree we could find. Oh, the excitement of adding lights, then the thrill of unboxing ornaments from years gone by. Memories flood my mind as each one is carefully placed upon the tree.

Christmas Eve is the most peaceful night of the year. Candlelight services offer a calm that you can only experience by knowing the true meaning of Christmas.

Tonight, do you feel the peace and calm as we await the birth of our Savior?

Today's Joy: And for tonight….. The night is calm; the stars are bright. I pray for peace tonight.

DECEMBER 25
REJOICE! IT'S CHRISTMAS DAY

I will celebrate with
love in my heart.

Let the trumpets sound. Halleluiah, our Christ, is born. Today is Christmas Day!

What a special day we are honored to enjoy. Time with our dearest family and friends over bountiful meals is our blessing this day.

Enjoy the moments with family gathered to open gifts and share meals. However, keep your focus on the very reason that we celebrate Christmas Day.

Take time to check on those who may be alone today. Or perhaps volunteer to serve a meal to those in need.

Raise your voice and your heart in praise to your God. Give Him thanks for your abundant blessings. Let all you do today be for the honor and glory of Christ, our Savior.

Today is a time for us to celebrate both peace and joy.

I am wishing you love and joy on this Christmas Day from my heart and home to you and yours! Much love always.

Today's Joy: "Glory to God in the highest and on earth peace, good will toward men." Luke 2:14 KJV

DECEMBER 26
THE ONE AFFIRMATION YOU NEED

I am enough.

Louise Hay was the queen of affirmations. She is the person that brought affirmations to the forefront of our everyday lives.[17]

And one affirmation that she used variations of was, "I am enough."

If you think about it, that one affirmation covers everything in our lives. It is the encouragement we need to overcome anything.

I am smart enough.
I am skinny enough.
I am loved enough.
I am worthy. It is enough.
I know enough to handle this situation.
My life is enough.
I am strong enough.
I am healthy. I am enough.
I am doing the best I can, and it is enough.
I will always be enough.

Always remind yourself that you are enough no matter what. It is ok—all is well.

Do you make a practice of saying affirmations? Do you know that you are enough just the way you are?

Today's Joy: "I exist as I am; that is enough."—Walt Whitman[18]

DECEMBER 27
ABUNDANCE

My life is brimming with abundance.

Each of our lives is chock-full of abundance if we take time to recognize it.

Today, as I sat watching the ocean waves roll in, I realized that my abundant life includes a tiny cottage by the sea, dinner with my family tonight, and my best friend who lives one island over.

You are also abundantly blessed if you have love, peace, truth, compassion, and harmony in your life. Manifesting abundance is the process of being grateful for what you already have. Every time you say, "Thank you," you are attracting more abundance.

As I sat by the sea today, I said to no one, but to everyone, "Thank you," for the ocean waves rolling in and ears to hear them. Thank you for the sea grass blowing in the breeze, and eyes to see it. Thank you for the clouds and the birds and the bench I'm sitting on.

The list is endless, and abundance is yours.

What are you attracting into your life today? What are you thankful for?

Today's Joy: "Abundance is not something we acquire. It is something we tune into."—Wayne Dyer[19]

DECEMBER 28
ONE WAY TO HAPPINESS

I seek happy friends.

There are many things you can do to increase your happiness. I just purchased a game for my family to play at a gathering later this week. I can already imagine the laughter that will accompany this game and our time together.

You can watch some television shows that make you laugh out loud. Engage in fun activities with family and friends. Play tennis or croquet. Bake and decorate cookies.

We've already talked about being grateful. It does reinforce all that you have and makes you a happier and kinder person.

Think back to happy moments in your life. Reliving these good times brings happiness to you all over again. Reminisce over times gone by with family and friends.

However, one of my favorite ways to increase happiness is to spend time around other happy people. Their good-natured spirit will also boost your happiness quotient. You will smile more and laugh often if your contact list is filled with happy faces.

How do you maintain happiness in your life? Which of your friends can you depend on to bring a smile to your face?

Today's Joy: Let happiness be your superpower.

DECEMBER 29
HAPPY PLACE

My soul is nourished.

Do you have a happy place to escape to whether it be a real place or one you can hold in your imagination?

My husband and I decided to spend the week of New Years at our seaside home. This morning, I'm sitting by the window as the ocean waves come crashing in. There are only a few fluffy clouds in the sky, and the sun is glistening on the water. I often sit here for many hours at a time, totally mesmerized by the ocean and the magic it holds. This is my happy place!

Taking a break at your favorite getaway is good for your body, your mind, and your soul. Stress just seems to dissipate. It clears your mind and helps you to refocus your energies. Your happy place is also your healing place.

Where is your happy, healing place? Do you go there often, even if only in your mind?

Today's Joy: All is well in my happy place!

DECEMBER 30
SOME FINAL WORDS

I always do my best.

As another year comes to a close, take time to think back over this past year.

> What did you accomplish?
> What did you learn?
> Did you love enough?
> Did you share enough?
> How much did you laugh?
> What are you grateful for?
> What are you most proud of?
> Did you forgive those who wronged you?
> Did you share your talents?
> Are you happy?

This is your time to evaluate the good and the not-so-good for the year. Make plans now for things you want to improve on in the coming year.

You can be or do whatever you want. You just have to take the first step forward.

Personally, I'll take time to answer these questions myself. And I'll use my responses to plan my goals for next year. Will you join me in the process?

Today's Joy: "Take the first step in faith. You don't have to see the whole staircase, just take the first step."—Martin Luther King Jr[20]

DECEMBER 31
HOW FAR CAN I GO?

I am an achiever.

"Thinking back over this year past, I have realized that I never have to doubt just how far I can go!

Looking forward, I only need to remember how far I have already come, everything I have faced, battles (often with myself) I have won, and best of all, the fears I have overcome."[21] This came to me from my friend, Laura, last year.

Laura's statement is a powerful message that is fitting for all of us. We have also faced battles and fears and won.

We are stronger than we give ourselves credit. We have accomplished so much in our lives already. Armed with those positive thoughts, we are ready for anything that life throws at us.

And *you* are capable of whatever your heart desires. How far will you dare to go?

I'm wishing for you a safe New Years' Eve and a wonderfully blessed year ahead!

December Challenge Follow-Up: December was the month to build up your joy and use it to carry you through the coming year. Do you feel your heart overflowing with joy? Are you the master of your joy?

Today's Joy: You are the captain of your own destiny. Set sail for all the possibilities!

DISCOVER YOUR JOY

WINTER SOLSTICE & CHRISTMAS

Rejoicing with Christmas Joy

Afterword

My dear readers, we have come to the end of this calendar year together. I hope you were able to truly *Discover your Joy* through these daily inspirations.

I thought of you each day as I wrote. Also, I prayed for each of you: the battles you've faced, the obstacles you've overcome, and the glorious light in your life.

As you continue to go forth each day, let your joy and light shine for others to see.

Sending you joyful blessings.

Louise

"Always be joyful." 1 Thessalonians 5:16 NLT
"You are the light of the world…" Matthew 5:14 NIV

Resources

January

1. January 4: Gibran, Kahlil, accessed December 11, 2020, https://www.quotespedia.org/authors/k/kahlil-gibran/kindness-is-like-snow-it-beautifies-everything-it-covers-kahlil-gibran/.

2. January 5: Williamson, Marianne, accessed December 11, 2020, https://www.goodreads.com/quotes/20300-joy-is-what-happens-to-us-when-we-allow-ourselves.

3. January 6: Theroux, Paul. Accessed December 11, 2020, https://www.brainyquote.com/quotes/paul_theroux_598564.

4. January 7: Johnson, Lady Bird, accessed December 11, 2020, http://www.ladybirdjohnson.org/quotes.

5. January 14: Scriven, Joseph M, From the hymn, *"What a Friend we Have in Jesus."*, accessed December 11, 2020, https://hymnary.org/text/what_a_friend_we_have_in_jesus_all_our_s.

6. January 16: Bennett, Roy T, *The Light in the Heart*, accessed December 11, 2020, https://www.goodreads.com/quotes/8110740-count-your-blessings-not-your-problems-count-your-own-blessings.

7. January 18: Inspired by https://www.lawofattractionresourceguide.com/the-30-day-better-feeling-thought-process/, accessed December 26, 2020.

8. January 21: Author Unknown, accessed December 11, 2020, https://www.dailyinspirationalquotes.in/2017/06/sometimes-life-just-need-hug-no-words-no-advice-just-hug-make-feel-matter/.

9. January 23: Author Unknown, accessed December 11, 2020, http://www.theglassgoddess.co.uk/journal/those-we-love-dont-go-away-author-unknown.

10. January 24: Roosevelt, Eleanor, accessed December 11, 2020, https://www.goodreads.com/quotes/190577-with-the-new-day-comes-new-strength-and-new-thoughts.

11. January 30: Mother Teresa of Calcutta. Accessed December 11, 2020, https://quotefancy.com/quote/869027/Mother-Teresa-There-is-no-key-to-happiness-the-door-is-always-open.

12. January 31: Karletta Marie, Creator of Daily Inspired Life at https://dailyinspiredlife.com, message to author, December 7, 2020.

February

1. February 1: Pagels, Douglas, *What is a Sister*, accessed December 17, 2020, http://www.imgag.com/product/full/ap/3033411/.

2. February 2: Walford, William, From the hymn *Sweet Hour of Prayer*, accessed December 17, 2020, https://hymnary.org/text/sweet_hour_of_prayer_sweet_hour_of_pray.

3. February 3: Twain, Mark, accessed December 29, 2020, https://www.goodreads.com/quotes/550436-give-every-day-the-chance-to-become-the-most-beautiful.

4. February 4: Boatright, Windy Gail, Out of My Mind: The Mutterings and Musings of a Free Spirit, accessed December 29, 2020, https://windygail68.com/, message to author.

5. February 8: WebMD, accessed December 29, 2020, https://www.webmd.com/a-to-z-guides/organ-transplant-donor-information#1.

6. February 9: Gibran, Khalil, accessed December 29, 2020, https://www.goodreads.com/quotes/11751-the-deeper-that-sorrow-carves-into-your-being-the-more-joy.

7. February 10: Warren, Rick, *The Purpose Driven Life: What on Earth am I Here for?*, accessed December 29, 2020, https://www.goodreads.com/quotes/234195-time-is-your-most-precious-gift-because-you-only-have.

8. February 12: Meyer, Joyce, accessed December 29, 2020, https://www.brainyquote.com/quotes/joyce_meyer_565202.

9. February 13: Author Unknown, accessed December 29, 2020, https://www.allgreatquotes.com/rose-speaks-of-love-silently/.

10. February 13: Emerson, Ralph Waldo, accessed December 29, 2020, https://www.goodreads.com/quotes/32931-nature-always-wears-the-colors-of-the-spirit.

11. February 15: Mother Teresa of Calcutta, accessed December 29, 2020, https://www.goodreads.com/quotes/355722-spread-love-everywhere-you-go-let-no-one-ever-come.

12. February 16: Inspired by https://www.abraham-hicks.com/, accessed December 29, 2020.

13. February 17: Carly Marie, accessed December 29, 2020, https://www.hathorsorganicsco.com/hathor-blog/https/algae-tomato-pl2wsquarespacecom/config/pages/5dcaf9d0bca658495d09dab4-1.

14. February 19: Corona, E, accessed December 29, 2020, https://www.greatesttweets.com/and-the-bravest-of-souls-are-those-who-choose-love-over-and-over/love/.

15. February 19: Kuypers, John, *The Non Judgmental Christian: Five Lessons That Will Revolutionize Your Relationships*, accessed December 29, 2020, https://www.goodreads.com/quotes/585363-when-you-have-nothing-but-love-you-have-everything-this.

16. February 20: Roosevelt, Eleanor, accessed December 29, 2020, https://www.goodreads.com/quotes/40249-many-people-will-walk-in-and-out-of-your-life.

17. February 21: Morely, Robert, accessed December 29, 2020, https://www.huffpost.com/entry/12-inspiring-quotes-about_b_5381155?guccounter=1&guce_referrer=aHR0cHM6Ly93d3cuZ29vZ2xlLmNvbS8&guce_referrer_sig=AQAAADN4Y2ls9kUKfnYOMmdCY4T-vWDgfiV0SgAMzkPG0LGs8CBCdzG4M1bIjin-IDpixx-0hJswlIYXqKoM8QzXTRot1AX0DnWd9M3JH8npG-Cu0sRDyzkj7V5OkvW4oOnuEdlRM-DU6nUwcLGAn-LAY-1O_-XXySjVM62KFwLwex2edcKr

18. February 23: Lama, Dalai XIV, accessed December 29, 2020, https://www.goodreads.com/quotes/125985-remember-that-sometimes-not-getting-what-you-want-is-a.

19. February 24: Cachola, Janna, accessed December 29, 2020, https://www.goodreads.com/quotes/8062113-eyes-are-the-windows-to-the-soul-a-smile-is.

20. February 25: Mother Teresa of Calcutta, accessed December 29, 2020, https://www.goodreads.com/quotes/20324-it-s-not-how-much-we-give-but-how-much-love.

21. February 26: Mridha, Debasish, accessed December 29, 2020, https://www.goodreads.com/quotes/4111313-the-moon-is-the-reflection-of-your-heart-and-moonlight.

22. February 27: Thomas, Gary L, *A Lifelong Love: What If Marriage is about More Than Just Staying Together?*, accessed December 29, 2020, https://www.goodreads.com/quotes/6475342-a-good-marriage-isn-t-something-you-find-it-s-something-you.

23. February 28: Cole, Nat King, accessed December 29, 2020, https://www.goodreads.com/quotes/214154-the-greatest-thing-you-ll-ever-learn-is-just-to-love.

March

1. March 1: Proverb, accessed December 29, 2020, https://grammarist.com/proverb/you-reap-what-you-sow/.

2. March 1: Mote, Edward, *My Hope is Built on Nothing Less*, accessed December 29, 2020, https://hymnary.org/text/my_hope_is_built_on_nothing_less.

3. March 2: Cathy, Truett, accessed December 29, 2020, https://www.azquotes.com/quote/582673.

4. March 2: Author Unknown, accessed December 29, 2020, https://quoteinvestigator.com/2013/10/26/kindness-see/.

5. March 5: Gospel Song, accessed December 29, 2020, https://en.wikipedia.org/wiki/This_Little_Light_of_Mine.

6. March 5: King, Martin Luther Jr , *A Testament of Hope: The Essential Writings and Speeches*, accessed December 29, 2020, https://www.goodreads.com/quotes/943-darkness-cannot-drive-out-darkness-only-light-can-do-that.

7. March 6: Sherman, James, accessed December 29, 2020, https://checkyourfact.com/2019/07/26/fact-check-cs-lewis-cant-go-back-change-beginning-start-ending/.

8. March 8: Anthony, Mark, *The Beautiful Truth*, accessed December 29, 2020, https://www.goodreads.com/quotes/9128902-and-one-day-she-discovered-that-she-was-fierce-and.

9. March 9: Boatright, Windy Gail, Out of My Mind: The Mutterings and Musings of a Free Spirit, accessed December 29, 2020, https://windygail68.com/, message to author.

10. March 10: Tamayo, Ro, accessed December 29, 2020, https://www.liveyourbestselfie.com/, message to author.

11. March 10: Sochnlin, Jenn, Embracing This Special Life, accessed December 29, 2020, https://www.goodreads.com/quotes/9726092-embrace-the-unique-way-your-child-is-blooming----even.

12. March 15: Mote, Edward, My Hope is Built on Nothing Less, accessed December 29, 2020, https://hymnary.org/text/my_hope_is_built_on_nothing_less.

13. March 16: Bassett, Wendy, accessed December 29, 2020, https://wednesdaymorningwhispers.com/, message to author.

14. March 17: Harnisch, Jonathan, The Brutal Truth, accessed December 29, 2020, https://www.goodreads.com/quotes/7515312-the-strongest-people-are-not-those-who-show-strength-in.

15. March 18: Author Unknown, accessed December 29, 2020, https://www.dailyinspirationalquotes.in/2019/02/sometimes-miracles-are-just-good-people-with-kind-hearts/.

16. March 20: Twin, Mark, accessed December 29, 2020, https://www.goodreads.com/quotes/69144-humor-is-mankind-s-greatest-blessing.

17. March 21: Springsteen, Bruce, Across the Border, accessed December 29, 2020, https://www.lyrics.com/track/856869/Bruce+Springsteen/Across+the+Border.

18. March 22: Larson, Christian D, accessed December 29, 2020, https://www.goodreads.com/quotes/210975-believe-in-yourself-and-all-that-you-are-know-that.

19. March 23: Beethoven, Ludwig van, accessed December 29, 2020, https://en.wikipedia.org/wiki/Symphony_No._9_(Beethoven).

20. March 26: Lama, Dalai XIV, The Art of Happiness, accessed December 29, 2020, https://www.goodreads.com/quotes/33159-love-and-compassion-are-necessities-not-lux-uries-without-them-humanity.

21. March 27: Inspired by https://www.abraham-hicks.com/, accessed December 29, 2020.

22. March 29: Pather, Poovanesh, accessed December 29, 2020, https://familygrowthlife.com/, contributed to this page.

23. March 29: Ziglar, Zig, accessed December 29, 2020, https://www.ziglar.com/quotes/sometimes-adversity/.

24. March 30: Robbins, Tony, accessed December 29, 2020, https://www.tonyrobbins.com/career-business/where-focus-goes-energy-flows/

25. March 31: Reeve, Christopher, accessed December 31, 2020, https://www.goodreads.com/quotes/263437-once-you-choose-hope-anything-s-possible.

April

1. April 2: Emerson, Ralph Waldo, accessed January 1, 2021, https://www.goodreads.com/quotes/64541-the-purpose-of-life-is-not-to-be-happy-it.

2. April 3: Hay, Louise, accessed January 1, 2021, https://www.louisehay.com/affirmations/.

3. April 4: Aquinas, Thomas, accessed January 1, 202, https://quotes.yourdictionary.com/author/thomas-aquinas/613150.

4. April 4: Barnard, Celeste, accessed January 1, 2021, https://www.countryliving.com/life/g5138/friendship-quotes/?slide=10.

5. April 4: Davis, Mary, accessed January 1, 2021, https://www.facebook.com/everydayspirit1/photos/now-more-than-ever-we-need-our-friends-to-field-our-doubts-and-fears-and-to-shar/2806338406117685/.

6. April 4: Author Unknown, accessed January 1, 2021, https://tinybuddha.com/wisdom-quotes/friendship-isn-t-a-big-thing-it-s-a-million-little-things/.

7. April 5: accessed January 1, 2021, https://authoracademyelite.com/.

8. April 5: Callaway, Naeem, accessed January 1, 2021, https://www.goodreads.com/quotes/8401191-sometimes-the-smallest-step-in-the-right-direction-ends-up.

9. April 7: Smith, Louise, accessed January 1, 2021, https://www.quotespedia.org/authors/l/louise-smith/you-cant-reach-for-anything-new-if-your-hands-are-still-full-of-yesterdays-junk-louise-smith/#:~:text=You%20

can't%20reach%20for,%2D%20Louise%20Smith%20
%2D%20Quotes%20Pedia.

10. April 8: Eckhart, Meister, accessed January 1, 2021, https://
    www.goodreads.com/quotes/631934-and-suddenly-you-
    know-it-s-time-to-start-something-new.

11. April 9: Langner, Sarah, Owner of A Great Big Beautiful,
    message to author.

12. April 11: Hume, Basil, accessed January 1, 2021, https://
    www.brainyquote.com/quotes/basil_hume_262981#:~:-
    text=Basil%20Hume%20Quotes&text=The%20
    great%20gift%20of%20Easter%20is%20hope%20
    %2D%20Christian%20hope%20which,love%2C%20
    which%20nothing%20can%20shake.

13. April 13: Emerson, Ralph Waldo, accessed January 1, 2021,
    https://www.goodreads.com /quotes/16878-do-not-go-
    where-the-path-may-lead-go-instead.

14. April 14: Newton, Isaac, accessed January 1, 2021, https://
    www.brainyquote.com/quotes/isaac_newton_129998.

15. April 15: Diana, Princess of Wales, accessed
    January 1, 2021, https://www.goodreads.com/
    quotes/484811-only-do-what-your-heart-tells-you.

16. April 16: Roosevelt, Eleanor, accessed January 1, 2021,
    https://www.goodreads.com/quotes/44539-you-can-often-
    change-your-circumstances-by-changing-your-attitude.

17. April 17: Emerson, Ralph Waldo, accessed January
    1, 2021, https://www.brainyquote.com/quotes/
    ralph_waldo_emerson_104452.

18. April 19: Buddha Groove, accessed January 1,
    2021, https://www.buddhagroove.com/blog/
    theme-of-the-week-clarity/.

19. April 20: Hepburn, Audrey, accessed January
    1, 2021, https://www.goodreads.com/
    quotes/831377-to-plant-a-garden-is-to-believe-in-tomorrow.

20. April 21: Emerson, Ralph Waldo, accessed January 1, 2021,
    https://www.goodreads.com/quotes/18830-finish-each-day-
    and-be-done-with-it-you-have.

21. April 21: Roosevelt, Eleanor, accessed January 1, 2021,
    https://www.quotespedia.org/authors/e/eleanor-roosevelt/
    with-the-new-day-comes-new-strength-and-new-thoughts-
    eleanor-roosevelt/.

22. April 23: Hale, Mandy, accessed January 1, 2021, https://www.goodreads.com/quotes/7140087-you-don-t-always-need-a-plan-sometimes-you-just-need.

23. April 25: Oberbrunner, Kary, accessed January 1, 2021, https://yoursecretname.com/.

24. April 25: Angelou, Maya, accessed January 1, 2021, https://www.goodreads.com/quotes/11877-my-mission-in-life-is-not-merely-to-survive-but.

25. April 27: Angelou, Maya, accessed January 1, 2021, https://www.goodreads.com/quotes/5934-i-ve-learned-that-people-will-forget-what-you-said-people.

May

1. May 3: Our State Magazine, accessed January 2, 2021, https://www.ourstate.com/bringing-back-the-sunday-supper/.

2. May 3: Child, Julia, accessed January 2, 2021, https://www.goodreads.com/quotes/814094-people-who-love-to-eat-are-always-the-best-people.

3. May 4: Lee, Becca, accessed January 2, 2021, https://www.goodreads.com/quotes/8009112-the-purpose-of-this-glorious-life-is-not-simply-to.

4. May 4: Native American Proverb, accessed January 2, 2021, https://www.quotes.net/quote/39139.

5. May 5, Chase, Nichole, *Recklessly Royal*, accessed January 2, 2021, https://www.goodreads.com/quotes/1199099-blood-doesn-t-make-someone-family-love-is-what-makes-a.

6. May 11: Caroll, Lewis, *Through the Looking Glass*, accessed January 2, 2021, https://www.goodreads.com/quotes/9151957-in-the-gardens-of-memory-in-the-palace-of-dreams.

7. May 12: Blackwelder, Jill, accessed January 2, 2021, https://www.louisepistole.com/the-ultimate-gift/.

8. May 16: Gandhi, Mahatma, accessed January 2, 2021, https://www.goodreads.com/quotes/11416-the-best-way-to-find-yourself-is-to-lose-yourself.

9. May 19: Ocean, Saratoga, accessed January 2, 2021, https://saratogaocean.com/.

10. May 20: Deschene, Lori, accessed January 2, 2021, https://tinybuddha.com/wisdom-quotes/

life-balance-dont-always-need-getting-stuff-done-some-
times-perfectly-okay-absolutely-necessary-shut-kick-back-
nothing/.

11. May 22: Orloff, Judith MD, accessed January 2, 2021,
    https://drjudithorloff.com/anchor-magazine/#:~:tex-
    t=Having%20empathy%20means%20putting%20
    yourself,don't%20agree%20with%20them.&text=Empa-
    thy%20is%20the%20sacred%20medicine,naturally%20
    able%20to%20provide%20it.

12. May 23: Beyonce, accessed January 2, 2021, https://www.
    goodreads.com/quotes/7308512-i-don-t-like-to-gamble-
    but-if-there-s-one-thing.

13. May 24: Jobs, Steve, accessed January 2, 2021, https://
    www.goodreads.com/quotes/445286-have-the-courage-to-
    follow-your-heart-and-intuition-they.

14. May 27: Author Unknown, accessed January 2, 2021,
    https://www.quotespedia.org/authors/u/unknown/home-is-
    where-love-resides-memories-are-created-friends-and-fami-
    ly-belong-together-and-laughter-never-ends-unknown/.

15. May 28: Inspired by Abraham Hicks, *Rampage of
    Appreciation*, accessed January 2, 2021, https://www.abra-
    ham-hicks.com/.

16. May 31: Satir, Virginia, accessed January
    12, 2021, https://www.goodreads.com/
    quotes/98328-we-need-4-hugs-a-day-for-survival-we-need.

June

1. June 5: Mridha, Debasish, accessed January 4, 2021,
   https://www.goodreads.com/quotes/3237934-let-happiness-
   bloom-in-the-freshness-of-your-mind-in.

2. June 7: Wilder, Laura Ingalls, accessed
   January 4, 2021, https://www.goodreads.com/
   quotes/27079-i-am-beginning-to-learn-that-it-is-the-sweet.

3. June 9: Disney, Walt, accessed January 4, 2021, https://
   www.goodreads.com/quotes/5616-laughter-is-timeless-
   imagination-has-no-age-and-dreams-are.

4. June 10: Wilson, E O, accessed January 4, 2021, https://
   www.goodreads.com/quotes/419449-we-are-drowning-in-
   information-while-starving-for-wisdom-the.

5. June 11: Pather, Poovanesh, accessed January 4, 2021, https://familygrowthlife.com/ contributed to this page.

6. June 13: Gilbert, Elizabeth, *Big Magic*, accessed January 4, 2021, https://www.elizabethgilbert.com/books/big-magic/.

7. June 13: Gregory, Brittany, Leeann Minton Virtual Assistance, contributed to this page.

8. June 14: Randolf, G, accessed January 4, 2021, https://www.goodreads.com/quotes/562151-truly-great-friends-are-hard-to-find-difficult-to-leave.

9. June 15: Fargo, Tim, accessed January 4, 2021, https://www.goodreads.com/quotes/1197607-who-you-are-tomorrow-begins-with-what-you-do-today.

10. June 16: Yearwood, Trisha, accessed January 4, 2021, https://www.goodreads.com/quotes/22566-what-s-meant-to-be-will-always-find-a-way.

11. June 18: Brown, Brene, accessed January 4, 2021, https://www.goodreads.com/quotes/330217-i-now-see-how-owning-our-story-and-loving-ourselves.

12. June 20: Hill, Napoleon, accessed January 4, 2021, https://www.goodreads.com/quotes/search?utf8=%E2%9C%93&q=self+discipline%2C+napoleon+hill&commit=Search.

13. June 23: Angelou, Maya, *I Know Why the Caged Bird Sings*, accessed January 4, 2021, https://www.goodreads.com/quotes/512-there-is-no-greater-agony-than-bearing-an-untold-story.

14. June 25, Stanley, Bessie Anderson, *More Heart Throbs Volume Two in Prose and Verse Dear to the American People and by them contributed as a Supplement to the original $10,000 Prize Book HEART THROBS*, accessed January 4, 2021, https://www.goodreads.com/work/quotes/10928238-more-heart-throbs-volume-two-in-prose-and-verse-dear-to-the-american-peo.

15. June 25: Pather, Poovanesh, accessed January 4, 2021, https://familygrowthlife.com/ contributed to this page.

16. June 25: Mann, Thomas, *The Magic Mountain*, accessed January 4, 2021, https://www.goodreads.com/quotes/695018-laughter-is-a-sunbeam-of-the-soul.

17. June 26: Tracy, Brian, accessed January 4, 2021, https://www.goodreads.com/quotes/292879-make-your-life-a-masterpiece-imagine-no-limitations-on-what.

18. June 27: Brown, Leon, accessed January 4, 2021, https://www.azquotes.com/quote/751613.

19. June 28: Flanery, Sean Patrick, accessed January 4, 2021, https://www.goodreads.com/quotes/7022248-do-some-thing-today-that-your-future-self-will-thank-you.

July

1. July 1: Nelson, Russell M, accessed January 5, 2021, https://www.goodreads.com/quotes/8063058-the-joy-we-feel-has-little-to-do-with-the.

2. July 2: Claire, December 5, 2019 message to author.

3. July 5: Lincoln, Jeff, accessed January 5, 2021, https://www.housebeautiful.com/home-remodeling/interior-designers/a13046952/jeff-lincoln-west-palm-beach-interview/.

4. July 6: Shakespeare, William, accessed January 5, 2021, https://www.goodreads.com/quotes/1334069-the-earth-has-music-for-those-who-listen.

5. July 7: Adelaja, Sunday, *The Mountain of Ignorance*, accessed January 5, 2021, https://www.quoteslyfe.com/quote/You-may-be-the-change-and-light-30909.

6. July 8: Mipham, Sakyong, *Running with the Mind of Meditation: Lessons for Training Body and Mind*, accessed January 5, 2021, https://www.goodreads.com/work/quotes/18329458-running-with-the-mind-of-meditation-lessons-for-training-body-and-mind.

7. July 10: Bevins, Winfield Dr, accessed January 5, 2021, https://asburyseminary.edu/students/chapel/prayers-for-turbulent-times/.

8. July 11: Abraham Hicks, accessed January 5, 2021, https://www.abraham-hicks.com/.

9. July 11: Brown, Brene, *Daring Greatly: How the Courage to be Vulnerable Transforms the Way We Live, Love, Parent, and Lead*, accessed January 5, 2021, https://www.goodreads.com/author/quotes/162578.Bren_Brown?page=11#:~:text=%E2%80%9CJoy%20comes%20to%20us%20in,joy%20is%20not%20a%20constant.%E2%80%9D.

10. July 12: Geiger, John, *The Angel Affect*, accessed January 5, 2021, https://www.goodreads.com/

quotes/1199311-a-beautiful-day-begins-with-a-beautiful-mindset-every-day.

11. July 14: Breathnach, Sarah Ban, accessed January 5, 2021, https://www.goodreads.com/quotes/14096-learning-to-live-in-the-present-moment-is-part-of.

12. July 18: Nelson, Russell M, accessed January 5, 2021, http://www.the-living-prophets.com/Russell-M-Nelson.html.

13. July 20: Uchtdorf, Dieter F, accessed January 5, 2021, https://www.churchofjesuschrist.org/study/general-conference/2015/10/a-summer-with-great-aunt-rose?lang=eng.

14. July 21: Nouwen, Henri J M, accessed January 5, 2021, https://www.goodreads.com/quotes/396401-joy-does-not-simply-happen-to-us-we-have-to.

15. July 22: Collette, Amy, *The Gratitude Connection: embrace the positive power of thanks,* accessed January 5, 2021, https://www.goodreads.com/quotes/8133906-gratitude-is-a-powerful-catalyst-for-happiness-it-s-the-spark.

16. July 24: Blake, Jenny, accessed January 5, 2021, https://www.pinterest.com/pin/129056345560674790/#:~:text=%22Radiate%20joy%20from%20the%20inside,Positive%20Quotes%20%7C%20Kara%20Evans%20Photographer.

17. July 25: Atherton, Amy, accessed January 5, 2021, https://amyshealthybaking.com/blog/2017/12/16/sunday-spotlight-84/.

18. July 29: Pather, Poovanesh, accessed January 5, 2021, https://familygrowthlife.com/, contributed to this page.

19. July 29: Barrymore, Drew, accessed January 5, 2021, https://www.instyle.com/news/drew-barrymores-flower-cosmetics-happiness-best-makeup.

20. July 31: Warren, Kay, accessed January 5, 2021, http://kaywarren.com/article/choose-joy-because-happiness-isnt-enough/.

August

1. August 3: Osteen, Joel, accessed January 5, 2021, https://www.facebook.com/JoelOsteen/posts/all-of-your-days-have-already-been-written-in-gods-book-when-you-go-through-a-di/10152974125265227/.

2. August 7: D'Angelo, Anthony J, accessed January 5, 2021, https://www.goodreads.com/author/quotes/14892. Anthony_J_D_Angelo.

3. August 10: Author Unknown.

4. August 19: DevelopGoodHabits.com, accessed January 5, 2021, https://www.developgoodhabits.com/self-love-affirmations/.

5. August 21: Osteen, Victoria, accessed January 5, 2021, https://www.barrypopik.com/index.php/new_york_city/entry/turn_your_worry_into_worship.

6. August 23: Weiland-Crosby, Angie, accessed January 5, 2021, https://www.momsoulsoothers.com/love-quotes-to-romance-the-soul/.

7. August 28: Marek, Denise, accessed January 5, 2021, https://www.healyourlife.com/climbing-your-own-everest.

8. August 28: Frost, Robert, *A Servant to Servants*, accessed January 5, 2021, https://www.bartleby.com/118/9.html.

9. August 30: Karletta Marie, Creator of Daily Inspired Life at https://dailyinspiredlife.com/, message to author December 7, 2020.

September

1. September 1: From the hymn, *I've Got Peace Like a River*, Author of the hymn is Unknown, accessed January 6, 2021, https://hymnary.org/tune/peace_like_a_river.

2. September 2: Louise Hay 2019 Calendar of Affirmations.

3. September 4: Sangster, Margaret E, accessed January 6, 2021, https://quoteinvestigator.com/2015/12/24/joy-give/#:~:text=long%20year%20thru%2C,The%20joy%20that%20you%20give%20to%20others%20is%20the%20joy,%E2%80%94Whittier.

4. September 5: Adam, David Rev, *A Celtic Prayer*, accessed January 6, 2021, https://holycelticchurch.weebly.com/green-chapel/a-celtic-prayer-by-revd-david-adam.

5. September 9: Nilakshi at MerakiMusings.org, accessed January 7, 2021, https://merakimusings.org/how-to-raise-your-vibration-despite-any-situation/?fbclid=I-wAR20_suf8lZmRODOaRRsusqF8Hu1X7iS5uu6qP-wty13XkSyzpmJMOyOlfr8.

6. September 9: Aristotle, *The Philosophy of Aristotle*, accessed January 7, 2021, https://www.goodreads.com/quotes/101859-the-energy-of-the-mind-is-the-essence-of-life.

7. September 10. Outka, Linda, message to author, August 1, 2020.

8. September 12: Mother Teresa of Calcutta, accessed January 7, 2021, https://www.quotetab.com/quote/by-mother-teresa/there-is-no-key-to-happiness-the-door-is-always-open.

9. September 13: Ziglar, Zig, accessed January 7, 2021, https://www.powerofpositivity.com/difficult-roads-lead-beautiful-destinations/.

10. September 14: Roosevelt, Eleanor, accessed January 7, 2021, https://www.brainyquote.com/quotes/eleanor_roosevelt_100940.

11. September 14: Disney, Walt, accessed January 7, 2021, https://www.goodreads.com/quotes/24673-if-you-can-dream-it-you-can-do-it-always.

12. September 21: Kennedy, John F, accessed January 7, 2021, https://www.csmonitor.com/USA/Politics/Decoder/2013/1111/JFK-assassination-President-Kennedy-s-last-Veterans-Day.

13. September 22: Boggs, Wade, accessed January 7, 2021, https://customerthink.com/creating-a-positive-attitude-chain-reaction/#:~:text=Former%20Red%20Sox%20third%20baseman,of%20positive%20attitude%20in%20others.

14. September 27: Spafford, Horatio, *It Is Well With My Soul*, accessed January 7, 2021, https://www.thebereantest.com/horatio-spafford-it-is-well-with-my-soul.

15. September 27: Bhagavati, Ma Jaya Sati, *The 11 Karmic Spaces: Choosing Freedom from the Patterns That Bind You,* accessed January 7, 2021, https://www.goodreads.com/work/quotes/18517574-the-11-karmic-spaces-choosing-freedom-from-the-patterns-that-bind-you.

16. September 28: Alcott, Louisa May, *Little Women*, accessed January 7, 2021, https://www.goodreads.com/quotes/19092-i-am-not-afraid-of-storms-for-i-am-learning.

17. September 30: Pather, Poovanesh, accessed January 7, 2021, https://familygrowthlife.com/, contributed to this page.

October

1. October 4: National Council on Aging, accessed January 7, 2021, https://www.ncoa.org/news/resources-for-reporters/get-the-facts/economic-security-facts/.

2. October 4: Mother Teresa of Calcutta, accessed January 7, 2021, https://www.goodreads.com/quotes/664276-it-is-not-how-much-we-do-but-how-much.

3. October 5: McClendon, Shayne, *Always the Good Girl*, accessed January 7, 2021, https://www.goodreads.com/quotes/7122225-i-will-breath-i-will-think-of-solutions-i-will.

4. October 8: Enns, Adrienne, *Intentional Days: Creating Your Life on Purpose*, accessed January 7, 2021, https://www.goodreads.com/quotes/tag?utf8=%E2%9C%93&id=joyful.

5. October 9: Spurgeon, Charles, *Christ's Prayer for His People*, accessed January 7, 2021, https://www.spurgeon.org/resource-library/sermons/christs-prayer-for-his-people/.

6. October 10: Wright, Frank Lloyd, accessed January 7, 2021, https://www.goodreads.com/quotes/194857-study-nature-love-nature-stay-close-to-nature-it-will.

7. October 11: Craig, Will, *Living the Hero's Journey*, accessed January 7, 2021, https://www.goodreads.com/author/quotes/17325522.Will_Craig_Living_the_Hero_s_Journey.

8. October 13: Santilli, Elyse, accessed January 7, 2021, https://elysesantilli.com/best-quotes-on-self-love/.

9. October 16: Gaiman, Neil, *Make Good Art*, accessed January 7, 2021, https://www.goodreads.com/quotes/858367-now-go-and-make-interesting-mistakes-make-amazing-mistakes-make.

10. October 17: Robbins, Tony, accessed January 7, 2021, https://www.goodreads.com/quotes/8561116-whatever-you-hold-in-your-mind-on-a-consistent-basis.

11. October 18: Boom, Corrie Ten, accessed January 7, 2021, https://www.goodreads.com/quotes/264407-faith-is-like-radar-that-sees-through-the-fog---.

12. October 19: Stevenson, Robert Louis, accessed January 7, 2021, https://www.goodreads.com/quotes/31-don-t-judge-each-day-by-the-harvest-you-reap-but.

13. October 19: Fredrickson, Fabienne, accessed January 7, 2021, https://www.quotespedia.org/authors/f/

fabienne-fredrickson/the-day-you-plant-the-seed-is-not-the-day-you-eat-the-fruit-be-patient-and-stay-the-course-fabienne-fredrickson/.

14. October 20: Goether, Johann wolfgang von, accessed January 7, 2021, https://www.goodreads.com/quotes/4140-the-greatest-thing-in-this-world-is-not-so-much.

15. October 23: Mathews, Nanette, accessed January 7, 2021, https://www.goodreads.com/quotes/tag/choose-wisely.

16. October 24: Emerson, Ralph Waldo, accessed January 7, 2021, https://www.goodreads.com/quotes/6957-dare-to-live-the-life-you-have-dreamed-for-yourself.

17. October 26: Rohn, Jim, accessed January 7, 2021, https://www.goodreads.com/quotes/6957-dare-to-live-the-life-you-have-dreamed-for-yourself.

18. October 27: Meyer, Joyce, accessed January 7, 2021, https://www.quotespedia.org/authors/j/joyce-meyer/a-positive-attitude-gives-you-power-over-your-circumstances-instead-of-your-circumstances-having-power-er-over-you-joyce-meyer/.

19. October 28: Weedn, Flavia, accessed January 7, 2021, https://www.goodreads.com/author/quotes/179541.Flavia_Weedn.

November

1. November 6: Renta, Oscar de la, accessed January 8, 2021, https://www.azquotes.com/quote/594838.

2. November 6: Stieglitz, Edward J, accessed January 8, 2021, https://quoteinvestigator.com/2012/07/14/life-years-count/.

3. November 7: Rowling, J K, accessed January 8, 2021, https://www.goodreads.com/quotes/657790-i-do-believe-something-very-magical-can-happen-when-you.

4. November 8: Roosevelt, Theodore, accessed January 8, 2021, https://www.goodreads.com/quotes/tag/comparing.

5. November 13: Mother Teresa of Calcutta, accessed January 8, 2021, https://www.goodreads.com/quotes/33359-let-no-one-ever-come-to-you-without-leaving-better.

6. November 15: Gregory, Brittany, Leeann Minton Virtual Assistance, contributed to this page.

7. November 18: Winfrey, Oprah, accessed January 8, 2021, https://www.goodreads.com/quotes/2646-the-more-you-praise-and-celebrate-your-life-the-more.

8. November 24: Oatman, Johnson, *Count Your Blessings*, accessed January 8, 2021, https://hymnary.org/text/when_upon_lifes_billows_you_are_tempest.

9. November 25: Northrup, Christiane, *Why Practicing Gratitude is Good for your Health*, accessed January 8, 2021, https://www.drnorthrup.com/giving-thanks/.

10. November 25: Author Unknown, accessed January 8, 2021, https://www.goodreads.com/work/quotes/21392943-the-gratitude-journal-a-21-day-challenge-to-more-gratitude-deeper-rela.

11. November 27: Roosevelt, Eleanor, accessed January 8, 2021, https://www.goodreads.com/quotes/46578-since-you-get-more-joy-out-of-giving-joy-to#:~:text=Quotes%20%3E%20Quotable%20Quote-,%E2%80%9CSince%20you%20get%20more%20joy%20out%20of%20giving%20joy%20to,you%20are%20able%20to%20give.%E2%80%9D.

12. November 28: Alexander, Cecil Frances, *All Things Bright and Beautiful*, accessed January 8, 2021, https://hymnary.org/text/each_little_flower_that_opens.

13. November 29: Angelou, Maya, accessed January 8, 2021, https://www.goodreads.com/quotes/67751-nothing-can-dim-the-light-which-shines-from-within.

December

1. December 4: Old English Nursery Rhyme Poem, accessed January 8, 2021, https://www.chegg.com/homework-help/questions-and-answers/monday-s-child-poem-old-english-nursery-rhyme-poem-first-recorded-1838-monday-s-child-fair-q44010527.

2. December 7: Schwarm, Betsy, accessed January 14, 2021, https://www.britannica.com/topic/The-Nutcracker.

3. December 7: Pfeiffer, Lee, accessed January 14, 2021. https://www.britannica.com/topic/Its-a-Wonderful-Life.

4. December 10: Dickens, Charles, *A Christmas Carol*, accessed January 8, 2021, https://www.goodreads.com/

quotes/494832-i-will-honour-christmas-in-my-heart-and-try-to.

5. December 11: Watts, Isaac, *Joy to the World*, accessed January 8, 2021, https://hymnary.org/text/joy_to_the_world_the_lord_is_come.

6. December 13: Tolle, Eckhart, accessed January 8, 2021, https://www.goodreads.com/quotes/222733-always-say-yes-to-the-present-moment-what-could-be.

7. December 14: Pather, Poovanesh, accessed January 8, 2021, https://familygrowthlife.com/, contributed to this page.

8. December 14: Palahniuk, Chuck, accessed January 8, 2021, https://www.goodreads.com/quotes/7029064-find-joy-in-everything-you-choose-to-do-every-job.

9. December 15: Churchill, Winston, accessed January 8, 2021, https://allauthor.com/quotes/3949/.

10. December 18: Holmes, Marjorie, accessed January 8, 2021, https://www.goodreads.com/quotes/957767-at-christmas-all-roads-lead-home.

11. December 18: Gannon, Kim and Kent, Walter, *I'll Be Home for Christmas*, accessed January 8, 2021, https://en.wikipedia.org/wiki/I%27ll_Be_Home_for_Christmas.

12. December 19: Roman Catholic Traditional Prayer, accessed January 8, 2021, https://en.wikipedia.org/wiki/Angel_of_God.

13. December 20: German Christmas Carol by and Unknown writer, accessed January 14, 2021, https://www.sharefaith.com/guide/Christian-Holidays/holiday-songs/o-christmas-tree-the-song-and-the-story.html.

14. December 21: Roosevelt, Eleanor, accessed January 8, 2021, https://www.goodreads.com/quotes/46578-since-you-get-more-joy-out-of-giving-joy-to.

15. December 23: Richie, Lionel and Jackson, Michael, *We are the World*, accessed January 8, 2021, https://www.rollingstone.com/music/music-features/we-are-the-world-a-minute-by-minute-breakdown-54619/.

16. December 23: Pather, Poovanesh, accessed January 8, 2021, https://familygrowthlife.com/, contributed to this page.

17. December 26: Hay, Louise, accessed January 8, 2021, https://www.louisehay.com/.

18. December 26: Whitman, Walk, accessed January 8, 2021, https://www.goodreads.com/quotes/7604-i-exist-as-i-am-that-is-enough-if-no.

19. December 27: Dyer, Wayne, accessed January 8, 2021, https://www.goodreads.com/quotes/7085897-abundance-is-not-something-we-acquire-it-is-something-we

20. December 30: King, Martin Luther Jr, *Let Nobody Turn Us Around: Voices on Resistance, Reform, and Renewal an African American Anthology,* accessed January 8, 2021, https://www.goodreads.com/quotes/199214-take-the-first-step-in-faith-you-don-t-have-to.

21. December 31: Calhoun, Laura, message to author, January 18, 2019.

Author, Louise Pistole is a

Joy-Fanatic!

Discover true joy, no matter where you are on life's journey!

Are you experiencing a season of darkness or trial? Do you find it impossible to *Rejoice Always*, as 1 Thessalonians 5:16 commands?

Louise Pistole understands all too well!

Called to share what she's learned along the way, Louise is convinced true joy is available and waiting for you!

Through her writing, coaching and speaking, Louise offers encouragement and inspiration to women worldwide.

Connect with Louise!
https://www.louisepistole.com

Discover Your Joy

Now Available for Speaking Engagements

Dates are filling up quickly!

Topics Include:

- How to open your mind and heart to miraculous joy
- Finding inspiration to survive your battles and seek joy every day
- Aligning your heart and soul to become your best self
- Centering your thoughts to restore peace to your soul

For a Deeper Dive into these and other topics through Personalized Coaching Sessions, contact Louise at Louise@LouisePistole.com.

Discover Your Joy! Newsletter

Subscribe!

Delivered to your inbox each month, you'll find valuable tips and practical ways to:

- Overcome life's many challenges
- Experience miraculous transformation
- Discover lasting joy and happiness

Connect with Louise on a deeper level at https://www.LouisePistole.com. There you'll find daily inspiration from her blog and other resources to *Discover Your Joy*.